Scarecrow Professional Intelligence Education Series
Series Editor: Jan Goldman

In this post–September 11, 2001 era, there has been rapid growth in the number of professional intelligence training and educational programs across the United States and abroad. Colleges and universities, as well as high schools, are developing programs and courses in homeland security, intelligence analysis, and law enforcement, in support of national security.

The Scarecrow Professional Intelligence Education Series (SPIES) was first designed for individuals studying for careers in intelligence and to help improve the skills of those already in the profession; however, it was also developed to educate the public in how intelligence work is conducted and should be conducted in this important and vital profession.

1. *Communicating with Intelligence: Writing and Briefing in the Intelligence and National Security Communities* by James S. Major. 2008.
2. *A Spy's Résumé: Confessions of a Maverick Intelligence Professional and Misadventure Capitalist* by Marc Anthony Viola. 2008.
3. *An Introduction to Intelligence Research and Analysis* by Jerome Clauser, revised and edited by Jan Goldman. 2008.
4. *Writing Classified and Unclassified Papers for National Security: A Scarecrow Professional Intelligence Educational Series Manual* by James S. Major. 2009.
5. *Strategic Intelligence: A Handbook for Practitioners, Managers, and Users*, revised edition by Don McDowell. 2009.
6. *Partly Cloudy: Ethics in War, Espionage, Covert Action, and Interrogation* by David L. Perry. 2009.

PARTLY CLOUDY

Ethics in War, Espionage, Covert Action, and Interrogation

David L. Perry

Jan Goldman
Series Editor

Scarecrow Professional Intelligence Education Series, No. 6

The Scarecrow Press, Inc.
Lanham, Maryland • Toronto • Plymouth, UK
2009

SCARECROW PRESS, INC.

Published in the United States of America
by Scarecrow Press, Inc.
A wholly owned subsidiary of
The Rowman & Littlefield Publishing Group, Inc.
4501 Forbes Boulevard, Suite 200, Lanham, Maryland 20706
www.scarecrowpress.com

Estover Road
Plymouth PL6 7PY
United Kingdom

British Library Cataloguing in Publication Information Available

Library of Congress Cataloging-in-Publication Data
Perry, David L. , 1959–
  Partly cloudy : ethics in war, espionage, covert action, and interrogation /
David L. Perry.
     p. cm. – (Scarecrow professional intelligence education series ; No. 6)
  Includes bibliographical references.
  ISBN 978-0-8108-6758-1 (pbk. : alk. paper) – ISBN 978-0-8108-6306-4
(ebook)
  1. Military ethics–United States. 2. War–Moral and ethical aspects–United
States. 3. Espionage, American–Moral and ethical aspects. 4. Military
interrogation–Moral and ethical aspects–United States. I. Title.
  U22.P45 2009
  172'.42–dc22   2008052812

I dedicate this book to my parents, Janice and Glenn; to my sister-in-law, Lisa, and my nephews, Drew, Scott, and Eric; to the memory of my late brother, Bruce; and to the memory of my late mentor and friend, David Knutson.

CONTENTS

EDITOR'S FOREWORD

Intelligence professionals require attributes common to many other professions, including excellent verbal and oral communication skills and a currency of knowledge. For example, intelligence professionals must know the latest techniques and methods used in the profession, as well as the trends and patterns of new knowledge. Since the end of the Cold War, the threat to U.S. national security has shifted from conventional warfare to asymmetrical warfare. Instead of collecting information on tanks and aircraft, the intelligence community is looking for terrorist encampments in extremely rugged terrain.

The aim of this series is to provide publications that enable individuals entering the profession, as well as those already in it, to develop and sharpen their skills and knowledge. As in any true profession, ethical engagement between individuals and their work must be brought to the forefront if that profession seeks to garner the respect of those served by the intelligence community. It is also extremely important for intelligence professionals to think about their individual conduct and how far they are willing to go in pursuit of their professional objectives.

Partly Cloudy is the first book in this series to address ethical issues in intelligence in great depth. But it is not the first book in that field from this publisher: Scarecrow Press in 2006 published a 400-page anthology that I edited called *Ethics of Spying: A Reader for the Intelligence Professional*, which included essays across a wide spectrum of intelligence work.

One of the contributors to that volume was David L. Perry, whose article, "'Repugnant Philosophy': Ethics, Espionage, and Covert Action," had previously appeared in *Journal of Conflict Studies*. In *Partly Cloudy*, Perry has greatly expanded the topics and arguments he addressed in that earlier article, often examining along the way other essays that appeared in *Ethics of Spying*.

Perry's expertise in moral philosophy and theology, combined with his years of research in open-source material on the work of intelligence and military personnel, his conversations with members of those professions, and his careful and balanced ethical analysis, provide a uniquely rich and valuable perspective. I trust that readers will come away from this book more knowledgeable and wise about some vitally important ethical issues facing some of our key government servants, and better able to engage in their own ethical reflections and decision-making.

Jan Goldman, Ed.D.
Washington, D.C.

PREFACE

Igrew up in the great Pacific Northwest, more specifically the Puget Sound area, Tacoma to be precise. It rains frequently there, and even when it's not raining, it's often overcast. I didn't find that nearly as depressing as some other residents do, especially those raised in sunnier climates, but I certainly looked forward to days when it was only *partly* cloudy, when blue sky, mountains, and sea were at least occasionally visible.

The title of this book is meant to suggest by analogy a few things about ethics, particularly ethics in war and foreign intelligence operations. Some people want their moral lives to be perfectly clear, with obvious differences between light and dark throughout; moral duties for them must be absolute or they fear they'll evaporate. Other people see ethics as completely gray, like a relentlessly overcast winter; for them there's no clarity possible in ethics, only shades of ambiguity.

I'm convinced that neither of those perspectives comprehensively captures the nature of our moral choices or the ethical principles that bind us. As I hope to demonstrate, some ethical situations are opaque, some ethical dilemmas and issues truly intractable, even when subjected to our most diligent ethical scrutiny; but other ethical choices are uncontroversial, while still others can be clarified and resolved in spite of their complexity. In other words, even in regard to war, espionage, covert action, and interrogation, our moral choices on the whole are only partly cloudy.

This book is primarily intended to inform the ethical deliberations of U.S. military and intelligence officers, as well as relevant policymakers and lawmakers in our executive and legislative branches. But it ought also to be of interest to any citizens who care about the ethical challenges faced by public servants who execute policy in their name and ostensibly on their behalf. In addition, I hope that instructors will find this book useful in courses on normative or practical ethics, political philosophy, political science, military leadership, intelligence studies, and international relations.

Chapter 1, "An Introduction to Ethical Reasoning," begins by exploring the nature and scope of ethics, distinguishing between normative and empirical disciplines, and noting similarities and differences between ethics, law and etiquette. Next, a framework for analyzing ethical theories and claims is outlined and used to categorize many illustrative ethical issues in war and intelligence operations. Some challenges to the objectivity of morality are then described, and the reasons why all of those challenges fail are summarized. A list of objective ethical principles is proposed. The question of whether any such principles are absolute is examined, and a theory of *prima facie* duties is explained. A mundane illustration of my approach is narrated. The chapter concludes with some essentials for cultivating moral wisdom.

The second chapter, "Comparative Religious Perspectives on War," examines ethical views on killing and war in Hinduism, Buddhism, Judaism, Christianity, and Islam. It shows how moral values and beliefs in each of those traditions exhibit a surprisingly wide range of stances, from pacifism to just/limited war to total/unlimited war, but the chapter ends by proposing a series of ethical principles regarding war that I think conscientious members of all of those faith traditions (or of no religious faith) can and should affirm.

Chapter 3, "Just and Unjust War in Shakespeare's *Henry V*," is meant to serve as a literary interlude. I interpret Shakespeare's play in light of the just-war criteria of just cause, proportionality, legitimate authority, and noncombatant immunity. I've found the play to evoke profound emotions, thereby enriching the study and understanding of ethics in war.

In the fourth chapter, "Anticipating and Preventing Atrocities in War," I use the case of the My Lai Massacre to reflect on factors in human nature that make atrocities more common in war than we might expect. I note insights from Stanley Milgram's experiments on obedience to authority to show that even conscientious people are prone to commit atrocities under certain social conditions. I use testimony from combat veterans to illustrate such factors as emotional distancing. I then draw on studies of primate behavior to ponder our genetic inheritance of aggression and cruelty. Finally, I recommend a number of practical steps military leaders can take to prevent atrocities from being committed by their own troops.

Chapter 5, "The CIA's Original 'Social Contract,'" marks a shift in the book's focus from military to intelligence operations. It considers whether secret intelligence is compatible with American democracy and how and why the CIA first developed its covert action mission. Its conclusions provide a political–philosophical and historical foundation for the chapters that follow.

The sixth chapter, "The KGB: The CIA's Traditional Adversary," provides a broad history of Russian and Soviet intelligence and addresses the question, What role did the prior history of the Soviet KGB play in the CIA's development of covert action capabilities and their justification?

Chapter 7, "Espionage," analyzes a broad range of ethical issues in the recruitment and handling of foreign agents, including those who are "witting" or voluntary, others who are deceived about the role they are playing, and others who are blatantly coerced into being agents. I draw to a great extent on memoirs and interviews of former intelligence officers. The chapter concludes with a discussion of whether the CIA ought to spy on behalf of U.S. corporations.

The eighth chapter, "Covert Action," narrates and evaluates specific historical cases of U.S. covert operations under three categories: secret support for foreign political leaders and parties, covert coups against unfriendly governments, and assassinations and other targeted killings.

Chapter 9, "Interrogation," examines a series of wrenching questions that emerged in the wake of the 9-11 attacks and continue to provoke debate today: Do ruthless enemies warrant ruthless interrogation methods? Does torture ever work? Is a right not to be tortured absolute, or can it be overridden by more important rights, or forfeited? Can torture be limited in practice? What consequences would occur from formally renouncing the Geneva and Torture conventions? The discussion ends with reflections on a Machiavellian temptation.

The final chapter, "Concluding Reflections," reviews some key elements of sound ethical reasoning and outlines some character traits and practices conducive to peacemaking.

In exploring diverse ethical issues, principles, arguments, and related stories, I feel akin to a guide leading the reader through a series of trails in a thick wood. Some of those trails will have familiar names, but my job is to introduce the reader to previously unknown twists and turns, to show the origins of those trails, to explain who cleared them and subsequently improved them, and to reveal parallel trails or branch paths that may have become overgrown and obscured. At other times my objective is to persuade readers that a trail that may appear to be an efficient way of reaching a desired destination actually leads to a dead end or into deadly quicksand. In rare instances, I force readers to a dangerous precipice to point out the grim topography of the abyss below, which can only be perceived from the cliff's edge.

Ethics is part of the essential meaning and significance of human life. It is endlessly fascinating but not always pretty.

ACKNOWLEDGMENTS

This book was more than twenty years in the making, though not as a continuous project to the exclusion of other work. Most of my teaching and writing from 1989 to 2003 focused instead on biomedical and business ethics. In the early 1980s, at the University of Chicago Divinity School, I was introduced to the history of Western ethical theory and political philosophy (including Christian and secular ethical perspectives on war) by professors Robin Lovin and James Gustafson, and I began writing a doctoral dissertation, *Covert Action: An Exploration of the Ethical Issues* (Chicago: University of Chicago Divinity School, 1993). Dissertation research in Washington, D.C., was enabled by a fellowship from the University of Chicago's Program in Arms Control and International Security, funded by the MacArthur Foundation. I benefited greatly in Washington from the knowledgeable staff and impressive range of intelligence literature at the Library of Congress, the Russell Bowen special collection at Georgetown University, the Radio Free Europe/Radio Liberty Research Institute, and the National Archives. I'm also very grateful to William Colby, B. Hugh Tovar, James McCargar, William Hood, David Whipple, Neil Livingstone, Michael Thompson, Peter Savage, Tom Reckford, Jim Barry, Michael Briggs, Robin Lovin, John Langan, Dan Dombrowski, and Rob Deltete for their thoughtful comments on draft dissertation chapters.

Some former CIA officers spoke and wrote to me on condition that their comments would not be attributed to them in my publications. I've honored their request by citing them in the endnotes as "confidential interviews." At the time of those conversations, I did not hold a security clearance, and my interlocutors knew that; I don't believe that any of them revealed classified information to me, even inadvertently. And since being granted a security clearance in 2003, I have been scrupulous in protecting all classified information.

The core of chapters 5–8 first appeared in my doctoral dissertation. Some ideas from that treatise were previously published as "'Repugnant Philosophy': Ethics, Espionage, and Covert Action," *Journal of Conflict Studies* 15, no. 1 (Spring 1995): 92–115, and reprinted in *Ethics of Spying: A Reader for the Intelligence Professional*, ed. Jan Goldman (Lanham, Md.: Scarecrow Press, 2006), 221–47. I'm indebted to David Charters for publishing my 1995 article and to Jan Goldman not only for including the piece in his 2006 anthology but for encouraging me to complete this book. Insightful comments on drafts of chapter 9 on interrogation were provided by Jim Burk, Michael Skerker, Jack DeFreytas, Loch Johnson, George Reed, and Mike Hargis.

Many of the ideas explored in the first four chapters originated in lecture notes I developed while teaching ethics courses at Seattle University (1993–1999) and Santa Clara University (1999–2003). Early versions of those chapters were published as "Killing in the Name of God: The Problem of Holy War," Markkula Center for Applied Ethics, Santa Clara University, September 2001, http://www.scu.edu/ethics/publications/submitted/Perry/holywar.html (23 November 2008); "The Problem of Total War in Judaism, Christianity, and Islam" and "Our Accountability for Afghan Civilian Deaths: Some Insights from Shakespeare's *Henry V*," both in *Journal of Lutheran Ethics* 2, no. 11 (2002); "Ethics and War in Comparative Religious Perspective," March 2003, on my personal website, http://home.earthlink.net/~davidlperry/relwar.htm (23 November 2008); "How Ethics Is Taught at the U.S. Army War College," *Military Ethics in Professional Military Education–Revisited*, ed. Edwin Micewski and

Hubert Annen (Frankfurt am Main: Peter Lang, 2005), 152–71; "Using Shakespeare's *Henry V* to Teach Just War Principles," *Teaching Ethics*, January 2005, www.ethicsineducation.com/HenryV.pdf (23 November 2008); and "Why Hearts and Minds Matter: Chivalry and Humanity, Even in Counterinsurgency, Are Not Obsolete," *Armed Forces Journal*, September 2006, 40–44. I'm grateful to all of the respective editors for allowing me to incorporate in this book revised versions of articles that they previously published. In part because the original versions of chapters 1–4 were written for different audiences, the revised versions here may read in some respects more like an anthology than as a single continuous/extended argument.

In June 2004, I had the privilege of participating in a four-week scholarly symposium on "War and Morality," convened at the U.S. Naval Academy in Annapolis, Maryland, and funded by the National Endowment for the Humanities. I'm indebted to George Lucas and Al Pierce, who hosted that symposium. Along with Shannon French, Martin Cook, Michael Walzer, James Turner Johnson, Anthony Hartle, John Kelsay, and Sohail Hashmi, they have strongly influenced my thinking about military ethics and the just-war tradition. My chapters on war can in no way replace or substitute for their incredible contributions to that subject and are not remotely intended to do so, but I hope that my work will at least complement and augment theirs.

Many of the arguments presented in this book were honed in lively discussions at academic conferences hosted by the following institutions and associations: Seattle University, Santa Clara University, Pacific Lutheran University (thanks to Mark Brocker and Pauline Kaurin), Dickinson College, Southern Methodist University (thanks to Robin Lovin and Tom Mayo), Roskilde University in Denmark (thanks to Jacob Dahl Rendtorff), Davenport College, the U.S. Air Force Academy, the U.S. Naval Academy, the U.S. Army War College, the French military academy at Saint-Cyr (thanks to Henri Hude), the Austrian National Defense Academy in Vienna (thanks to Edwin Micewski), the Society of Christian Ethics, the Conference on the Study of Government Ethics, the International Studies Association, the Shakespeare Association of America (thanks to Scott

Newstok), the American Association of University Women, and the Inter-University Seminar on Armed Forces and Society.

My reflections have also been enriched during the past 16 years by conversations with my students, who now number in the thousands. From bright undergrads at Seattle University and Santa Clara University to dedicated and patriotic colonels at the U.S. Army War College, they've all challenged me to refine my formulations and applications of ethical principles in the context of concrete experience, especially in military and intelligence operations. I've further benefited from the insights of many faculty colleagues at those institutions.

Finally, I'm extremely grateful for the altruism and fortitude exhibited by Fred Close, G. K. Cunningham, Craig Nation, John Tisson, and Jan Goldman in reviewing the entire book manuscript.

No one but me should be blamed for any mistakes that I may have made in this book. And although I am currently professor of ethics at the U.S. Army War College, none of my views should be construed necessarily to reflect those of the U.S. government.

1

AN INTRODUCTION TO ETHICAL REASONING

We are discussing no small matter, but how we ought to live.

—Socrates[1]

[M]oral thinking is analogous to hypotheses in science that are tested, modified, or rejected through experience and experimental thinking.

—Tom Beauchamp and James Childress[2]

Consider two scenarios: 1) A man points a gun at another man and shoots him dead. 2) A woman lies to her family and friends about her occupation. Do those scenarios raise moral or ethical concerns? Obviously. Are the actions that they describe unethical/immoral? Most readers would probably respond, yes, at least at first glance (prima facie). But now consider the following permutations of those scenarios:

1a. The man is a soldier shooting an armed enemy soldier in combat. Or,
1b. The man is a soldier shooting an enemy soldier, but after he's surrendered and thrown down his weapon.
2a. The woman is a Central Intelligence Agency (CIA) clandestine service officer. Or,

2b. The woman is a member of an underground terrorist organization.

I assume that readers would say that the details in these permutations dramatically affect how the original scenarios would be interpreted ethically/morally. But why would they matter? And what makes these scenarios and permutations interesting in an ethical sense? More broadly, what does the ethical realm encompass, and how might we successfully navigate its territory?

THE NATURE AND SCOPE OF ETHICS

The words *ethics* and *morality* have Greek and Latin origins, respectively. Traditionally, they referred to customary values and rules of conduct—meanings we retain in such terms as "cultural ethos" and "social mores"—as well as insights about what counts as human excellence and flourishing. Ethics and morality sometimes have different connotations in everyday conversation—one of my former students quipped that ethics is about money while morality is about sex! But we often use *ethics* and *morality* interchangeably as well, for example, we can usually call a moral issue an ethical issue with no change in meaning. Ethics also refers to moral philosophy, that is, the discipline of critical analysis of the meaning and justification of moral beliefs and arguments; the present book is an example of ethics in that sense.

Ethics and morality are essentially *normative*, that is, they *prescribe* human behaviors as obligatory (must do), prohibited (must not do), permissible (may do), or ideal (admirable but not mandatory). By contrast, many disciplines like the natural sciences, psychology, history and economics are *empirical*, meaning that they attempt to *describe*, *explain*, or *predict* events or motives or actions. In general, empirical disciplines deal with facts and probabilities, while normative disciplines promote or assess values or state obligations.[3]

Empirical disciplines study what exists, what happened, or what tends to happen under certain conditions; their claims can at least in theory be tested using controlled scientific methods or in light of the best available evidence. For example, the dud rate for a certain type of cluster munition can be reliably predicted by testing a randomly selected, statistically significant sample.

Moral principles state how human beings ought to treat one another. Moral beliefs can be surveyed empirically: that's what many sociologists and anthropologists do. (This is sometimes termed *descriptive ethics*.) But moral claims cannot be proven or disproven by empirical means alone; no data about what people believe to be ethical is sufficient by itself to prove what truly (objectively) is ethical (more on this point later).

Ethical arguments often rely on one or more empirical premises, however. For example, in deciding whether it would be ethical to use cluster munitions against enemy tanks or soldiers in combat, the dud rate would be vitally important information to have, as well as the likely proximity of civilians, the potential risks to one's own troops from unexploded ordnance, and so forth. Also, military leaders hoping to reinforce high standards of ethical conduct by their troops in combat and counterinsurgency would do well to understand the social–psychological factors that can lead otherwise decent people to commit atrocities, factors that are the subject of empirical research. (See chapter 4, "Anticipating and Preventing Atrocities in War.")

There's considerable overlap between ethics and other normative/prescriptive realms like *law* and *etiquette*. Much of the law embodies ethical principles, for example, respect for basic rights to life and property and to participate in political life. It's usually unethical to break the law. A lie can rise to the level of criminal fraud, and a broken promise can be "actionable" as a breach of contract. A breach of etiquette can also be unethical if it is done intentionally to offend someone simply for one's own amusement.

Ethics/morality and etiquette differ from law in that they can have authority and influence even if they haven't been formally codified or approved by a government. But ethics goes beyond etiquette (whose rules typically differ in relation to particular cultures) to include matters that every human society considers significant: such actions as lying, breaking a promise, or killing someone are more serious than social faux pas. Ethics regards some actions as ideal or admirable, but not strictly mandatory, further distinguishing it from both law and etiquette. Ethics also has to do with human character and motivation, which in many cases are irrelevant to etiquette and law. And law and etiquette can sometimes be criticized on moral grounds: consider laws and customs in this country and elsewhere that have historically treated women and minorities as less than full citizens (to say the least).

I assume that most readers of this book have developed what might be called the "standard equipment" of ethics: sympathy with the suffering of others, a sense of fairness and injustice, and habits of telling the truth and keeping promises even when doing so is not personally convenient; in short, a conscience.[4] To put it another way, I assume that my readers are neither coldly scheming manipulators nor psychopaths; I'd need to assume differently were I writing for a reading audience of convicted felons.

But then, you might wonder, what is the point of reflecting on ethics as an adult, let alone a member of a profession, if the "standard equipment" is already in place? Well, one reason is that people don't always take the time to scrutinize their moral beliefs or the alternatives available to them in their ethical decisions, and as a result they sometimes make costly mistakes that they might otherwise have avoided. Also, when a genuine moral dilemma arises where two important ethical principles point us in different directions, our unaided consciences may be unable to prescribe a clear resolution to the problem. Occasionally, especially in the uses of military or intelligence assets, we can face tragic decisions where each of the available options will result in serious harm, and we must therefore choose the lesser of evils. And people of integrity sometimes disagree fundamentally about what's right and wrong, so it won't quite do at that point simply to encourage them to obey their individual consciences. We need wisdom and critical thinking as well as a good conscience. We need to find some way to judge which moral views are most sensible. Moral philosophy can be helpful in these respects.

Ever since the ancient Greek philosopher Socrates, ethicists have tried to construct a unified vision of the moral life and a rational means of testing the adequacy of moral claims and resolving conflicts among important moral values. Moral philosophy often proceeds by proposing an ethical principle, or identifying one that is implied by a particular action or policy, then testing that principle to see if it is vulnerable to counterexamples, and if so, revising the principle or proposing a new one that is less vulnerable to objection. (That approach is evident throughout this book.) Moral philosophy can't guarantee infallible decisions, but it ought to reduce the likelihood of making bad choices due to lack of careful reflection.

Among theories and principles of ethics, there is an important distinction between 1) those which consider only the consequences of alternative actions in determining whether those actions are morally right or wrong (i.e., *consequentialist* or *teleological*); 2) those which give moral weight to aspects of actions other than their consequences or in addition to them (i.e., *nonconsequentialist* or *deontological*); and 3) those which focus on motives and character traits rather than right or wrong actions. William Frankena, in his classic book *Ethics*[5], called the latter *aretaic* approaches, drawing on an ancient Greek concept of excellence of character. Now while classifying an ethical claim one way or the other is never enough to prove or disprove it, grasping this tripartite classification framework can enable us to fruitfully examine all sorts of ethical claims and arguments, as well as to avoid getting stuck in one category at the exclusion of the others, which can lead to serious mistakes in ethical judgment and deliberation. (I make frequent use of those categories throughout this book.)

ETHICAL ISSUES IN WAR AND INTELLIGENCE OPERATIONS

To indicate how the headings teleological, deontological, and aretaic can be useful in analyzing ethical issues in war and intelligence operations, here are some illustrative questions:

A. *Teleological* considerations (i.e., focusing on the beneficial and harmful consequences of alternative actions):
1. Given war's destructive potential, how far should a government pursue alternative means of achieving strategic objectives, instead of or prior to going to war? (E.g., diplomatic pressure, economic sanctions. In just-war terms, this is a *jus ad bellum* matter, i.e., a moral concern bearing on deliberations by government leaders whether to declare war.)
2. If covert action to undermine or overthrow a hostile or tyrannical foreign government would be less harmful than war, would that be sufficient to justify it?
3. If a nation's reasons for going to war are just, does that permit it to use any weapons and tactics available to it to win, or are there some weapons and tactics that should never be used because they would inevitably produce excessive noncombatant deaths?
4. Is it ethical to threaten to use weapons that would probably be immoral to use, if such a threat would be more effective in preventing war than any alternative action or policy? (Consider strategic nuclear deterrence.)
5. Can a preventive war satisfy an evaluation of its likely consequences in comparison with its alternatives (e.g., economic sanctions or deterrence)?
6. When noncombatant lives are at risk from a proposed attack by our military forces against a legitimate enemy military target, how should our commanders weigh those potential harms against the risk to their military personnel when evaluating alternative tactics and weapons? (In just-

war terms, this is a question of *jus in bello* proportionality, i.e., a moral concern bearing on the conduct of war, more specifically in this case, force protection versus minimizing indirect harms to noncombatants.)

B. *Deontological* considerations (i.e., distinct from the consequences of actions and from personal character):

1. Do human beings have a basic right not to be killed? (Why is killing people generally wrong?) If so, is that right absolute, or can it be overridden by other moral factors, such as self-defense or the defense of other innocent people?

2. What might count as just cause for waging war? Defense against invasion? Retaliation or retribution after being invaded or attacked? Preempting an imminent threat? Preventing a grave but less imminent threat? Protecting foreign civilians (humanitarian intervention)?

3. Who has the right to declare war and authorize military forces to wage it? Any supreme authority in a state (including a dictator/tyrant)? Only political leaders in democratic republics, acting in accord with their constitutional mandate? Revolutionary leaders?

4. Can a "coalition of the willing" have as much legitimacy as the United Nations Security Council (UNSC) in deciding to wage war? What if the UNSC refuses to authorize a humanitarian intervention, as in the 1994 Rwandan genocide, or a preventive war, as in the 2003 invasion of Iraq?

5. Should civilians have the right to refuse to serve the war effort? Would it be wrong to compel a pacifist to join the military?

6. Should soldiers have the right to refuse to serve in particular wars that they consider to be unjust? That is, should we permit *selective* conscientious objection?

7. Do some people (e.g., children, the elderly, or other adults in certain occupations or places) have an absolute right never to be intentionally attacked in war? (This is a *jus in bello* question of noncombatant immunity.)

8. Do soldiers fighting in a just cause have more rights than soldiers fighting for an unjust cause? Should we hold the latter accountable for the decisions of their leaders? Or should all soldiers have the same prima facie rights in war, such as those governing prisoners of war and the wounded?

9. How badly must a government treat its citizens before it forfeits the right not to be overthrown? How many internal efforts at reform or regime change must fail before other countries may intervene paternalistically (humanitarian intervention)? Is it right to compel our own troops to risk their lives for another country's citizens, if that country poses no threat to our nation or our allies?

10. Should we uphold ethical and legal rules in war even if our enemy does not? (Do such rules lose their force if not reciprocated?) For example, would we be justified in violating the UN's *Convention against Torture and Other Cruel, Inhuman, and Degrading Treatment or Punishment* in cases of captured insurgents or terrorists? In light of the U.S. Constitution, does the president have the prerogative to override that treaty without the consent of the Senate?

11. Apart from what the law might permit or require, do insurgents and terrorists have an absolute moral right not to be tortured? Or do their murderous acts/plans cause them in effect to forfeit that right?

12. Do the citizens of foreign countries have a right not to be recruited by our intelligence officers to betray their countries' secrets as espionage agents? Do they have a right not to be the targets of CIA covert action? Can such rights be overridden in the interest of U.S. national defense? Could espionage or covert action against tyrannical regimes be justified in terms of the hypothetical consent of their citizens?

C. *Aretaic* considerations (i.e., focusing on personal character, dispositions, and attitudes):

1. What dispositions are essential to being an effective soldier? Which ones does the experience of war tend to inculcate in soldiers? (Note that those are empirical questions, not moral

ones per se.) Which dispositions are morally admirable? Neutral? Troubling? (Consider: obedience to military authorities; loyalty to comrades; courage under fire; efficiency in killing enemy soldiers; risk of increasing indifference to the suffering and death of enemy soldiers and civilians; desire to inflict gratuitous suffering, destruction, rape.)

2. What does military honor require before, during, and after battle?

3. How can military commanders train, lead, and manage soldiers in ways that will help prevent them from developing immoral dispositions, without making them ineffective in battle? (Another empirical question, albeit with obvious moral significance.)

4. Should soldiers love their enemies (a duty found in the teachings of Jesus, Mahatma Gandhi, and Martin Luther King Jr.)? Can soldiers plausibly (psychologically) do that while using deadly force against their enemies?

5. Paul Seabury claimed, "The exercise of power does not necessarily corrupt. The craft of intelligence can have as its practitioners those who were able to maintain their integrity while being liars and obfuscators."[6] Was he right? Is integrity compatible with deception?

6. What dispositions and skills are essential to being an effective interrogator of suspected terrorists? Would a policy permitting the torture of such suspects inevitably entail moral corruption of the interrogators? Would the answer to that question determine whether torture should be allowed at all? Or must the issue be resolved in terms of the contending rights, benefits, and harms at stake for all who are potentially affected?

IS MORALITY OBJECTIVE?

In other words, are there moral obligations that apply to all of us, even if we don't recognize them as such? Consider some theories that deny that there are any such obligations and some compelling reasons why those theories fail. It's important to address such theories early in this book, because they're widely assumed to be true even by well-educated people and because they're a deadly impediment to sound ethical reasoning. (I draw frequently in this section on James Rachels, *Elements of Moral Philosophy*.[7])

Psychological Egoism: *We Can't Avoid Being Selfish*

This theory claims that all free actions are selfishly motivated: Even ostensibly compassionate or self-sacrificial actions are really selfish, since they are done to satisfy the agent's desires. Psychological egoism (PE) is an empirical theory rather than a normative one, since it attempts to explain motives and behavior rather than prescribe them. If it were a cogent theory, though, it would have profound implications for normative theories: If we can only be selfish, if there's no such thing as an unselfish motive, then it makes no sense to pretend we're capable of ethical conduct or debate the merits of various normative principles or theories, all of which assume that we can be moral.

To be sure, selfishness can sometimes masquerade as altruism. Psychological egoism may be useful as a reminder that ostensibly moral motives can also be mixed with self-interested motives. But PE is not plausible as an explanation of all moral motives: As Rachels points out, it assumes that any satisfaction of one's desires is *selfish*, but some desires can be *self-interested* without being selfish, and other desires are not even self-interested. Even if showing kindness toward others makes you happy, that isn't necessarily *why* you do it. Soldiers who throw themselves on live grenades to save their buddies don't do so to be posthumously awarded the Congressional Medal of Honor. Although we are clearly selfish some of the time, we can have unselfish motives, too. We can be concerned about others for their own sake and not simply for what they can do for us.[8]

Incidentally, it's sometimes said that nation–states and corporations are inherently self-interested and incapable of real altruism. I think it's safe to assume that most public commitments by countries and companies to ethical conduct have an element of "self"-interest, in that it can serve their interests to have a reputation for being ethical. But that doesn't mean that states or corporations are necessarily or thoroughly "selfish": They—or rather their individual human representatives—can act in ways that respect the interests of others as well as their own.

Normative Egoism: *I Have No Moral Obligations to Anyone Else; Only My Interests Count in Deciding What I Should Do*

Unlike psychological egoism, this theory prescribes a principle of conduct instead of explaining behavior or motivation. Normative egoism (NE) argues that one ought only to act in ways that promote one's own interests, even when they conflict with others' interests. Normative egoists are not necessarily unconcerned with long-term consequences, nor do they necessarily behave in an obviously selfish way—hence the term *enlightened egoist*. Egoists might want to keep their NE philosophy secret, though, since others would be unlikely to trust them if they knew they're only really concerned about themselves.

But there are important questions about the logical consistency of NE: If another person's interests are identical to those of the egoist in all relevant respects, on what grounds could the egoist's have preferential status? In other words, as Rachels argues, if I give my own interests greater standing than anybody else's simply because they're mine, that's arbitrary and thus logically untenable.[9]

Subjective Relativism: *Ethics Is Relative to Individual Beliefs; Whatever You Believe Is Right Is Right "for You"*

Many people automatically fall back on a subjective relativist viewpoint in situations of moral controversy, partly because they worry about "imposing" values on other people. But few people are comfortable sticking with subjective relativism (SR) after some of its implications are recognized. Consider cases of rape, child abuse, and slavery. Even if the perpetrators of such things believe them to be okay, that doesn't *make* them right. Those actions are immoral or unethical in spite of what their perpetrators might believe. When we arrest and punish rapists and murderers, we're not unfairly "imposing" our values on them.[10]

Cultural Relativism: *Ethics Is Relative to Cultural Beliefs*

Clearly some moral differences among cultures are significant, for example, the status of women or how the elderly are treated. But many moral values and rules are shared across cultures, such as prohibitions on lying, stealing, and murder. In other words, cultural relativism (CR) tends to overstate the moral differences between cultures.

But more importantly, the refutation of cultural relativism is like that of SR: A culture's belief in something doesn't make it true "for them." (Rachels asks rhetorically, Is the earth really flat for people who believe that it's flat?) Moral disagreement between cultures doesn't prove by itself that there's no objectively true morality.

Conversely, as Rachels also notes, we certainly ought to resist bigotry and ethnocentrism and not assume that everything our culture believes must be right. But we shouldn't be afraid to challenge cultural beliefs and practices (including our own) that can be shown to clearly violate basic human rights and universal (objective) obligations. Rejecting SR and CR need not lead to arrogance or imperialism, since our own views are subject to rational critique and revision as much as everyone else's. The point is to stand by those ethical principles that have the best reasons supporting them and to refine or reject principles that exhibit bad reasoning.[11]

WHAT ARE SOME OBJECTIVE ETHICAL PRINCIPLES?

The failure of the theories I've summarized does not by itself show that there *are* objective ethical principles; a proof like that would require a lengthier argument than I can provide here.[12] At this point,

I will simply assume that there are such principles, that is, ones that apply to all rational human beings even if everyone doesn't recognize them as such. But you might test the plausibility of the ones I propose below by asking yourself: What would be the logical and practical consequences of *rejecting* these principles? Would doing so necessarily have such alarming implications that it would be ridiculous to deny that they apply objectively to us all? If you are tempted to deny that they apply to you, would you want to live in a world where no one else was obliged to take seriously your rights and well-being either?

1. Compassion: concern for the well-being of others; avoiding inflicting suffering; preventing and alleviating others' suffering; meeting the needs of the most vulnerable; promoting others' happiness (teleological)
2. Fairness: treating people the way they deserve to be treated, as having equal rights unless merit or need justifies special treatment, or if their criminal acts cause them to forfeit such rights (deontological)
3. Respect for individual autonomy; not manipulating rational people even for their own good (deontological)
4. Respect for laws enacted by legitimate governing bodies (deontological)
5. Honesty: not deceiving anyone who deserves to know the truth; not making promises that we don't intend to keep (aretaic and deontological)
6. Courage in opposing injustice, defending the innocent from harm, and so forth (aretaic)
7. Integrity: upholding our obligations in spite of personal inconvenience; keeping promises that we have freely made (aretaic and deontological)

This list of ethical principles is intended to be suggestive rather than comprehensive. I doubt that many readers will object to them, but perceptive and reflective readers might imagine scenarios where these principles might conflict with one another, entailing mutually exclusive actions, in which case we'd need to figure out how to resolve the dilemma.

For military officers and soldiers, more specific obligations are entailed in the oaths they swear at commissioning or enlistment. Former West Point ethicist Anthony Hartle, in his impressive book *Moral Issues in Military Decision Making*, argues that American officers:

1. accept service to country as their primary duty and defense of the Constitution of the United States as their calling
2. conduct themselves at all times as persons of honor whose integrity, loyalty, and courage are exemplary
3. develop and maintain the highest possible level of professional knowledge and skill
4. take full responsibility for their actions and orders
5. promote and safeguard, within the context of mission accomplishment, the welfare of their subordinates as persons, not merely as soldiers, sailors, or airmen
6. conform strictly to the principle that subordinates the military to civilian authority
7. adhere to the laws of war and the regulations of their service in performing their professional functions[13]

Assumed along with those commitments (or implied by them) is a willingness to die in defense of the nation; moreover, if our country truly faced an existential threat demanding nothing less than the efforts of every able-bodied citizen in its defense, Hartle's list of military obligations might come to apply to us all, even if we hadn't explicitly and freely sworn to accept them. In that situation, the virtues of the good citizen and the good soldier would become virtually identical.

I acknowledge that such claims may be controversial or ambiguous, for example: Does "honor" have a clear and consistent meaning? (Consider how U.S. and Japanese officers and soldiers during World War II differed on its scope and requirements.[14]) Could we rightly demand national service from a strict pacifist, even in a grave national emergency? Should we permit our soldiers, whether volunteer or conscripted, to claim selective conscientious objection to participating in particular wars, for example, if they sincerely believe that U.S. involvement in a war is unjust, or if we are asking them to risk their lives in purely humanitarian missions on behalf of foreign citizens, where U.S. security or other vital interests are not at stake? But unfortunately I cannot pursue those important questions here in the depth that they deserve.[15]

We should recognize, though, that military officers might well find themselves having to choose between two or more of Hartle's principles, for instance, if given a legal order to launch an attack that they believe will result in a useless waste of their soldiers' lives (as illustrated in Stanley Kubrick's powerful film *Paths of Glory*); or if loyalty to the U.S. Constitution seems to conflict with loyalty to their superior officers, were the latter to order violations of the Geneva Conventions, which have the same status under the U.S. Constitution as any other ratified treaty; or if honesty toward Congress involved apparent disloyalty to the president, for example, if a general officer believes that a presidential decision to wage war is imprudent or unjust, and is questioned in that regard by a congressional committee.

ARE ANY ETHICAL PRINCIPLES ABSOLUTE?

A potential way to resolve moral dilemmas is to show that at least one of the relevant principles is absolute, that is, admitting of no exceptions and trumping all other moral considerations. Are there such absolutes?

Some readers might reply, "Yes, there are absolute moral principles, namely those commanded by God." In theory, every person might be able to hear the voice of God directly, in which case presumably everyone would hear the same general moral commands, or at least ones that were logically consistent. But religious believers often disagree amongst themselves, not only between religions but within the same religious tradition, on how one comes to know those commands and what they specifically require. And of course individuals can be mistaken about what God might be saying to them directly: Today we know that some of those errors can be due to wishful thinking, perceptual biases, schizophrenia, mind-altering drugs, and so forth.

Most of the faithful in fact tend to place greater trust in their sacred scriptures than in individual revelation, but as I argue in chapter 2, those scriptures can be inconsistent guides to action, even on a question as fundamental as whether it's ever right to kill people. For instance, if a Christian were trying to assess the ethics of killing, should he or she follow the teachings and example of Jesus, who seemed to advocate strict nonviolence, or some Old Testament writers, who urged strict retributive justice (including capital punishment), or Joshua, who slaughtered every last inhabitant of Jericho supposedly in obedience to God's order?

Attempts to explain away such contradictory ethical standards in foundational religious texts raise additional problems. If the conflicting scriptural commands are claimed to be appropriate for different eras, part of an unfolding divine plan, we're left wondering how a God who is said to be loving and just in some scriptural verses could elsewhere be said to demand the wholesale slaughter of men, women, and children—or cause death directly, as in Noah's flood.

Similarly, believers sometimes credit God with having miraculously rescued them from a natural disaster, plague, massacre, and so forth. But in doing so they fail to explain why that same (loving) God would permit the disaster, plague, or massacre to occur in the first place, killing many (other) innocent people. In other words, any claim that God has intervened benevolently in human history or natural processes must account for the times when God did *not* intervene, for example, to prevent slavery, the Holocaust, the 9-11 attacks, the 2004 tsunami, or the painful, daily deaths of young children from cancer, genetic disease, starvation, physical abuse, or neglect.

Now, it's possible to conceive of a God who would *require* the suffering and deaths of children and other innocents as part of some grand design, but while that kind of God would clearly merit our *fear*, how would such a God deserve our *love*? Alternatively, if

God's reasons for permitting radical evil are said by some believers to be beyond our ability to understand, that undermines their claim to know anything else about God's character or providential actions. The attempt to explain evil through an appeal to mystery is no explanation at all.[16] In short, religious believers cannot escape the necessity of wrestling with ethical challenges without strict or exclusive reliance on scriptural commands or stories.

Some philosophers have attempted to unify all moral obligations under one overarching principle or procedure. For example, utilitarian ethical theorists rely exclusively on a teleological/consequentialist principle, seeking the greatest balance of beneficial over harmful consequences among alternative actions or policies, while Immanuel Kant's theory is strictly deontological/nonconsequentialist, testing every potential moral rule as to whether it can be universalized without logical contradiction. Both utilitarians and Kantians also claim absolute status for their fundamental principles.

The strengths of utilitarian theory lie in its consideration of the well-being of all sentient beings potentially affected by proposed actions and its goals of ameliorating suffering and enhancing happiness. The chief virtue of Kantian ethics is its respect for individual human autonomy, dignity, and worth. Both of those theories have been highly influential, for good reasons, but many other ethicists have identified serious problems in them: utilitarianism is especially vulnerable to concerns about justice and basic rights, while Kantian ethics tends to undervalue the importance of compassion.[17]

A THEORY OF PRIMA FACIE DUTIES

A more promising approach was developed by W. David Ross, an important twentieth-century British philosopher. He proposed a mixed/pluralistic theory that sees consequentialist, nonconsequentialist, *and* aretaic concerns as important considerations in making moral decisions. Ross argued in *The Right and the Good*[18] that there are no absolute moral principles; rather, there is a cluster of prima facie duties, each of which has moral weight and may take precedence over others in different situations. (My list of objective ethical principles given earlier in this chapter is similar but not identical to Ross's own list. I think he'd approve of mine, though.)

Often our prima facie duties reinforce one another, for example, in ruling out cruel or purely egoistic actions. But when our obligations do conflict, there's no way to establish for all time which will take precedence: Ross believed that we must simply wrestle with every duty relevant to a particular situation and determine which is most weighty, that is, which prima facie duty is our *actual* duty then and there. In some cases, one's paramount moral duty will be to promote happiness; in others, to prevent or alleviate harm; in others, to protect rights, and so forth. The need for moral deliberation and wisdom is simply part of the human condition, in Ross's view.

The fact that one principle can give way to another does not mean that the less weighty one loses significance entirely. For example, deciding that I must break a promise to meet a friend to save the life of an accident victim whom I encounter on the way does not mean that my promise to my friend loses all moral value; I still regret breaking the promise even when it's the right thing to do. But Ross's principles apply universally, across cultures and apart from individual differences in preferences and tastes; Ross was not a relativist.

Ross was probably right in believing that our general moral obligations are a mixture of consequentialist, nonconsequentialist, and aretaic ones and that there's no clear hierarchy among prima facie duties that would apply to every possible ethical dilemma. But there may nonetheless be some absolute moral *rules.* Consider "Don't rape" and "Don't torture children or animals": there don't seem to be any credible exceptions to those rules, where they could justifiably be overridden by more important duties. (Of course, we'd need to define rape and torture in morally neutral ways if the rules I've suggested are to avoid begging the question.) The *jus in bello* rule of noncombatant immunity also seems to be a very good candidate for absolute status.

However, it's often very difficult to state other rules that aren't vulnerable to counterexamples: Consider "Don't kill." Never in self-defense? Never in defense of other innocent people? Or consider "Don't lie." Even to save lives or prevent other serious harm? Such counterexamples suggest that general rules against killing and lying are not absolute, a point that has obvious relevance to military and intelligence operations. (Recall the two scenarios and their permutations provided at the beginning of this chapter.)

Principles can sometimes be strengthened, though, by incorporating exceptional cases into them. For example, we might modify "Don't lie" in this way: "It's wrong to deceive people, unless 1) they have forfeited their right to know the truth, or 2) they lack the ability to make rational decisions, and telling them the whole truth would clearly hurt them more than it would help them." Of course, these specific exceptions are controversial, and it would take more complicated arguments to support them.

Tom Beauchamp and James Childress, whose ethical theory strongly reflects the influence of W. David Ross, helpfully described the ideal relationship between moral theories and concrete moral experiences and judgments:

> We develop theories to illuminate experience and to determine what we ought to do, but we also use experience to test, corroborate, and revise theories. If a theory yields conclusions at odds with our considered judgments . . . we have reason to be suspicious of the theory and to modify it or seek an alternative theory. We regard this dialectical strategy as a way to work toward coherence between particular and general judgments.[19]

A MUNDANE ILLUSTRATION

To further explain the ethical categories and principles that I've outlined, consider an everyday scenario of owning and driving a car. Anytime we turn our car's ignition key and release the parking brake, we take control of a potentially deadly weapon that could kill or seriously injure someone, so a *teleological* ethical principle of *nonmaleficence* (avoiding harms to others) clearly applies. That prima facie duty also demands that we maintain the car to keep it running safely, for example, by replacing worn tires and wiper blades. And it ought to warn us against such dangerous distractions as using cell phones while driving. Although we can't do away with our reliance on unconscious judgment and coordination, nonmaleficence may demand that we be more consciously and frequently mindful of safety.

If we wanted to completely eliminate the chance of hurting someone with our car, we could sell the car and walk or ride a bike instead. (We might need to move to a home closer to work, of course.) That would also reduce our "carbon footprint," our consumption of fossil fuels and contribution to harmful greenhouse gases (think nonmaleficence again). Individuals who willingly sacrifice certain luxuries on ethical grounds deserve our admiration, but we may be unable to live car-less without sacrificing many other important values, including holding a job that makes full use of our skills and education or that pays enough to buy food, heat during bitter winters, a decent home, medical care for our family, and so forth. Some of those values reflect teleological concerns, but others involve *deontological* commitments, like *keeping promises* to our spouse or *showing gratitude* to our parents, scholarship donors, and taxpayers for investing in our education. More broadly, our society cannot presently do away with fossil fuels in such essential sectors as transportation, defense, manufacturing, and so forth.

So let's keep our car for this scenario but complicate matters a bit. Imagine that you pull out of your driveway one morning aware that you're running late for an important appointment. You thus have an incentive to speed, and in your anxious state you might begin to speed without even being conscious of it. Frustration at drivers in front of you going slower than you want to go might also induce you to drive even more aggressively, but doing so raises obvious safety concerns. Now, it's sometimes possible to exceed a speed limit without putting anybody else in significantly greater danger, since some speed limits are set much lower than the road conditions permit. And if you're late to your appointments, you may fail to uphold one or more *promises* you freely made to others and give them the impression that you don't sufficiently value their time.

Mindful of those factors, then, could it be ethical to speed when you're running late? Well, there's a deontological obligation to *respect laws* created by legitimate governments, so speeding would violate that prima facie duty. And the *aretaic* concept of *integrity* doesn't condone our making an arbitrary exception for ourselves just for our convenience. So in most cases, our relevant prima facie ethical obligations will tend overall to forbid speeding.

However, that general prohibition might well be overridden in some cases, for example, if you needed to transport a pregnant woman in labor or a seriously injured accident victim to the hospital. In those situations, *nonmaleficence* takes precedence again, but this time potentially to *justify* speeding, albeit with considerable care to avoid harming others along the route. In that instance we might say (paraphrasing Paul Ramsey) that what permits also constrains.

CULTIVATING MORAL WISDOM

In the end, what does good ethical reasoning require? As I hope this chapter demonstrates, ethical decision making cannot be reduced to a short checklist or model. Fundamentally it requires a rich range of *moral emotions*, including empathy toward others' suffering and well-being, a sense of fairness and outrage against injustice, a desire not to incur shame and guilt from doing evil, and so forth. But since some of our gut-level feelings and judgments can be rooted in biased perceptions and ignorance (e.g., racism or sexism), we need to be able to reflect on whether they're sensible or not; this demands *mindfulness and self-awareness*. Good ethical decisions can also depend on *imagination*, both in anticipating the consequences of alternative actions/policies for everyone they'll affect and in creating new and better options. Sound ethical reasoning sometimes entails *hard intellectual work* to research relevant facts and probabilities, to identify which prima facie duties are at stake and to determine whether an ethical argument satisfies the canons of logic. And converting ethical reasoning to action may require *courage* to oppose powerful countervailing social, organizational, economic, or political pressures.

In some situations, when sufficient time is available before a decision must be made, people of integrity will need to draw upon all of those traits and skills. In other instances, though, such as dealing with a live grenade that's just been tossed into a moving vehicle by an insurgent, split-second decisions will not permit sophisticated analysis. We can educate and train people to make good decisions even in those cases, but at that point, they'll be relying largely on unconscious intuitions and judgments, not a deliberate decision-making model.

In military terms, by way of analogy, it's not possible to construct a rules-of-engagement card to cover all of life's moral challenges or a sequence of steps that would constitute the necessary and collectively sufficient conditions for sound ethical reasoning in every possible situation. To continue the military metaphor, that would be like trying to employ a narrowly tactical mindset at the operational or strategic level. (Checklists are sometimes unreliable even at the tactical level.) As Anthony Hartle wrote in his landmark book on military ethics, "No set of rules can provide answers in every case. We can only seek to understand the applicable moral principles clearly, weigh our experience and responsibilities, and determine which course of action is most defensible."[20]

The ancient Greek philosopher Aristotle expressed a similar note of caution in one of his lectures on ethics: "It is the mark of an educated person never to expect more precision in the treatment of any subject than the nature of that subject permits."[21] As his predecessor Socrates taught, what we really need is to *cultivate moral wisdom*, but there's no shortcut, no simple prescription or comprehensive fix for that; it's a lifelong, complex quest.

NOTES

1. Plato, *The Republic*, 352d.

2. Tom Beauchamp and James Childress, *Principles of Biomedical Ethics*, 4th ed. (New York: Oxford University Press, 1994), 22.

3. The two categories of empirical and normative are not meant to be comprehensive. There is at least a third important category that concerns a priori factors underlying and governing the other two, including the

fundamentals of mathematics and basic rules of logic, such as the law of noncontradiction.

4. On the normal development of moral emotions and reasoning in children and adolescents, see William Damon, *The Moral Child: Nurturing Children's Natural Moral Growth* (New York: Free Press, 1988).

5. William Frankena, *Ethics*, 2nd ed. (Upper Saddle River, N.J.: Prentice-Hall, 1973).

6. Paul Seabury, quoted in *Intelligence Requirements for the 1980s: Covert Action*, ed. Roy Godson (Washington, D.C.: National Strategy Information Center, 1981), 107.

7. James Rachels, *The Elements of Moral Philosophy*, 4th ed. (Boston: McGraw-Hill, 2003). After his death in 2003, his son Stuart published a 5th edition of that book, but I prefer the 4th in most respects.

8. Rachels, *The Elements of Moral Philosophy*, 4th ed., ch. 5, "Psychological Egoism."

9. Rachels, *The Elements of Moral Philosophy*, 4th ed., ch. 6, "Ethical Egoism."

10. Rachels, *The Elements of Moral Philosophy*, 4th ed., ch. 3, "Subjectivism in Ethics."

11. Rachels, *The Elements of Moral Philosophy*, 4th ed., ch. 2, "The Challenge of Cultural Relativism."

12. For an indication of how sophisticated such an argument can be, and perhaps needs to be at the level of metaethics, see Alan Gewirth, *Reason and Morality* (Chicago: University of Chicago Press, 1978).

13. Anthony Hartle, *Moral Issues in Military Decision Making*, 2nd ed. (Lawrence: University Press of Kansas, 2004), 73–74.

14. Shannon French, *The Code of the Warrior: Exploring Warrior Values Past and Present* (Lanham, Md.: Rowman & Littlefield, 2003), ch. 8 vividly described incidents of suicide by Japanese officers and soldiers who failed to accomplish military objectives (which obviously was not expected of U.S. troops similarly situated), drawing on an ancient samurai sense of honor. See also Paul Robinson, *Military Honour and the Conduct of War: From Ancient Greece to Iraq* (New York: Routledge, 2006). William Miller, *The Mystery of Courage* (Cambridge, Mass.: Harvard University Press, 2000), indicated that the concept of military courage can also be more ambiguous and elusive than we might expect.

15. On the history of conscientious objection in the United States, see Lillian Schlissel, ed., *Conscience in America: A Documentary History of Conscientious Objection in America, 1757–1967* (New York: E. P. Dutton, 1968), and John

Rohr, *Prophets without Honor: Public Policy and the Selective Conscientious Objector* (Nashville, Tenn.: Abingdon, 1971). Martin Cook, *The Moral Warrior: Ethics and Service in the U.S. Military* (Albany: State University of New York Press, 2004), 50–53, questioned the fairness of expecting one nation's soldiers to risk their lives on behalf of another nation's citizens if no (other) vital interests were at stake, for example, in humanitarian interventions in Haiti and Bosnia.

16. These concerns evoke the classic "problem of evil," that is, the difficulty of reconciling beliefs in God as omniscient, omnipotent, *and* compassionate without denying human freedom or the reality of evil. One of the most powerful expressions of this theological–ethical problem was stated in the "Rebellion" chapter of Fyodor Dostoevsky's novel *The Brothers Karamazov* by the character Ivan. A compelling philosophical analysis is J. L. Mackie, "Evil and Omnipotence," *Mind* 64 (1955): 200–212. Both of those texts are included in Michael Peterson's fine anthology, *The Problem of Evil: Selected Readings* (Notre Dame, Ind.: University of Notre Dame Press, 1992), 57–66 and 89–101, respectively. See also Rachels, *The Elements of Moral Philosophy*, 4th ed., ch. 4, "Does Morality Depend on Religion?" for an effective critique of the divine-command theory of ethics, drawing in part on Plato's dialogue, *Euthyphro*.

17. The scholarly literature by and about utilitarians and Kantians is immense; I can't remotely do it justice here. But concise analyses and insightful evaluations of their theories can be found in Rachels, *The Elements of Moral Philosophy*, 4th ed., chs. 7–10.

18. W. David Ross, *The Right and the Good* (New York: Oxford University Press, 1930).

19. Beauchamp and Childress, *Principles of Biomedical Ethics*, 4th ed., 23. These authors also draw on the concept of "reflective equilibrium" proposed by John Rawls, *A Theory of Justice* (Cambridge, Mass.: Harvard University Press, 1971, 2005). James Childress, "Just War Criteria," in *War or Peace? The Search for New Answers*, ed. Thomas Shannon (Maryknoll, N.Y.: Orbis, 1980), 40–58, applied Ross's theory to the just-war tradition.

20. Hartle, *Moral Issues in Military Decision Making*, 2nd ed., 180. Note, however, that Hartle was not encouraging his readers to take shortcuts out of frustration with the complexity of ethical decisions or to rely unreflectively on their raw intuitions. He made the comments I quoted only after 180 pages of careful reasoning about the foundations and content of ethical principles in military service and just prior to his analysis and evaluation of a series of challenging cases.

21. Aristotle, *Nichomachean Ethics*, 1:3.

COMPARATIVE RELIGIOUS PERSPECTIVES ON WAR

The LORD is gracious and merciful, slow to anger, and abounding in steadfast love.

—Psalm 145:8[1]

Joshua defeated the whole land . . . [and] left no one remaining, but utterly destroyed all that breathed, as the LORD God of Israel commanded.

—Joshua 10:40

This chapter highlights a wide range of ethical views on killing and war in the world's major religious traditions. One can learn a lot about a religion or culture by paying close attention to how it answers the question, Is it ever right to kill?[2] People raised within particular religious faiths are sometimes led to believe that their tradition has always held a consistent set of ethical principles, but what we find when we look closely at virtually any religious tradition are teachings that are at least paradoxical and in some cases downright contradictory. Every major religious faith regards life (especially human life) as sacred in some sense and affirms mercy and compassion as basic human obligations, but sacred scriptures and influential religious authorities have also taught that it's sometimes right to kill other human beings. Some have gone so far as to rationalize wars of annihilation against heretics and infidels.

Religion is clearly not the only catalyst of total war and other forms of indiscriminate violence: People seem prone to inventing all sorts of rationales for mass killing without necessarily feeling the need to cite the will of God. Some of the most appalling atrocities in history have been rooted not in religion per se but rather in racial or class hatred: think of the twentieth-century victims of Hitler, Stalin, Mao, and Pol Pot. There may even be a genetic tendency in our species, like that of our chimpanzee relatives, to fear, hate, attack, and kill others for no reason than that they aren't "one of us."[3] (More about that in chapter 4.)

But religious violence can take on a particularly intense and ruthless character, if the objects of that violence are seen as blaspheming or insulting God, and thus as enemies of God who must be humbled or destroyed.[4] I'm confident, though, that some ethical principles to limit violence can be affirmed by all of the world's major religions, even if the use of deadly force cannot—or should not—be completely prohibited.

Obviously I cannot do complete justice to the complexity of any significant religious tradition's ethical views in a short chapter like this.[5] But I hope nonetheless to illuminate some important similarities and differences among the major faiths on pacifism, limited war, and total war. I also hope that readers will profit from this chapter in the following ways: first, in recognizing the diversity of teachings within their own religion, especially its moments of violent intolerance of other faiths, they ought to be less likely to proclaim their country's wars as divinely ordained struggles against "infidels" who might be denied basic rights as a result; second, in learning to appreciate certain ethical values and precepts in other traditions as similar to those of their own, they will be better able to support diplomatic initiatives between countries and cultures to reduce the likelihood of war and lessen its severity; and third, specifically in "the battle for hearts and minds" in such places as Afghanistan and Iraq today, they may learn ways to ally with moderates against the murderous ideologies of Al Qaeda and the Taliban.

EASTERN TRADITIONS

One of the oldest living religions is Hinduism. The Hindu tradition reveres all of life and affirms an ethical principle of *ahimsa*, or avoiding injury to any sentient creature.[6] This ethic has often led Hindus to adopt vegetarianism and strict pacifism and has been especially strong in Buddhism and Jainism, both offshoots of Hinduism. The pacifist ethic nurtured by these faiths lives today amongst the followers of Mahatma Gandhi and such renowned Buddhist teachers as the Dalai Lama of Tibet, Thich Nhat Hanh of Vietnam, and Maha Ghosananda of Cambodia.[7]

According to Gandhi, who drew on multiple religious traditions to formulate his core ethical teachings, the moral implications of *ahimsa* are profound and holistic, encompassing attitudes and dispositions as well as decisions and actions:

> In its negative form, [*ahimsa*] means not injuring any living being, whether by body or mind. . . . In its positive form, *ahimsa* means the largest love, the greatest charity. If I am a follower of *ahimsa*, I must love my enemy. . . . When a person claims to be nonviolent, he is expected not to be angry with one who has injured him. He will not wish him harm; he will wish him well. . . . He will put up with all the injury to which he is subjected by the wrongdoer. Thus nonviolence is complete innocence. Complete nonviolence is complete absence of ill will against all that lives.[8]

Similarly, a sacred Jain text says, "One may not kill, ill-use, insult, torment, or persecute any kind of living being."[9] Buddhism stresses the need for people to constantly be aware of how hateful and greedy emotions can arise to avoid being controlled by them and lashing out violently against others. Buddhism seeks to undermine social divisions (including the Hindu caste system), while at the same time reinforcing its virtue of compassion and the obligation of noninjury. As a result, the duty not to kill people or other sentient animals applies to all Buddhists, though as an absolute duty it has often been restricted in practice to Buddhist monks and nuns.[10] Former Burmese prime minister U Nu even renounced the use of force by the state, claiming that Buddhism "cannot sanction even such acts of violence as are necessary for the preservation of public order and society."[11]

How would pacifists within those faiths respond to a concern that nonviolence might have little or no persuasive effect on a ruthless enemy and could result in the destruction of their community? Some contend that violence only seems to be effective but usually ends up merely producing more violence: Gandhi has often been quoted as saying, "An eye for an eye makes the whole world blind." Others would admit that nonviolence sometimes does not succeed in deterring or ending violence but claim that success is not as important as doing the right thing. The Christian pacifist Theodore Koontz stated that point in a manner that would be affirmed by many Hindus and Buddhists as well: "Although pacifists know that sometimes turning the other cheek is effective in transforming the enemy, they tend to stress readiness to accept suffering as an essential part of the disarmed life."[12] A Vietnamese Buddhist group once proclaimed bravely, "We solemnly promise never to hate those who kill us, above all never to use violence to answer violence, even if the antagonists see us as enemies and kill until they annihilate us."[13]

Hindus and Buddhists believe in the Law of Karma, which rigorously enforces justice through an indefinite series of rebirths. So even if evil people succeed in their present lives, Karma will ensure that they'll pay for it in their next life. Trusting in the Law of Karma can help motivate adherents of these faiths to overcome selfishness and hostility and resist succumbing to violence.[14] (This functions similarly to the Western belief in a heavenly reward for living a devout and moral life, even if one suffers great injustice during one's earthly life at the hands of evil people.)

In practice, though, Eastern traditions often permit some exceptions to the general rule against killing. Even Gandhi found it difficult to consistently affirm a rule of strict *ahimsa* or nonviolence. During World War I, he openly supported the British war effort, enthusiastically recruiting Indians to serve as front-line troops. Apparently Gandhi believed that such support would prove to the British that India had earned its right to independence. He also claimed in 1918 that Indians might only inculcate the courage required for nonviolent civil disobedience and national independence by first acquiring military courage through the experience of combat. And after many decades of nonviolent resistance to British rule, by 1942 Gandhi reluctantly concluded, "We have to take the risk of violence to shake off the great calamity of slavery."[15]

For many centuries, the Hindu caste system included a distinct and honored caste of warriors, the *Ksatriyas*, whose role in defending the community with force was considered to be just as important as that of the Brahmin or priestly caste. If a Hindu man were born into the warrior caste, he could be obligated to kill enemy soldiers in defense of the community if so ordered; his social role would not permit him to be a pacifist. He must kill with the proper disposition, though, without greed or anger. (Read the "pep talk" given by the god Krishna to the reluctant warrior Arjuna in the *Bhagavad Gita*.) Some Hindu gods, like Indra, are believed to have warlike characteristics themselves and are praised for destroying the enemies of orthodox Hindu teachings and practices.[16] So justified war and holy war are not entirely foreign to Hinduism. And some contemporary Hindus cite traditional warrior values in support of India's possession of nuclear weapons.[17]

Conversely, *total* war in the sense of indiscriminate killing has typically been forbidden in the Hindu tradition. Hindu soldiers are not to kill unarmed prisoners or civilians, apparently due in part to a sense of chivalry: It is considered unprofessional for a Hindu soldier to harm defenseless people.[18] (Similar values of chivalry in the West helped ground the modern principle of noncombatant immunity. And Chinese strategist Sun Tzu also stipulates, "The king's army does not kill the enemy's old men and boys; it does not destroy crops. . . . In carrying out punitive expeditions, it does not punish the common people."[19])

From a comprehensive survey of Buddhist ethical traditions, Peter Harvey concluded:

> The Buddhist path aims at a state of complete nonviolence, based on insight and inner strength rooted in a calm mind. Yet those who are

not yet perfect, living in a world in which others may seek to gain their way by violence, still have to face the dilemma of whether to respond with defensive violence. Pacifism may be the ideal, but in practice Buddhists have often used violence in self-defense or defense of their country.[20]

Some Buddhists have argued that killing can be justified in rare cases as the lesser of evils, if the Buddhist community or other innocent people are threatened by violent attackers and if nonviolent means of persuasion and protest have not succeeded. Interestingly, even when war might be waged with just cause and as a last resort, Buddhists still regard it as inherently sinful; so just warriors might nonetheless expect to undergo karmic punishment.[21] (Medieval Christians held a similar view, requiring their soldiers to perform penitential acts upon their return from war, discussed later in this chapter.)

Sadly, Hindus and Buddhists have also resorted to total war and other indiscriminate killing on occasion. Some of their leaders have openly advocated aggressive violence against people of competing religions. Zen Buddhism was distorted in Japan to support a ruthless warrior ethic before and during World War II. Xenophobic Buddhists in Sri Lanka have promoted the "ethnic cleansing" of Hindu Tamils from the island. An influential Thai monk claimed in the 1970s that killing communists would actually produce karmic merit.[22] And the man who assassinated Gandhi in 1948 was a member of a radical Hindu sect that opposed any political compromise with Islam or other faiths.[23] But of course it's very difficult to see how such things can be justified in light of their religions' core values.

In the Western monotheistic religions of Judaism, Christianity, and Islam, we also encounter a mixture of moral values, some restraining war, others promoting it. I think it's fair to say, though, that the problem of total war has been more frequent in these faiths than in Eastern traditions, due to a more intense fear of unorthodox beliefs and idolatry (i.e., the worship of false gods).

JUDAISM

Frequently in the Hebrew Bible (or what Christians call the Old Testament), love of one's neighbor is said to be a fundamental duty; in fact, love is to extend beyond one's religious or ethnic kin to include resident aliens as well (Leviticus 19:17–18, 19:33–34). Murder and other forms of unjust violence are forbidden (Exodus 20:13). The primary moral arguments underlying or reflected in those commandments appear to be: 1) God is loving, so imitate God's love; 2) God has shown mercy to you, so show gratitude to God by being merciful to others; and 3) human beings are created in God's image, so treat them as such. (See Psalm 145:8–9; Micah 6:8; and Genesis 1:26–27, 9:6). If we considered those ideas in isolation from some other biblical values and commandments, we might derive an ethic of strict pacifism toward human beings,[24] an absolute duty not to kill people, since killing even a murderous attacker might be regarded as a kind of sacrilege as well as contradicting love.

But that's apparently not what the ancient Hebrews believed, since murder and other serious offenses (Exodus 21–22) were subject to capital punishment, a form of intentional killing. Genesis 9:6 says, "Whoever sheds the blood of a human, by a human shall that person's blood be shed; for in his own image God made humankind." I would interpret that to mean, all people have a basic right not to be killed, rooted in their having been created in God's image, but they can forfeit that right if they commit a serious enough offense.

So far, this would only permit those who are guilty of certain crimes to be executed, that is, strict retributive justice. Deuteronomy 24:16 states, "Parents are not to be put to death for their children, nor children for their parents; each one may be put to death only for his own sin." In addition, if this ethic permitted war at all, it would seem to limit it to the defense of the innocent against unjust invaders or in punishment of their atrocities.

But collective punishment and indiscriminate war were also commanded or approved in the Hebrew Bible, especially in cases of idolatry. The first of the Mosaic commandments prohibited the Israelites from worshipping anyone but Yahweh. God demanded purity and strict obedience; idolatry and blasphemy were punishable by death (Exodus 20:3, 20:5). Non-Israelites who lived within the area believed by the Hebrews to have been promised to them by God were seen to pose a great temptation to them to abandon their faith. This led them to rationalize the slaughter of entire communities (a combination of preventive war, holy war, and total war) in some of the most chilling passages in the Bible. Deuteronomy 20:16–18 says, "[In] the towns of the nations whose land the LORD your God is giving you as your holding, you must not leave a soul alive. . . . [Y]ou must destroy them . . . so that they may not teach you to imitate the abominable practices they have carried on for their gods." Joshua 6:21 and 10:40 claim that, "[Joshua's army killed everyone in Jericho], both men and women, young and old, oxen, sheep, and donkeys. . . . Joshua defeated the whole land . . . he left no one remaining, but utterly destroyed all that breathed, as the LORD God of Israel commanded."[25]

Similarly grim wars of annihilation attributed directly to God were portrayed in the Psalms:

I will sing praise to your name, O Most High. . . . The enemies have vanished in everlasting ruins; their cities you have rooted out; the very memory of them has perished. . . . The LORD will swallow [up his enemies] in his wrath, and fire will consume them. [He] will destroy their offspring from the earth . . . their children from . . . humankind. (Psalms 9:2, 9:6, 21:9–10)

However, in contrast to the exterminations prescribed for Israel's internal foes, Israel's external enemies were to be treated somewhat more leniently: They were first to be presented with peace terms, and if those were accepted, then the people would be subjugated, not killed; but if they rejected the terms, the men were to be slaughtered and the women and children enslaved (Deuteronomy 20:10–15). In those respects, the Hebrews were little different from other ancient cultures.

Later rabbinic commentators who compiled the Talmud relegated wars of annihilation and other indiscriminate killing solely to the specific divine commands connected with the ancient conquest of the Promised Land.[26] But theological questions about the consistency between indiscriminate war and God's ethical character remained, of course: How could a loving and just God ever order someone like Joshua to massacre whole communities? Even if all of their adults were guilty of "abominable practices," which itself is highly doubtful, how would that possibly justify killing their children and livestock as well? Apparently the Talmudic writers wrestled with such questions themselves, since they invented a story about King Saul in which he *refuses to obey* a divine command to slaughter Amalekite civilians indiscriminately, asking God rhetorically, "If the adults have sinned, what is the sin of the children?"[27]

But although the Talmud evinced scruples against wars of annihilation, it gave explicit permission for individuals to kill murderous pursuers either in self-defense or in defense of others, based primarily on Genesis 9:6 (though that verse seems to apply only to a murder that's already occurred). Maimonides even thought that killing in such cases could be *required*, in light of his reading of Leviticus 19:16: "Don't stand idly by the blood of your neighbor." Defensive war was permitted on those grounds as well and required if the survival of a Jewish state were threatened. Pacifism was only recommended as a prudential option, when using force against oppression or invasion would likely result in significantly more harm to the community.[28]

Even when just cause for war existed, though, Maimonides and most other rabbis urged that nonviolent efforts to achieve justice and maintain peace be pursued first. If war regrettably ensued in spite of such efforts, destruction should not exceed what was minimally necessary to achieve important military objectives. And innocent lives should be spared whenever possible.[29] As early as the first century C.E., Philo of Alexandria wrote:

> When [the Jewish nation] takes up arms, it distinguishes between those whose life is one of hostility and the reverse. For to breathe slaughter against all, even those who have done very little or nothing amiss, shows what I should call a savage and brutal soul.[30]

So in contrast to the ancient rationales for total war, the Jewish tradition developed ethical limits on war comparable to *jus ad bellum* proportionality (e.g., that war should only be a last resort), *jus in bello* proportionality (minimizing collateral damage), and noncombatant immunity.

Drawing in part on elements of the Jewish tradition, the contemporary code of ethics of the Israel Defense Forces (IDF)[31] requires soldiers to use minimally necessary force; to spare civilian lives; and to respect their dignity, property, values, and sacred sites. Clearly a war of annihilation like Joshua's would not be permitted under the IDF Code.

But in practice, the code has not always been upheld in Palestinian areas occupied by Israel since 1967 or during Israel's wars with Lebanon in the 1980s and 2006. Israeli military force is not always discriminate or proportionate: Whole families of individual terrorists have been punished collectively (e.g., their houses bulldozed) and Palestinian civilians intimidated and humiliated on a daily basis. However, many Jewish people have criticized those tactics, along with the policy of successive Israeli governments to build illegal Jewish settlements in the West Bank and defend them with IDF soldiers. Such critics have explicitly or implicitly drawn upon centuries of Talmudic affirmations of compassion, fairness, and respect for human dignity.[32]

CHRISTIANITY

One question that has been the subject of considerable debate in the Christian tradition is whether Jesus was a pacifist, in other words, whether he prohibited violence absolutely. Some passages in the Gospels seem to clearly imply that, but others are more ambiguous.

Matthew chapter 5 reports Jesus as saying: "You have heard that it was said, 'An eye for an eye and a tooth for a tooth.' But I say to you, Do not resist an evildoer. [I]f anyone strikes [or slaps] you on the right cheek, turn [and offer him] the other also. . . . You have heard that it was said, 'You shall love your neighbor and hate your enemy.' But I say to you, love your enemies and pray for those who persecute you."[33] Those sayings seem to imply a strict rule of nonviolence and have inspired Christian pacifists for nearly two millennia. C. John Cadoux inferred from such passages that, "Jesus adopted for himself and enjoined upon his followers principles of conduct which, in as much as they ruled out as illicit all use of violence and injury against others, clearly implied the illegitimacy of participation in war."[34]

On the other hand, when Jesus spoke with Roman soldiers, he did not recommend that they abandon their profession to serve God (Luke 7). Now, an argument from silence is logically weak: The fact that Jesus was never reported to have criticized soldiers as such doesn't entail that he supported their vocation. But it's puzzling how Jesus would have reconciled the military profession with nonresistance to evil and love of enemies.

The Gospels further portray Jesus as using some degree of intimidation or force to eject the merchants from the Temple in Jerusalem (John 2:13–16). There's also a story where Jesus seems to explicitly permit his disciples to carry swords, and by implication to use them in self-defense, though that passage appears only in Luke 22 and is very mysterious.

The apocalyptic book of Revelation even imagines the returning Christ as a mighty warrior, "just in war" and wielding "a sharp sword to smite the nations." But how can such passages be squared with Jesus' pacifist precept, "Do not resist an evildoer"?

Similar puzzles emerge from the stories of Jesus' arrest. The four Gospels agree that when Jesus was arrested by an armed group, one of his disciples drew a sword and wounded a servant of the high priest. This is startling by itself, in suggesting that at least one disciple apparently carried a deadly weapon while accompanying Jesus in his ministry and that Jesus by implication did not forbid or discourage that.

But the Gospels differ about what was said during that incident, and those differences are fascinating.

In Mark's version of the story (14:43–52), Jesus says nothing to the disciple who inflicts the wound. Mark's gospel is thought by scholars to be the earliest of the four and probably familiar at least to the writers of Matthew and Luke, but only Mark's gospel suggests that Jesus was silent at this point. Perhaps Mark meant to imply that Jesus was rendered speechless at the sight of one of his disciples lashing out violently, but we can't know for sure.

In Luke's account (22:47–51), alone among the gospels, Jesus' disciples first ask him, "Lord, should we strike with the sword?" But Jesus doesn't respond before one of them cuts the servant's ear off. (Perhaps he wasn't given enough time to reply.) Then Jesus says simply, "Stop! No more of that!" In Luke's version there's only that brief command, with no supporting reasons given. It might reflect an abhorrence of violence in general, but we might wonder why Luke's Jesus would permit his disciples to carry swords just a few verses earlier, yet forbid their use here in his defense.

In John's version of the arrest (18:3–11), the disciple who uses his sword is identified as Simon Peter, and the servant's name is said to be Malchus. (In the other Gospels they're nameless.) John quotes Jesus as saying to Peter, "Put your sword back into its sheath. Am I not to drink the cup that the Father has given me?" So John's focus is on the need to permit Jesus's divine mission to continue (which includes his arrest and crucifixion), not a specific opposition to violence per se. The contrast with Luke's version is remarkable.

Matthew's version of Jesus' statement is lengthier and more complex than the others (26:51–54): "Suddenly, one of those with Jesus put his hand on his sword, drew it, and struck the slave of the high priest, cutting off his ear. Then Jesus says to him, 'Put your sword back into its place; for all who take the sword will perish by the sword.[35] Do you think that I cannot appeal to my Father, and he will at once send me more than twelve legions of angels? But how then would the scriptures be fulfilled, which say it must happen in this way?'" Note that Jesus gives at least two rationales in Matthew against the disciple's use of his sword. One sounds like a piece of prudential advice: If you don't want to be killed yourself, don't use lethal weapons. (But then, wouldn't the disciple respond, "I'm perfectly willing to die to protect you"?) But the other rationale, like John's, might be restricted to this situation only: The disciple must not interfere with Jesus' mission. We might also wonder, though, how the legions of angel "reserves" are consistent with pacifism.

In light of this puzzling combination of texts, how did the early Christian community answer the question of whether force could ever be morally justified? Many of them seem to have affirmed a *dual* ethic, one for Christians and another for the state (which during their era was not favorably disposed toward Christianity). I'll use Paul, Tertullian of Carthage, and Origen of Alexandria to illustrate this thesis.

All three of those influential Christians interpreted Jesus' teaching and example to prohibit all uses of force by Christians, not only in personal self-defense but apparently even in defense of other innocent people. Paul wrote to Roman Christians (ch. 12): "Do not repay anyone evil for evil, but take thought for what is noble in the sight of all. . . . Beloved, never avenge yourselves, but leave room for the wrath of God." More than a century later, Tertullian wrote that when Jesus rebuked the disciple who defended him at his arrest, in effect he disarmed every soldier.[36] Tertullian explained to Roman rulers that Christians believe it's better for them to be killed than to kill and that they may never retaliate if injured by others.[37] And he stipulated that when soldiers convert to Christianity, they must leave the military, asking rhetorically, "Shall it be held lawful [for Christians] to make an occupation of the sword, when the Lord proclaims that he who uses the sword shall perish by the sword?"[38] His contemporary Origen also claimed that Jesus prohibited homicide, so Christians may never kill for any reason: "He nowhere teaches that it is right for His own disciples to offer violence to any one, however wicked."[39]

But all three of those early Christians, in spite of their apparently pacifist stances, also seemed to think that God authorized the state to use lethal force for certain purposes. Paul wrote in Romans 13,

> Let every person be subject to the governing authorities; for there is no authority except from God, and those authorities that exist have been instituted by God. Therefore whoever resists authority resists what God has appointed, and those who resist will incur judgment. For rulers are not a terror to good conduct, but to bad. Do you wish to have no fear of the authority? Then do what is good, and you will receive

its approval; for it is God's servant for your good. But if you do what is wrong, you should be afraid, for the authority does not bear the sword in vain! It is the servant of God to execute wrath on the wrongdoer.

I find it hard to conceive of a more conservative political philosophy than the one suggested here by Paul. Indeed, since he was himself persecuted by Roman authorities and knew that Jesus was executed by them, it's difficult to imagine him sincerely believing that rulers are never "a terror to good conduct." However, later Christians like Augustine who cited Romans 13 approvingly did not ponder such questions. Paul's words sadly served for many centuries as a "proof text" for the "divine right of kings" in Europe and thus ironically as a rationale for arbitrary royal power and tyranny.

Tertullian, in puzzling contrast to his strict pacifist sayings noted earlier, also wrote, "We [Christians] pray . . . for security to the empire; for protection to the imperial house; for brave armies."[40] Similarly, Origen claimed that although Christians won't serve in the military, they offer "prayers to God on behalf of those who are fighting in a righteous cause . . . that whatever is opposed to those who act righteously may be destroyed."[41]

Now, the combination of views drawn from Paul, Tertullian, and Origen is logically inconsistent: It's not possible to rule out killing entirely and then permit it on the part of the state. But it's important to recognize that those authors apparently thought strict pacifism to be the only acceptable ethic for followers of Jesus. As Cadoux concluded after a thorough examination of pertinent texts from that era, many other Christians shared that same view.[42] In light of their witness, no contemporary Christian should simply assume that Jesus clearly approved of the use of violence, even in defense of the innocent. Killing enemies to protect one's family, community, or nation may be morally justified (perhaps on nonreligious grounds), but doing so may well contradict the ethic of Jesus.

However, a significant shift in Christian thinking about war occurred in the fourth and fifth centuries, after Emperor Constantine began to use the Roman state to support the Church. According to an influential bishop named Eusebius, absolute nonviolence was from then on to apply solely to clergy, monks, and nuns; lay Christians could now be obligated to defend the empire with force.[43]

Ambrose, another important bishop of that era, thought that Christian love entailed a duty to use force to defend innocent third parties.[44] He also shifted the focus of Christian moral concern from the *act* of violence to the *attitude* of the agent: Christian soldiers should love their enemies even while using deadly force against them (a psychological state that I doubt is really possible in close combat).[45] In effect, Ambrose "baptized" ancient Roman patriotism and military virtues of courage, fortitude, and honor to encourage Christians to inculcate them.

Augustine, who was influenced by Ambrose in many ways, recognized that Jesus had taught things that seemed to entail strict nonviolence, but like Ambrose, he believed that they applied to dispositions rather than to actions. Christians, in his view, are not only permitted to use force in defense of the community, they're obligated to obey such orders from higher authorities. Augustine also came to accept the use of force against heresy, believing it to be consistent with a benevolent desire of the Church to correct its wayward children.[46] He thereby tragically established a precedent for "Christian" intolerance and violence that would infect Europe for more than a thousand years, fomenting inquisitions, crusades, and pogroms.

However, Ambrose[47] and Augustine[48] also believed that there should be moral limits on Christian uses of violence. Even in cases where Augustine considered war to be the lesser of evils, he regarded all killing as ultimately tragic, always requiring an attitude of mourning and regret on the part of Christians. Partly due to his influence throughout most of the medieval period, killing in war was considered a very serious sin: If a Christian soldier killed an enemy soldier, even in a war that his bishops had ruled to be just, he would have to do penance for the killing, often by fasting and prayer for a year or more.[49] (Recall a similar belief in Buddhism.)

We can also see Christian roots[50] of the modern principle of noncombatant immunity develop during the medieval period, when secular military ideals of chivalry combined with Christian decrees of protection for clergy, peasants, women, and others who usually did not take part in combat.[51] Thomas Aquinas added another important ethical consideration in stipulating that Christians may only use the minimal force needed to save lives from unjust attack,[52] an early version of the *jus in bello* principle of proportionality.

But the medieval period also witnessed the emergence of total war in the name of Christianity. First there was increasing glorification of the Christian knight and growing identification of military courage and honor with Christian virtue (though that originated with Ambrose, as indicated ealier). Consider how this German poem of the period drew on John's story of Jesus' arrest:

> Then boiled with wrath
> The swift sword wielder
> Simon Peter.
> Speechless he,
> Grieved his heart that any sought to bind his Master,
> Grim the knight faced boldly the servants,
> Shielding his Suzerain,
> Not craven his heart,
> Lightning swift unsheathed his sword,
> Strode to the first foe,
> Smote a strong stroke,
> Clave with the sharp blade
> On the right side the ear from Malchus.[53]

The glorification of Peter here is rather ironic, in that (as we've seen) most of the gospels report Jesus as rebuking his disciple for using his sword, but the poem no doubt stirred its audience to imagine that if they had been with Jesus at his arrest, they might have hoped to have the disciple's courage and sense of moral outrage.

Now, military courage and honor by themselves might help to reinforce *limits* on war conduct, for example, in protecting noncombatants from gratuitous harm, but many of the traditional restraints on war advocated by the Church started to erode in the medieval period.

In the ninth century, the Vatican declared that death in battle could be spiritually beneficial for Christian soldiers: Their sins could be erased if they died in defense of the Church, and they would be guaranteed entry into heaven.[54] (A similar belief developed in Islam, as we'll see.)

Ken Ringle has described some additional factors that led to the period of the Crusades:

> European Christians had been making pilgrimages to the Holy Land since the 4th century. Generally they were unmolested, but things changed abruptly in 1009, when the caliph of Egypt [its Muslim political/religious leader], in a fit of madness, ordered the destruction of the Holy Sepulcher in Jerusalem, where Christians believe Jesus was [temporarily] entombed. For much of the rest of the century, Christian pilgrims were sporadically set upon, first by Arabs, then by Muslim Turks who replaced the Arabs as rulers of Syria and Palestine.[55]

In the year 1095, apparently in response to a request for aid from the Byzantine Emperor against his Muslim enemies, Pope Urban II launched what later came to be called the First Crusade, urging Frankish knights to rescue the Holy Land from its infidel occupiers. The Pope was quoted by witnesses to his speech as referring to Muslims as a "vile race" and an "unclean nation" who had polluted Christian holy places; moreover, killing Muslims became a way for Christians to obtain remission of their sins.[56] Moral rules governing the conduct of war were abandoned: No one was immune from attack by Christian crusaders; captured Muslim soldiers and defenseless civilians were indiscriminately slaughtered. Even Jews in Germany were massacred by crusaders on their way to Palestine.[57]

Thus, ironically and tragically, a religion that began with the largely nonviolent teachings and example of Jesus evolved in its first millennium to the point where Christians were waging total, indiscriminate war against their enemies. In the wake of a later series of devastating wars in Europe between Catholics and Protestants, such Christians as Francisco de Vitoria concluded that mere difference of religion should no longer be considered just cause for war.[58] Most Christians today find total war morally repugnant, of course, especially if waged in the name of God. Some even continue in the ancient path of pacifism in obedience to Jesus' sayings on love of enemies and nonretaliation against evil.[59] But total holy war against infidels also remains a continuing temptation for Christians.[60]

ISLAM

The Qur'an, the most sacred Muslim text, repeatedly refers to God as compassionate and just. It also insists that "there is no compulsion in religion" (2:256), meaning that authentic submission to God must be freely and sincerely chosen, not forced.[61] (The word "Islam" means submission.) The Qur'an urges Muslims to use "beautiful preaching" to persuade people to accept Islam and to "argue nicely" with Jews and Christians who are seen as worshipping the same God as their own (16:125, 29:46).[62]

Those ideas taken in isolation might tend to preclude holy war, and perhaps even ground a pacifist prohibition of war entirely. Indeed, the Prophet Muhammad was said to have practiced nonviolence during the first twelve years of his prophetic career, even in the face of serious persecution by polytheists in Mecca.[63] The Prophet's stance during that early Meccan period eventually served as the model for a nonviolent Islamic movement in twentieth-century Afghanistan led by Abdul Ghaffar Khan, a friend and admirer of Gandhi.[64]

But after the Prophet's emigration to Yathrib (Medina) in 622, he came to believe that God permitted and even commanded the use of force in defense of his growing religious community. (Unlike Jesus, Muhammad not only inspired and led a new religious movement, he also became a civil lawmaker, an administrator, a diplomat, and a military commander.) Qur'an 22:39–40 says, "Permission is given to those who fight because they have been wronged . . . unjustly expelled from their homes only because they say, 'Our Lord is Allah.'"[65] Like the Hebrew Bible, the Qur'an mandates capital punishment for certain offenses, though it also urges mercy and forgiveness in other cases. Muhammad often urged diplomacy rather than war to resolve disputes.[66]

Furthermore, certain verses in the Qur'an and other sayings of the Prophet seemed to go beyond defensive and retributive uses of force to permit *offensive* jihad to expand the territory of Islam. Qur'an 9:5 says, "[K]ill the idolaters wherever you find them, and seize them, beleaguer them, and lie in wait for them in every stratagem (of war)." Qur'an 9:73 exclaims, "O Prophet! Strive against the unbelievers and the dissenters, and be ruthless with them." Although some early Muslim jurists (such as Shaybani) interpreted Qur'an 2:190 to mean "Don't initiate hostilities," analogous to a *jus ad bellum* prohibition on offensive/aggressive war, the dominant interpretation of that verse became "Don't transgress limits" or "Don't exceed the bounds," which is more vague but understood as "Don't violate traditional standards of conduct in war" (*jus in bello*), not as a ban on offensive war.[67]

The root meaning of the Arabic word *jihad*, by the way, is effort, striving, or struggle. Jihad can refer to the struggle of the individual Muslim to conform his or her will to Allah's, or to a peaceful effort to persuade others to accept Islam. But jihad can also mean holy war. In fact, there's a sense in which the only completely just war in Islamic terms is a holy war, since it has to be approved by proper religious authorities and waged to defend or promote Islam or the Muslim community.[68] And very early in the developing tradition, Muslim soldiers who died in defense of the faith were praised as martyrs and promised the benefits of Paradise.[69]

In spite of the Qur'anic statement against forcing religion on others, Muslim leaders have sometimes threatened to kill unbelievers if they did not accept Islam. Muhammad himself was said to condemn Muslims to death if they abandoned their faith. Some of the early Muslim raids out of Medina against trading caravans are hard to interpret as strictly defensive, and although Islam eventually spread to such parts of the world as Indonesia mainly by means of "beautiful preaching," much of its expansion elsewhere was due to offensive war, first by Muhammad to unify Arabia, then by his successors in conquering Palestine, Syria, Persia, Egypt, North Africa, Spain, Sicily, and so forth.[70] In fact, for centuries the caliphs were expected to wage offensive jihad at least once a year.[71]

However, Islam adopted moral limits on war conduct similar to Christian *jus in bello* very early in its history, in part because Muslim military leaders were able to draw upon some pre-Islamic principles of Arab chivalry against killing defenseless people. Muhammad and his successors insisted that women, children, and the elderly were not to be intentionally killed in battle, though they could be enslaved; monks, nuns, and the disabled were also to be spared.[72] In other words, Islamic holy wars were never supposed to be total wars involving indiscriminate killing and scorched-earth tactics, in spite of what the contemporary leaders of Al Qaeda, Hamas, or Hizbollah might say to the contrary.[73]

Conversely, Muslim military leaders were explicitly permitted by Muhammad to kill all captured enemy soldiers and most adult male civilians if they were polytheists or even if they were Jews or Christians but had fought rather than agreed to pay the poll tax. In practice, post-battle mass-slaughter seems to have been rare, but that might have been due not only to chivalrous or humanitarian scruples against killing the defenseless but also to the practical advantages of keeping alive a fresh supply of slaves, sources of long-term tax revenue or potential recruits into Muslim armies.[74] In any case, Islam traditionally did not affirm a *comprehensive* principle of noncombatant immunity. Also, if civilians were likely to be killed in attacks on military areas, Muslim ethics permitted that as regrettable but necessary "collateral damage"—in fact, the moral blame was said to rest entirely on the enemy leaders for putting their citizens in harm's way.[75]

But many contemporary Muslim officials and imams strongly advocate noncombatant immunity, as well as a duty to minimize harm to civilians in otherwise legitimate military attacks, that is, *jus in bello* proportionality. Such leaders have also condemned terrorism committed in the name of Allah, including the 9-11 attacks against the United States. For example, Abdulaziz Al-Ashaykh, the chief religious leader of Saudi Arabia, declared on 15 September 2001, "[T]he recent developments in the United States, including hijacking planes, terrorizing innocent people, and shedding blood, constitute a form of injustice that cannot be tolerated by Islam, which views them as gross crimes and sinful acts." Similarly, Muhammad al-Sabil, a member of the Saudi Council of Senior Religious Scholars, stated a few months later, "Any attack on innocent people is unlawful and contrary to *shari'a* (Islamic law). . . . Muslims must safeguard the lives, honor, and property of Christians and Jews. Attacking them contradicts *shari'a*."[76] Nevertheless, the contemporary challenge facing moderate Muslims to counter the misguided ethic of Muslim extremists can hardly be overestimated,[77] especially in regard to the bizarre distortion of Islamic martyrdom in the cult of "suicide bombers."[78]

CONCLUSION

Tragically, some advocates of aggressive religious war can still be found today in all of the world's major religions. What they cannot legitimately claim, though, is that their position is *the* authentic expression of their faith: Each of the traditions I've discussed contains ethical principles that are incompatible with total war.

But in order for members of those faith communities to continue to believe that God is *compassionate and just*, they must repudiate claims and values in their own scriptures and traditions that are incompatible with those ideas. That may seem sacrilegious, but in fact it does not blaspheme or insult God to believe that God's actions are limited by objective moral principles. To say that God would *never* condone or command total war, cruelty, or the intentional killing of innocent people does not represent a significant limit on God's power; furthermore, if God truly is compassionate and just, then attributing indiscriminate slaughter to God or God's commands, even when such ideas originate in scripture, strikes me as itself a kind of blasphemy.

All members of the U.S. military, like any other country's soldiers bound to uphold the Geneva Conventions, are strictly prohibited from directly and intentionally harming noncombatants. But imagine that some military personnel were to believe (based on biblical stories like those in Joshua) that God has at one time or another ordered the mass killing of noncombatants: In principle, they must also believe that God might do so again (unless they think that God's moral character can change, which seems unlikely), indeed, that in theory God might someday order *them* personally to slaughter noncombatants (for being tainted by idolatry, say). But since obeying that kind of divine command would violate their obligations under the laws of armed conflict, why should the American people trust anyone holding such beliefs about God to uphold their constitutional oath whenever it might conflict with divine orders? When someone swears to uphold the U.S. Constitution, they may not secretly cross their fingers on the chance that God might order them to violate that oath.

To put the question more starkly and broadly, how can any of us consistently condemn and combat terrorism if we believe that God has practiced and mandated terrorism?

I sincerely hope that people of many different faiths as well as those of no religious faith might concur with the following ethical principles and rules, though some will not be acceptable to strict pacifists:

1. All people have a prima facie right not to be killed. This right can only be forfeited if they intentionally try to kill innocent people or while they are combatants in war.
2. Given the immense destruction and loss of life that war usually brings, all nonviolent means of realistically achieving just objectives should first be attempted.
3. War should only be waged when necessary to protect the rights and welfare of the innocent.
4. Innocent civilians should not be directly targeted.
5. Weapons and tactics should not be used against military targets in ways that are certain to cause civilian casualties, unless that is the only way to protect one's own soldiers or civilians. Even then, harms to enemy civilians should be minimized.
6. Captured soldiers should not be tortured or summarily executed but treated humanely.
7. Each side should be held accountable for any atrocities committed by its military forces.

Similar principles and rules arose out of the Western just-war tradition and have been incorporated into such international treaties as the Hague, Geneva, and Torture conventions. But as I have suggested throughout this chapter, such principles and rules are not unique to the West or Christianity in particular: Every major religious tradition has developed comparable ones. It ought to be possible for people of all faiths to work in concert to implement them, without first having to agree on which views of God are best. In fact, when Christian armies and Muslim armies, for example, have clashed in the past, they have typically not resorted to total war, but rather more often have showed mercy toward civilians and captured soldiers, respected truce agreements, and even expressed admiration for heroism and generosity displayed by the other side. And today, the 194 nations that are parties to the Geneva Conventions represent cultures spanning the full spectrum of major religious traditions: Hindu, Buddhist, Jewish, Christian, and Muslim.[79]

The just-war tradition rejects strict pacifism as insufficient to protect the innocent from unjust attack, but just-war rules, at least when applied in a careful and honest way, also guard against total war waged in the name of religion or any other cause. Religious communities can help ensure that political and military leaders abide by these rules and inculcate respect for them in the training and management of soldiers. But just as importantly, faith communities can nurture firmly rooted habits and dispositions of compassion and nonviolence, reducing the likelihood and severity of war by dispelling the ignorance, fear, and hatred that too often inspire and escalate it.

NOTES

1. Biblical quotes in this essay are from *The New Oxford Annotated Bible: New Revised English Bible with the Apocrypha* (New York: Oxford University Press, 2001), and *The Oxford Study Bible: Revised English Bible with the Apocrypha* (New York: Oxford University Press, 1989).

2. Although that question is foundational to the ethics of war (in that if the answer were a categorical "No" then war would be absolutely forbidden),

the scope of the question clearly goes well beyond war. A comprehensive treatment of it (which I will not attempt here) would necessitate exploring capital punishment, euthanasia, abortion, meat-eating versus vegetarianism, and so forth.

3. Richard Wrangham and Dale Peterson, *Demonic Males: Apes and the Origins of Human Violence* (Boston: Houghton Mifflin, 1996).

4. J. Glenn Gray, *The Warriors: Reflections on Men in Battle* (New York: Harcourt, Brace, 1959; Lincoln: University of Nebraska Press, 1998), ch. 5, "Images of the Enemy," offers many relevant insights.

5. John Ferguson, *War and Peace in the World's Religions* (New York: Oxford University Press, 1978), provided a lengthier overview of each tradition than I can afford to offer here. Roland Bainton, *Christian Attitudes toward War and Peace* (Nashville, Tenn.: Abingdon, 1960), focused primarily on one tradition but in considerably greater historical detail. *Ethics and Weapons of Mass Destruction: Religious and Secular Perspectives*, eds. Sohail Hashmi and Steven Lee (New York: Cambridge University Press, 2004), is an excellent contemporary anthology, reflecting the tremendous amount of scholarship that has occurred since Ferguson and Bainton. In this chapter, I often take scripture and other religious sources at face value for my ethical analysis, thereby ignoring some crucial historical questions like whether such figures as Joshua, Jesus, Muhammad, or Pope Urban II actually said or did what has been attributed to them.

6. Klaus Klostermaier, "*Himsa* and *Ahimsa* Traditions in Hinduism," in *The Pacifist Impulse in Historical Perspective*, ed. Harvey Dyck (Toronto: University of Toronto Press, 1996), 227–39.

7. As the ethic and example of each of these men suggest, pacifism should not be equated with passivity. Ferguson, *War and Peace in the World's Religions*, 36–40, helpfully summarized Gandhi's philosophy and practice of nonviolent civil disobedience (which strongly influenced Martin Luther King Jr.). Many influential Buddhist pacifists are described in Peter Harvey, *An Introduction to Buddhist Ethics* (New York: Cambridge University Press, 2000), ch. 6.

8. Mahatma Gandhi, "On *Ahimsa*" and "Nonviolence," in his *Selected Political Writings*, ed. Dennis Dalton (Indianapolis, Ind.: Hackett, 1996), 40–41.

9. *Ayaramgasutta*, cited in Ferguson, *War and Peace in the World's Religions*, 32.

10. Harvey, *An Introduction to Buddhist Ethics*, ch. 6. See also David Chappell, "Buddhist Perspectives on Weapons of Mass Destruction," in *Ethics and Weapons of Mass Destruction*, ed. Hashmi and Lee, 214–17.

11. Cited in Ferguson, *War and Peace in the World's Religions*, 58.

12. Theodore Koontz, "Christian Nonviolence: An Interpretation," in *The Ethics of War and Peace: Religious and Secular Perspectives*, ed. Terry Nardin (Princeton, N.J.: Princeton University Press, 1996), 170. Mennonite ethicist John Howard Yoder defended a similar point in many of his books.

13. School of Youth for Social Service, South Vietnam, ca. 1967, quoted in Chappell, "Buddhist Perspectives on Weapons of Mass Destruction," 232.

14. Harvey, *An Introduction to Buddhist Ethics*, 11–31.

15. Manfred Steger, *Gandhi's Dilemma: Nonviolent Principles and Nationalist Power* (New York: St. Martin's, 2000), 141–55, 170.

16. Klostermaier, "*Himsa* and *Ahimsa* Traditions in Hinduism," 228, 231–33.

17. Katherine Young, "Hinduism and the Ethics of Weapons of Mass Destruction," in *Ethics and Weapons of Mass Destruction*, ed. Hashmi and Lee, 277–307.

18. Klostermaier, "*Himsa* and *Ahimsa* Traditions in Hinduism," 230–31; Ferguson, *War and Peace in the World's Religions*, 31.

19. Sun Tzu, "Debating Military Affairs," cited in C. A. J. Coady, *Morality and Political Violence* (New York: Cambridge University Press, 2008), 109.

20. Harvey, *An Introduction to Buddhist Ethics*, 249.

21. Harvey, *An Introduction to Buddhist Ethics*, 135–38.

22. Harvey, *An Introduction to Buddhist Ethics*, 255–70. For further details on militant forms of Japanese Buddhism, see Brian Victoria, *Zen at War* (New York: Weatherhill, 1997).

23. Dennis Dalton, "Introduction," in Gandhi, *Selected Political Writings*, ed. Dalton, 21.

24. In contrast to Hinduism, Buddhism, and Jainism, the Abrahamic faiths of Judaism, Christianity, and Islam have traditionally not regarded nonhuman sentient animals as falling within the scope of their rules against killing.

25. See Reuven Firestone, "Conceptions of Holy War in Biblical and Qur'anic Tradition," *Journal of Religious Ethics* 24, no. 1 (Spring 1996): 105–7. Most historians doubt that the ancient Hebrews actually engaged in many wars of annihilation against their immediate neighbors; the book of Judges suggests that they often tended toward peaceful coexistence.

26. Reuven Kimelman, "Judaism, War, and Weapons of Mass Destruction," in *Ethics and Weapons of Mass Destruction*, ed. Hashmi and Lee, 363–64.

27. Cited in Michael Walzer, "War, Peace, and the Jewish Tradition," in *Ethics of War and Peace*, ed. Nardin, 102. The chutzpah of the Talmudic Saul (admirable, in my view) in arguing with God has biblical roots in Abraham's attempt to persuade God not to destroy a city if that meant killing the righteous along with the wicked, and in Job's heretical questioning of God's justice in allowing innocent people to suffer and evil people to prosper. An excellent treatment of Job's righteous anger is John Wilcox, *The Bitterness of Job: A Philosophical Reading* (Ann Arbor: University of Michigan Press, 1994).

28. Michael Broyde, "Fighting the War and the Peace: Battlefield Ethics, Peace Talks, Treaties, and Pacifism in the Jewish Tradition," in *War and Its Discontents*, ed. J. Patout Burns (Washington, D.C.: Georgetown University Press, 1996), 1–30.

29. Broyde, "Fighting the War and the Peace," 1–30, and Kimelman, "Judaism, War, and Weapons of Mass Destruction," 367–78.

30. Walzer, "War, Peace, and the Jewish Tradition," 107.

31. Israel Defense Forces, "The Spirit of the IDF: The Ethical Code of the Israel Defense Forces," www.jewishvirtuallibrary.org/jsource/Society_&_Culture/IDF_ethics.html (23 November 2008).

32. See for example: Jacobo Timmerman, *The Longest War: Israel in Lebanon* (New York: Knopf, 1982); Tzvi Marx, "A Post-Hebron Letter to My Son Michael Who Just Went from Yeshiva to Basic Training," *Tikkun* 9, no. 3 (1994): 40–46, 95; Gidon Remba, "Jewish Ethics and the Palestinian-Israeli Problem," *Tikkun* 12, no. 4 (1997), www.tikkun.org/archive/backissues/tik0797/tik16.html (23 November 2008); Firestone, "Our Own House Needs Order," *Shma: A Journal of Jewish Responsibility*, December 2001, 4–5; Anna Badkhen, "Israel's Reluctant Reservists Torn: 'Brutal Campaign' Weighs Heavily," *San Francisco Chronicle*, 18 April 2002, A1; Wendy Pearlman, *Occupied Voices: Stories of Everyday Life from the Second Intifada* (New York: Nation Books, 2003); Saul Landau, "Israel Is Bad for Jewish Ethics," *Counterpunch*, 30 June 2007, www.counterpunch.org/landau06302007.html (23 November 2008).

33. The meaning of those verses is examined in considerable detail in Willard Swartly, ed., *The Love of Enemy and Nonretaliation in the New Testament* (Louisville, Ky.: Westminster/John Knox, 1992). I'm aware that there is an important and vigorous debate among New Testament scholars as to whether any of the sayings of Jesus in the gospels can be confidently attributed to the historical Jesus, but I'm not qualified to adjudicate that dispute.

34. C. John Cadoux, *The Early Christian Attitude to War* (London: Headly Bros., 1919; New York: Seabury, 1982), 244.

35. Later Christian interpretations of that saying of Jesus differed in curious ways: Tertullian saw it as forbidding any use of force by Christians, which is plausible in its context, though it seems on its face to be merely a prudential warning that the gospel writer imported from some other setting. Ambrose limited its prohibitive scope to killing in self-defense, even though the disciple in the story was defending Jesus, not himself. Augustine regarded the saying not as a comprehensive criticism of Christian violence but as an instance where Jesus did not specifically authorize the disciple to use his sword. Thomas Aquinas, who drew on John's gospel in naming Peter as the sword-wielder, claimed that Peter represented bishops and priests and concluded that Jesus was therefore only forbidding Christian clergy from bearing arms. Christian proponents of just war have usually felt compelled to acknowledge Jesus' hard sayings at some point in their arguments, but they have sometimes shamelessly ignored their obviously pacifist implications.

36. Tertullian, *On Idolatry*, www.newadvent.org/fathers/0302.htm (23 November 2008).

37. Tertullian, *Apology*, www.newadvent.org/fathers/0301.htm (23 November 2008).

38. Tertullian, *On the Crown*, www.newadvent.org/fathers/0304.htm (23 November 2008). Compare the equally strict precepts stipulated by another contemporary, Hippolytus of Rome: "A soldier in the lower ranks shall kill no one. If ordered to do so, he shall not obey. . . . A catechumen or a member of the faithful who wants to join the army should be dismissed because he has shown contempt for God." Cited in Louis Swift, *The Early Fathers on War and Military Service* (Wilmington, Del.: Michael Glazer, 1983), 47.

39. Origen, *Against Celsus*, www.newadvent.org/fathers/0416.htm (23 November 2008). See also his *Commentary* on Matthew 26:47ff., www.newadvent.org/fathers/1016.htm (23 November 2008): "We must beware of unsheathing the sword simply because we are in the army, or for the sake of avenging private injuries, or under any other pretext, because Christ's teaching in the Gospels considers all of these uses an abomination." Lactantius, in his *Divine Institutes*, similarly claimed that, "it is always unlawful to put to death a man, whom God willed to be a sacred animal," www.newadvent.org/fathers/0701.htm (23 November 2008). Thus, drawing from the creation story in Genesis 1, Lactantius inferred a different

ethical principle regarding capital punishment than the ancient Hebrews evinced in Genesis 9:6.

40. Tertullian, *Apology*.

41. Origen, *Against Celsus*.

42. Cadoux, *Early Christian Attitude to War*, 49–160, carefully examined the relevant writings of Tertullian, Origen, Clement of Alexandria, Hippolytus of Rome, Cyprian, Arnobius, Lactantius, and others.

43. Eusebius, *Demonstration of the Gospel*, cited in Swift, *The Early Fathers on War and Military Service*, 88–89.

44. Ambrose, *Duties of the Clergy*, www.newadvent.org/fathers/34011 .htm (23 November 2008). He even went so far as to claim in that text, "He who does not keep harm off a friend, if he can, is as much in fault as he who causes it"—a striking judgment, but one that I think unfairly equates a malicious, unjust attacker with a third party who might simply be lacking in courage.

45. Ambrose, cited in Swift, *The Early Fathers on War and Military Service*, 96–110.

46. See Augustine's *Letter to Publicola*, *Against Faustus*, *Letter to Marcellinus*, and *Letter to Vincentius*, all at www.newadvent.org/fathers (23 November 2008).

47. Ambrose, *Duties of the Clergy*.

48. Augustine, *Letter to Boniface*, www.newadvent.org/fathers (23 November 2008).

49. Bernard Verkamp, *The Moral Treatment of Returning Warriors in Early Medieval and Modern Times* (Scranton, Pa.: University of Scranton Press, 1993), chs. 1–2.

50. Except for Origen of Alexandria, whom I mentioned previously, I've ignored Eastern Orthodoxy here, partly because it apparently never developed a tradition of careful just-war analysis like the West's. According to Paul Robinson, "On Resistance to Evil by Force: Ivan Il'in and the Necessity of War," *Journal of Military Ethics* 2, no. 2 (2003): 145–59, Orthodox writers tend to use "necessary war" as a substitute for "just war," even though that dangerously conflates many important ethical issues in *jus ad bellum* and *jus in bello*.

51. James Turner Johnson, *The Holy War Idea in Western and Islamic Traditions* (University Park: Penn State Press, 1997), 102–11; Maurice Keen, *The Laws of War in the Late Middle Ages* (London: Routledge and Kegan Paul, 1965), ch. 11; Robert Stacey, "The Age of Chivalry," in *The Laws of War: Constraints on Warfare in the Western World*, ed. Michael Howard

and George J. Andreopoulos (New Haven, Conn.: Yale University Press, 1994), 27–39.

52. Thomas Aquinas, "Whether It Is Lawful to Kill a Man in Self-Defense," *Summa Theologica*, http://newadvent.org/summa/3064.htm (23 November 2008). A vivid if crude way of expressing that Thomistic rule might be, "Don't use a shotgun when a baseball bat will suffice."

53. Quoted in Bainton, *Christian Attitudes toward War and Peace*, 103–4.

54. Pope Leo IV, "Forgiveness of Sins for Those Who Die in Battle with the Heathen," and Pope John VIII, "Indulgence for Fighting the Heathen," online at Paul Halsall, "Internet Medieval Sourcebook: The Crusades," www.fordham.edu/halsall/sbook1k.html (23 November 2008).

55. Ken Ringle, "The Crusaders' Giant Footprints: After a Millennium, Their Mark Remains," *Washington Post*, 23 October 2001, C1.

56. James Brundage, *Medieval Canon Law and the Crusader* (Madison: University of Wisconsin Press, 1969), 149–54.

57. Multiple accounts of Urban's speech and the First Crusade are available at Halsall's online "Crusades" site, but even the eyewitness versions were apparently written a few years after Urban's call to arms in 1095, so their accuracy is disputed. Some scholars believe that Christian limits on war conduct at that time did not apply in wars against non-Christian enemies, which calls into question my claim that moral rules were abandoned in the First Crusade.

58. Francisco de Vitoria, *On the Law of War* (1539), in *Vitoria: Political Writings*, ed. Anthony Pagden and Jeremy Lawrance (New York: Cambridge University Press, 1991), 293–327.

59. Any list of prominent Christian pacifists in the modern era should at least include Leo Tolstoy, Dorothy Day, Martin Luther King Jr., and John Howard Yoder.

60. Martin Cook, "Christian Apocalypticism and Weapons of Mass Destruction," in *Ethics and Weapons of Mass Destruction*, ed. Hashmi and Lee, 200–210. David Kirkpatrick, "Wrath and Mercy: The Return of the Warrior Jesus," *New York Times*, 4 April 2004, D1, noted some particularly bloodthirsty visions of the fate of non-Christians in the popular *Left Behind* series of novels by Tim LaHaye and Jerry Jenkins.

61. Abdullah Yusuf Ali, *The Meaning of the Holy Qur'an* (Beltsville, Md.: Amana, 1989).

62. Reuven Firestone, *Jihad: The Origin of Holy War in Islam* (New York: Oxford University Press, 1999), 52, 72.

63. Sohail Hashmi, "Interpreting the Islamic Ethics of War and Peace," in *Ethics of War and Peace*, ed. Nardin, 152–53; John Kelsay, *Islam and War* (Louisville, Ky.: Westminster/John Knox, 1993), 21. Firestone, *Jihad*, challenged the theory that Muhammad's ethic evolved in the ways I'm assuming it did. He may be right, but I'm more interested in identifying pacifist, just-war, and total-war elements in Islam than in defending any particular story of how and when those ideas emerged.

64. Eknath Easwaran, *Nonviolent Soldier of Islam* (Tomales, Calif.: Nilgiri, 1999).

65. Firestone, *Jihad*, 53–54; Hashmi, "Interpreting the Islamic Ethics of War and Peace," 150.

66. Hashmi, "Interpreting the Islamic Ethics of War and Peace," 153, 155.

67. I'm grateful to Asma Afsarrudin for pointing out the early Hanafi interpretation of Qur'an 2:190. On the dominant interpretation, see Firestone, *Jihad*, 55–56. The translation of part of that verse as "do not exceed the bounds" is from John Kelsay, *Arguing the Just War in Islam* (Cambridge, Mass.: Harvard University Press, 2007), 107.

68. Kelsay, *Islam and War*, 34–35, 53.

69. Michael Bonner, *Jihad in Islamic History: Doctrines and Practice* (Princeton, N.J.: Princeton University Press, 2006), 72–76.

70. Bonner, *Jihad in Islamic History*, 58–59.

71. Johnson, *Holy War Idea*, 91.

72. Hashmi, "Interpreting the Islamic Ethics of War and Peace," 152, 161–63.

73. Kelsay, *Islam and War*, chs. 4–5; Hashmi, "Islamic Ethics and Weapons of Mass Destruction: An Argument for Nonproliferation," in *Ethics and Weapons of Mass Destruction*, ed. Hashmi and Lee, 321–52; Kelsay, "'Do Not Violate the Limit': Three Issues in Islamic Thinking on Weapons of Mass Destruction," *Islam and War*, 353–62; Kelsay, *Arguing the Just War in Islam*, 106–9, 141–50.

74. Bonner, *Jihad in Islamic History*, 84–93.

75. Ibn Rushd and Ibn Tamiya, cited in Rudolph Peters, *Jihad in Classical and Modern Islam* (Princeton: Markus Wiener, 1996), 31, 33, 49–50; Kelsay, *Islam and War*, ch. 4; Hashmi, "Interpreting the Islamic Ethics of War and Peace," 162–63.

76. Cited in Charles Kurzman, "Islamic Statements against Terrorism in the Wake of the September 11 Mass Murders," www.unc.edu/~kurzman/terror.htm. (23 November 2008). See also Caryle Murphy, "U.S. Muslim

COMPARATIVE RELIGIOUS PERSPECTIVES ON WAR

Scholars to Forbid Terrorism," *Washington Post*, 28 July 2005, A11. Murphy noted that American Muslim leaders had publicly condemned terrorism well before 2005.

77. Alfonso Chardy, "Palestinian Parents Step In to Stop Suicide Bombing by Kids," *Seattle Times*, 28 May 2002, A1; Neil MacFarquhar, "Muslim Scholars Increasingly Debate Unholy War," *New York Times*, 10 December 2004, A1; John Broder, "For Muslim Who Says Violence Destroys Islam, Violent Threats," *New York Times*, 11 March 2006, A1; Walter Pincus, "U.S. Working to Reshape Iraqi Detainees: Moderate Muslims Enlisted to Steer Adults and Children Away from Insurgency," *Washington Post*, 19 September 2007, A1; Katherine Zoepf, "Deprogramming Jihadists," *New York Times Magazine*, 9 November 2008, 50–56.

78. A good summary of the ideological roots of violent extremism in contemporary Islam, along with some recommended counterstrategies, are in Dale Eikmeier, "Qutbism: An Ideology of Islamic-Fascism," *Parameters* 37, no. 1 (Spring 2007): 85–97. See also Robert Pape, *Dying to Win: The Strategic Logic of Suicide Terrorism* (New York: Random House, 2006); Farhad Khosrokhavar and David Macey, *Suicide Bombers: Allah's New Martyrs* (London: Pluto, 2005); Mark Juergensmeyer, *Terror in the Mind of God: The Global Rise of Religious Violence*, 3rd ed. (Berkeley: University of California Press, 2003).

79. The International Committee of the Red Cross lists the Geneva Conventions and their state parties at www.cicr.org/ihl.nsf/ CONVPRES?OpenView (23 November 2008).

3

JUST AND UNJUST WAR IN SHAKESPEARE'S *HENRY V*

[N]ever two such kingdoms did contend
Without much fall of blood, whose guiltless drops
Are every one a woe

—Henry V, 1.2

Most of us assume that we have a basic right not to be killed. We might not consider that to be an absolute right—since that would entail strict pacifism—but rather what philosophers call a prima facie right (as explained in chapter 1). For example, we might be said to *forfeit* our right not to be killed if we commit a particularly heinous crime, like aggravated murder. Or we might *waive* that right if we suffer from a terminal illness and can't end our own life without assistance from others. And any right that can be forfeited or waived cannot be absolute. But we're certainly on solid ground in believing that we have to have very serious moral reasons to justify killing people.

In the Western just-war tradition, war is thought to be morally acceptable if it can satisfy certain ethical and procedural criteria, but that tradition also regards war as potentially causing so much suffering, death, and destruction that leaders must carefully weigh those harms against the goals they hope to achieve through war. Even if one's country has been seriously harmed, one's soldiers or other citizens unjustly killed by foreign powers or terrorists, leaders still face significant moral constraints under just-war criteria on what they may do in response. Having just cause to go to war, for example, does not permit one to wage total war.

How is William Shakespeare relevant in this context? Legal historian Theodor Meron has written:

> War provided Shakespeare with a dramatic vehicle through which his characters could highlight and praise such concepts as honor, courage, and patriotism. In addition, it was the ideal setting for an articulation of ethical and humanitarian attitudes toward war.[1]

In particular, Shakespeare's play about King Henry V of England,[2] loosely based on historical events in the early 1400s, provides an especially rich source of ethical issues in warfare and military leadership. In what follows, I'll explain how I've found Shakespeare's play to be helpful in illustrating specific just-war concerns.

JUS AD BELLUM: JUST CAUSE, RIGHT INTENTION, PROPORTIONALITY, AND LEGITIMATE AUTHORITY

Henry V was not only heir to the English throne but was also descended from a French king and had other claims to parts of France through other ancestors as well as some recent treaties.[3] At the beginning of Shakespeare's play, Henry is deliberating with his close advisors about whether his claim on the French throne is strong enough to justify his going to war against the French if they refuse to recognize him as their true king. Henry asks the archbishop of Canterbury for an assessment of his claim and warns him to be scrupulously honest:

> God forbid, my dear and faithful lord,
> That you should fashion . . . or bow your reading. . . .
> For God doth know how many now in health
> Shall drop their blood in approbation

Of what your reverence shall incite us to.
Therefore take heed how you impawn our person,
How you awake our sleeping sword of war. . . .
For never two such kingdoms did contend
Without much fall of blood, whose guiltless drops
Are every one a woe, a sore complaint
'Gainst him whose wrongs gives edge unto the swords
That makes such waste in brief mortality.[4] (1.2)

In this moving passage, Henry indicates that he is keenly aware of the high cost of war in innocent human lives, therefore the moral importance of sincere and careful appraisal of the reasons offered in support of war.[5] He later expresses great affection and admiration for his troops, for example, at the battles of Harfleur (3.1) and Agincourt (4.3), where he even praises the courage of the lower-class yeomen and calls them his brothers: "We few, we happy few."

In teaching the play, I've found it intriguing to compare Henry's deliberations with the advice of Francisco de Vitoria, who lived after the real Henry but before Shakespeare. Meron has doubted that Shakespeare knew the work of Francisco de Vitoria or other just-war theorists like Francisco Suarez or Alberico Gentili (though the latter were his contemporaries and Gentili even taught at Oxford), but Meron has inferred from the play that Shakespeare was quite familiar with existing laws of war as well as the customary ways in which royals deliberated about war.[6]

According to Vitoria, when a head of state is trying to determine whether there is just cause to go to war, "One must consult reliable and wise men who can speak with freedom and without anger or hate or greed. . . . [I]f he is in doubt about his rightful title [to a particular region, e.g.] he must carefully examine the case and listen peacefully to the reasons of the other side, to see if a clear decision can be reached in favor of himself or the other party."[7] Unfortunately, Shakespeare's Henry V has surrounded himself with advisors who are all biased in favor of war, and the archbishop whom Henry trusts to provide an objective opinion has a hidden agenda—to fund Henry's war in France in the hope of quashing a parliamentary bill that would have taken enormous tracts of church land (1.1).[8]

The archbishop effectively refutes the French argument against Henry's claim via his female ancestor (1.2), but he ignores the fact that there have been nearly 100 years of rule by another family line in France, making French nobles and commoners unlikely to want to shift their allegiance abruptly to Henry. Furthermore, was it realistic to believe that people speaking different languages and separated by the Channel could become a unified nation under Henry V? Shakespeare implies otherwise in his striking insertion of a comic scene in 3.5, with its dialogue almost entirely in the French language. The conversation there also focuses on words for body parts, which Shakespeare may have meant to hint that Katherine, the French king's daughter, would be treated as a form of property, part of the spoils of Henry's military victories, and there's an analogy drawn in 5.2 between virgins and fortified towns ("girdled with maiden walls"). Shakespeare may have intended these elements of the play to remind his audience that the French were conquered against their will and that Henry's invasion was akin to the rape of a virgin. Then again, it's tempting but quite possibly anachronistic to imagine Shakespeare as a feminist ahead of his time: Shakespeare and his audience may have assumed that Henry was merely taking what was his by right anyway, whether it was French land or the daughter of the French king.

Returning to Henry's initial deliberations about whether to war against France, his other advisors suggest that European monarchs will expect him to enforce his claims, as his ancestors did, and they appeal to his warlike courage and youthful desire to expand his power. None of them urges caution or careful consideration of French counterclaims. All of this has the effect of persuading Henry to go to war: "France being ours, we'll bend it to our awe or break it all to pieces" (1.2).[9]

He then receives a message from the French dauphin (the crown prince), who repudiates Henry's demands and offers in their place a "treasure" of tennis balls, an insulting reference to Henry's former reputation as a rowdy, irresponsible playboy. Even though it's not clear that this message was sent with the knowledge or permission of the French king, Henry is deeply insulted by it and says to the French ambassador:

> Tell the pleasant Prince this mock of his
> Hath turned his balls to gunstones, and his soul
> Shall stand sore charged for the wasteful vengeance
> That shall fly from them—for many a thousand widows
> Shall this his mock mock out of their dear husbands,
> Mock mothers from their sons, mock castles down (1.2)

Here Henry seems to have allowed a personal insult to cloud his objective moral assessment of *jus ad bellum*. His anger and obsession with winning the French crown overwhelm the more humane disposition he exhibited at the beginning of the scene, when he worried about war's "guiltless drops" of blood, "every one a woe." In just-war terms, he's not clearly satisfied the criteria of just cause, right intention, or proportionality. He's hurtling headlong into war.[10] (According to Peter Saccio, the tennis-ball incident never actually occurred,[11] but no matter, as it reminds us how personal animosities between national leaders can sometimes drive or exacerbate momentous international crises.)

Just before Henry leads his army against the French, an assassination attempt sponsored by them is uncovered (2.2). The real Henry V did indeed quash an assassination plot, but the conspirators didn't need French money to have a motive for deposing him: They sought to replace him with someone whom they believed had a stronger claim to it than Henry, due to his father's usurpation of the crown from Richard II. In other words, the assassination was rooted in a controversy concerning Henry's legitimate authority, not foreign intervention.[12] The only hint of this in the play occurs on the eve of the battle of Agincourt, when Henry prays that God will be with his troops and not hold his father's sin against him (4.1).

Curiously, Shakespeare doesn't portray Henry as holding a grudge against the French for trying to assassinate him, even though that would have dramatically strengthened his rationale for war. In other words, having invented a French role in the conspiracy to murder him, Shakespeare subsequently forgets all about it. In Act V, Henry treats the French king—the sponsor of his would-be assassins—with surprising cordiality as his new father-in-law.

After Henry lands in France with his invading army, his relative, Exeter, delivers an ultimatum directly to the French king, similar in its ominous tone to Henry's earlier retort to the dauphin:

> [King Henry bids you to] deliver up the crown, and to take mercy
> On the poor souls for whom this hungry war
> Opens his vasty jaws; and on your head
> [Are laid] the widows' tears, the orphans' cries,
> The dead men's blood, the pining maidens' groans,
> For husbands, fathers, and betrothed lovers
> That shall be swallowed in this controversy. (2.4)

Note that like Henry's retort to the dauphin's insult, and in contrast to his initial warning to his archbishop, with Exeter's ultimatum ("on your head") Henry has completely shed any sense of personal responsibility for the destruction that the war will cause. *All of its carnage will be the fault of the French.* Now there's obviously an important sense in which those who launch an unnecessary war are primarily responsible for the deaths that result. (I tend to see Henry as the real aggressor here anyway, not the French.) But it doesn't follow that the other side is not also accountable for at least some of those deaths. Rulers cannot use a righteous *jus ad bellum* to excuse their own indiscriminate killing of foreign civilians *in bello*, for example.

One additional topic relevant to Henry's authority to wage war and the justice of his cause concerns the conditions under which citizens must obey the order of their government to fight. This issue is wonderfully explored by Shakespeare in a conversation on the eve of the battle of Agincourt between Henry (in disguise) and some of his men (4.1):

Henry: "Methinks I could not die anywhere so contented as in the King's company, his cause being just and his quarrel honorable."

Williams: "That's more than we know."

Bates: "Ay, or more than we should seek after. For we know enough if we know we are the King's subjects. If his cause be wrong, our obedience to the King wipes the crime of it out of us."

Williams: "But if the cause be not good, the King himself hath a heavy reckoning to make, when all those legs and arms and heads chopped off in a battle shall join together at the latter day, and cry all, 'We died at such a place'—some swearing, some crying for a surgeon, some upon their wives left poor behind them, some upon the debts they owe, some upon their children rawly left. I am afeard there are few die well that die in a battle, for how can they charitably dispose of anything, when blood is their argument? Now, if these men do not die well, it will be a black matter for the King that led them to it—who to disobey were against all proportion of subjection."

Bates later pledges to fight "lustily" for Henry, but here he argues that because soldiers must obey their king, they can't be blamed if the king's reasons for going to war are unjust. Williams adds, though, that if the king's cause is truly unjust, he'll have a lot to answer for in terms of the unnecessary deaths of his soldiers and the effects on their wives and children. He also seems to imply that the Christian souls of soldiers are endangered in battle, perhaps because they can't maintain dispositions of Christian love and repentance while they're killing and thus may die in a sinful state. So even if soldiers are innocent in some sense, the king in effect forces them to incur a grave moral taint.[13]

These are important concerns that almost any soldier in combat might express, emphasized by Shakespeare with vivid and emotionally charged images. Unfortunately, the King's subsequent reply completely evades the issue of his responsibility in forcing his soldiers to kill and endanger their own lives and souls for a possibly unjust cause. Political leaders owe their troops much more careful consideration before placing them in harm's way.

Meron has noted an intriguing fact about Henry that Shakespeare apparently didn't know. After conquering Harfleur, Henry challenged the French dauphin to a duel, the result of which would determine which of them would rule France. Henry ostensibly sought to prevent further destruction, suffering, and loss of life that the war would continue to produce, which in itself would be attractive under *jus ad bellum* principles of proportionality and last resort. But the dauphin apparently never responded to the challenge, either because he feared losing his life to an older and stronger warrior, or because he would not wager the throne of France on such an unpredictable scenario, or perhaps because it would imply that the issue of just cause in that war was of no real consequence.[14]

JUS IN BELLO: NONCOMBATANT IMMUNITY AND PROPORTIONALITY

Under modern just-war criteria, soldiers are subject to being killed in combat until they surrender or are incapacitated by their wounds. The point is that combatants may justly be harmed only so long as they pose a credible threat to others. Most civilians pose no such threat and thus may not be intentionally killed except in rare circumstances (e.g., if and when they work in munitions factories); moreover, if civilian lives are thought to be at risk in legitimate military attacks, then officials must carefully consider whether the target needs to be hit at all. If so, it should involve the least destructive force necessary to do the job, to minimize "collateral damage." Those moral ideas are often encapsulated as rules of noncombatant immunity and proportionality and have been incorporated into such international treaties as the Hague and Geneva conventions. Even if our enemies do not hold themselves to those high standards, we cannot shirk our own responsibility to do so.

Of course, King Henry V lived well before the formulation in just-war theory or international law of a comprehensive principle of noncombatant immunity, not to mention technologies like satellite surveillance and smart weapons that help us to uphold such a principle. Many battles in Henry V's era involved sieges of fortified towns, which often led to horrific losses of both soldiers and civilians from indiscriminate weapons. Captured towns were also frequently subject to total annihilation.[15]

But even in Henry's day, it was understood that direct attacks on civilians violated Christian prohibitions on killing the innocent, as well as a secular code of chivalry among knights that ruled out intentional harms to defenseless people as unprofessional.[16] With that in mind, consider the frightening ultimatum[17] that Henry delivers to the fortified city of Harfleur, the first town that he attacks after landing in France.

How yet resolves the Governor of the town?
This is the latest parle we will admit [i.e., the last cease-fire we'll allow].
Therefore to our best mercy give yourselves,
Or like to men proud of destruction
Defy us to do our worst. For as I am a soldier. . . .
If I begin the batt'ry once again
I will not leave the half-achieved Harfleur
Till in her ashes she lie buried.
The gates of mercy shall be all shut up,
And the fleshed soldier, rough and hard of heart,
In liberty of bloody hand shall range
With conscience wide as hell, mowing like grass
Your fresh fair virgins and your flow'ring infants. . . .
What is't to me, when you yourselves are cause,
If your pure maidens fall into the hand
Of hot and forcing violation?
What rein can hold licentious wickedness
When down the hill he holds his fierce career. . . ?
Therefore, you men of Harfleur,
Take pity of your town and of your people
Whiles yet my soldiers are in my command,
Whiles yet the cool and temperate wind of grace
O'erblows the filthy and contagious clouds
Of heady murder, spoil, and villainy.
If not—why, in a moment look to see
The blind and bloody soldier with foul hand
Defile the locks of your shrill-shrieking daughters;

Your fathers taken by the silver beards,
And their most reverend heads dashed to the walls;
Your naked infants spitted upon pikes,
Whiles the mad mothers with their howls confused
Do break the clouds. . . .
What say you? Will you yield, and this avoid?
Or, guilty in defense, be thus destroyed? (3.4)

In sum, if Harfleur won't surrender, the English will do their worst and have no mercy. Henry's soldiers will rape women and slaughter infants and the elderly. He won't be able to stop them and doesn't much care to. In the end, he'll burn the city to the ground, and their destruction will be their own fault.

In the face of this ultimatum, Harfleur duly surrenders, and Henry then tells Exeter to "use mercy to them all." So was his ultimatum just a bluff? Possibly, since elsewhere (3.7) he set strict rules ordering his soldiers not to molest or plunder civilians and punished soldiers who broke those rules. In other words, he cared more about military ethics—and was better able to control his troops—than he let on in his ultimatum.[18]

On the other hand, his angry speech at Harfleur was consistent with his earlier threats against the French dauphin and king that innocent people would die if his rule in France was not accepted.[19] Meron noted an actual precedent for this in the year 1370, when the English massacred 3,000 unarmed French residents of Limoges after the town surrendered. After capturing Caen, Henry himself spared only its women, children, and priests; all other adult males were massacred. And in spite of his order in the play to "use mercy" against Harfleur, the real Henry expelled most poor people from the town.[20]

But even if Shakespeare intended for us to infer that Henry was bluffing at Harfleur in threatening atrocities, his ultimatum clearly went well beyond predicting "collateral damage" from his siege tactics. We might well question whether it was ethical for him to threaten something that would be immoral to do, even if the threat was intended to achieve a legitimate military goal. (Compare our possession of nuclear weapons as a deterrent against their use against us by other countries.)

During the battle of Agincourt, there is another powerful scene where marauding French soldiers are reported to have killed a group of English boys who had been assigned to guard the supplies (4.7). One of the English soldiers, outraged at the slaughter of the defenseless boys, cries that it's "expressly against the law of arms" and "an errant piece of knavery," implying a principle of noncombatant immunity, but no one, including Henry, evinces any regret or remorse at having brought the boys along on the campaign, thus placing their lives at risk.

Shakespeare's play also provokes ethical reflection on the proper treatment of prisoners of war. In the midst of the battle of Agincourt (4.6), Henry's army was well on its way to defeating a much larger French army, but he didn't yet know that, and fearing at one point that French forces were regrouping for a counterattack, he ordered his men to kill their prisoners. In the play, that line usually goes by so quickly that readers or viewers might completely miss its import, but Gary Taylor, in his scholarly edition of the play, claims that Shakespeare's original text gave an explicit stage direction, "The soldiers kill their prisoners," which when performed by the actors would have a much more powerful effect on audiences than simply hearing Henry's order by itself.[21] (Meron has pointed out that the real Henry V had to order his archers to kill the French prisoners because his own knights refused, either out of chivalry or because they would be unable to ransom their captives.[22])

Shortly thereafter, Henry demands that the French either renew the battle or "void the field," or else,

we'll cut the throats of those we have,
And not a man of them that we shall take
Shall taste our mercy. (4.6)

In other words, he'll renew the slaughter of prisoners and deny quarter to any other French warriors captured after that. (Unfortunately, Kenneth Branagh and Lawrence Olivier completely excised those scenes from their films of the play, perhaps because it would undermine their otherwise consistent portrayal of Henry as a noble hero.)

Today the international law of war explicitly prohibits the killing of prisoners:

> It is especially forbidden to kill or wound an enemy who, having laid down his arms, or having no longer means of defense, has surrendered at discretion. . . . A commander may not put his prisoners to death because their presence retards his movements or diminishes his power of resistance by necessitating a large guard, or by reason of their consuming supplies, or because it appears certain that they will regain their liberty through the impending success of their forces. It is likewise unlawful for a commander to kill his prisoners on grounds of self-preservation, even in the case of airborne or commando operations, although the circumstances of the operation may make necessary rigorous supervision of and restraint upon the movement of prisoners of war.[23]

But we might imagine ourselves in a situation similar to that of Henry V, commanding soldiers in the face of a much larger force. In spite of the strict legal regulations just cited, would it really be unethical to order that no quarter be given or that prisoners be killed, if we thought that our own soldiers were at risk of annihilation and we couldn't spare any of them to guard prisoners?[24] Granted that killing surrendered and disarmed soldiers is a horrific thing, bordering on murder, is it really fair to prohibit their captors from doing so in the heat of battle, if they have reason to fear that they themselves will otherwise be killed? These are questions I have often posed to my students in wrestling with the implications of the play.

NOTES

1. Theodor Meron, *Bloody Constraint: War and Chivalry in Shakespeare* (New York: Oxford University Press, 1998), 16.

2. Roma Gill's edition of Shakespeare's *Henry V* (New York: Oxford University Press, 2001) is an inexpensive version suitable for classroom use, but Gary Taylor's edition of the play (New York: Oxford University Press, 1998) is indispensable for teachers, due to the depth of his scholarly annotations.

3. Peter Saccio, *Shakespeare's English Kings* (New York: Oxford University Press, 2000), 75–79; Theodor Meron, *Henry's Wars and Shakespeare's*

Laws: Perspectives on the Law of War in the Later Middle Ages (New York: Oxford University Press, 1993), ch. 3.

4. Michael Walzer, *Just and Unjust Wars*, 4th ed. (New York: Basic Books, 2006), 52, used some of those lines to illustrate his point that, "Aggression opens the gates of hell."

5. John Mark Mattox, "Henry V: Shakespeare's Just Warrior," *War, Literature, and the Arts* 12, no. 1 (2000): 32–34.

6. Meron, *Henry's Wars and Shakespeare's Laws*, 10–11.

7. Francisco de Vitoria, *On the Law of War*, 307, 310.

8. Meron, *Bloody Constraint*, 21–27.

9. Mattox, "Henry V," 35–36, unfortunately ignored that ominous line in assessing whether Henry satisfied the criterion of right intention.

10. On this point I differ from Mattox, "Henry V," 34–35.

11. Peter Saccio, *Shakespeare's English Kings*, 80.

12. Saccio, *Shakespeare's English Kings*, 72–75.

13. On the need for medieval Christian soldiers to perform penance for killing enemy soldiers, even in a just war, see Bernard Verkamp, *Moral Treatment of Returning Warriors in Early Medieval and Modern Times* (Scranton, Pa.: University of Scranton Press, 1993), chs. 1–2.

14. Meron, *Henry's Wars and Shakespeare's Laws*, ch. 7. Meron, in *Bloody Constraint*, 88–89, noted an ancient precedent for this in Homer's *Illiad*, in which Paris challenges Menelaos to a dual for possession of Helen to end the Trojan War and save the lives of soldiers.

15. Meron, *Henry's Wars and Shakespeare's Laws*, ch. 6.

16. Meron, *Henry's Wars and Shakespeare's Laws*, 91–93.

17. An abridged version of this speech was delivered with chilling effect by the actor Kenneth Branagh in his 1989 film of the play.

18. Meron, *Bloody Constraint*, 158.

19. I don't believe that a close reading of the play supports Mattox's claim in "Henry V," 49, that Shakespeare sought to portray Henry V as a consistently just warrior.

20. Meron, *Henry's Wars and Shakespeare's Laws*, ch. 6.

21. Gary Taylor, *Henry V* (New York: Oxford University Press, 1998), 243.

22. Meron, *Bloody Constraint*, 119–20.

23. U.S. Army, *Field Manual 27-10: The Law of Land Warfare* (1976), 2.29, 3.85.

24. John Keegan, *The Face of Battle* (New York: Penguin Books, 1978), 108–12, connected that specific rationale with the killing of French prisoners at the actual battle of Agincourt.

4

ANTICIPATING AND PREVENTING ATROCITIES IN WAR

War is cruelty and you cannot refine it.

> —Gen. William Tecumseh Sherman[1]

I've seen my own men commit atrocities, and should expect to see it again. You can't stimulate and let loose the animal in man and then expect to be able to cage it up again at a moment's notice.

> —British colonel during World War I[2]

A warrior has to be ruthless in combat, but [also] have empathy.

> —U.S. Marine Gunnery Sgt. Hans Marrero[3]

WAR AND ATROCITY

If Gen. Sherman's claim (cited above) were true, then there would be no such thing as a distinct atrocity *in* war, because *war itself* and everything in it would constitute a cruel atrocity. It would also make no sense to condemn soldiers for any harms they inflicted on the enemy as long as the war lasted or to praise them morally for resisting the temptation to wage indiscriminate warfare. Those troubling implications ought to make us reconsider Sherman's generalization.

Now clearly the vast majority of deaths in any war are tragic in some sense. Even in the very rare cases when the only people who die in war are soldiers serving freely, their deaths are obviously still highly regrettable, since, apart from their honor, they were deprived of everything they valued and could have valued had they lived. From their perspective, dying in horribly painful ways from bombs, bullets, knives, gas, or fire, war must seem a cruel atrocity indeed. The families and friends of soldiers also suffer grievously from their deaths.

And there's an important sense in which an aggressive, unnecessary war is cruel and irresponsible on the whole for government leaders to start in the first place. Shakespeare's *Henry V* eloquently reminds us that war entails "much fall of blood, whose guiltless drops are every one a woe, a sore complaint 'gainst him whose wrongs gives edge unto the swords that make such waste in brief mortality."

But Gen. Sherman wasn't entirely correct: Not every case of killing in war is barbaric or cruel. We can and must "refine" war and insist that only some killing by our soldiers, and by enemy soldiers, is justified. We want them to kill only those who may legitimately be killed and to scrupulously avoid committing atrocities, for example, intentionally and directly killing unarmed civilians.

In fact, as Michael Walzer pointed out,[4] Gen. Sherman himself didn't really wage war entirely in the manner that his dark claim implied: Although his Union army devastated Confederate industrial and agricultural resources on its infamous March to the Sea, Sherman did not permit his soldiers to rape women, execute prisoners summarily, or slaughter civilians indiscriminately. But atrocity is sadly a common occurrence in the history of warfare. Is it inevitable? More broadly, how can social–psychological factors undermine ethical conduct in war? How might military commanders use the knowledge of such factors to minimize the likelihood of their own soldiers committing atrocities? The My Lai massacre provides a useful point of departure for our analysis.

WHAT HAPPENED AT MY LAI AND WHY?

On 16 March 1968, U.S. soldiers killed hundreds of unarmed Vietnamese in a set of hamlets known collectively as My Lai. Those general facts are well known to the American public even 40 years later, but many of the details of the massacre have been forgotten. One of the most thorough descriptions of what happened that day was narrated by British journalists Michael Bilton and Kevin Sim in their book *Four Hours in My Lai*.[5] Those authors also discussed some of the antecedent conditions that might help explain why it happened.

In chapters 4–5, they provided a nearly minute-by-minute account of the massacre. Rather than reconstruct their chronology here, I've found it helpful to classify the behaviors exhibited by the men of Charlie Company under the following eleven headings, ranging roughly from the most appalling to the most admirable. (Numbers in parentheses refer to the minimum number of soldiers and/or officers whose behavior at My Lai fit the categories listed, based on my reading of Bilton and Sim. Some soldiers' behaviors fit under more than one category.)

1. Gratuitous cruelty, mutilation, sexual assault (11)
2. Enthusiastic killing of noncombatants (3)
3. Shooting someone to "see what it felt like" (1)
4. Unfeeling, callous killing; accomplish the assigned task (8)
5. Shooting before determining whether someone's armed, for example, as they're running away (6)
6. Resigned or regretful killing; it's a dirty job, but we have to do it; "mercy killing" of wounded instead of applying first aid (6)
7. Agonized, strongly conflicted obedience (2)
8. Conscientious but covert noncompliance (10)
9. Active compassion, for example, aid to the wounded or urging others to flee or hide (3)
10. Open refusal to obey direct orders to kill civilians (5)
11. Active resistance, challenge, rebuke (4)

In sum, a few members of Charlie Company not only killed with enthusiasm but also raped and mutilated their victims. Others killed efficiently and without emotion, as if shooting infants and old people were just like any other task they might be asked to accomplish. Some killed initially out of fear but soon stopped in disgust or shame. Others went on killing even though they clearly felt anguished and sickened by it. Some showed compassion toward the wounded or warned villagers to flee. And some exhibited great courage in openly refusing to obey orders to slaughter clearly unarmed people, even when Lt. William Calley reportedly threatened to shoot them for disobedience.[6]

How were any of the men of Charlie Company capable of slaughtering unarmed civilians at close range? Did they just turn out to be more callous or cruel than the average American? Was it rooted in the particular nature of the war in Vietnam? Was it due to bad training or incompetent commanders? Are there tendencies in all or most people to do such things under similar conditions?

Bilton and Sim indicated that at least fourteen written directives had been issued by the U.S. Army prohibiting the killing of noncombatants by its soldiers in Vietnam.[7] Why then were those directives not always followed? What factors tended to undermine them?

Consider the tactics typically employed by the Viet Cong: using villages as bases of operation and fortifying them with mines and secret tunnels; dressing like civilians rather than in uniform; and attacking U.S. patrols from inside villages.[8] Such tactics tended to blur the line between combatant and noncombatant and threaten the lives of civilians.

But Bilton and Sim also raised serious concerns about the training that Charlie Company received. Briefings on respect for noncombatants were relatively superficial and often not taken seriously. A company sergeant claimed that he trained his men to obey orders without question and made it clear that disobedience would lead to serious consequences; he was actually *proud* of how his men performed at My Lai. Lt. Calley testified that he assumed all orders to be legal, only to be questioned (if ever) after they were carried out. Racist comments about the Vietnamese and warnings that none of them could be trusted were frequently voiced informally by officers and returning vets, undermining concern for Vietnamese noncombatants.[9]

The authors further questioned some wider strategies and tactics used by the United States in that war. The strong emphasis from the top on "body count" meant that there were constant pressures on the ground to meet the objective of a high "kill ratio" of Viet Cong dead to American dead, and since there was too often little real concern by superior officers to verify whether dead Vietnamese were Viet Cong, U.S. soldiers had an incentive to count *civilian* dead as Viet Cong and thus not to be very scrupulous about putting their lives at risk. Moreover, the standard U.S. response to sniper or mortar fire from Vietnamese villages tended to be massive retaliation with artillery and bombing runs, leading to enormous collateral damage. American forces also frequently designated large areas as "free-fire zones," ostensibly warning local civilians to leave but then subjecting those zones to indiscriminate strafing, shelling, and bombing.[10] These strategies and tactics almost inevitably led to violations of *jus in bello* criteria of noncombatant immunity and proportionality.[11]

Bilton and Sim also argued that many experiences of Charlie Company after they arrived in Vietnam made some sort of massacre almost inevitable. A formidable Viet Cong battalion was known to operate in and around My Lai; their weapons and tunnels were discovered in the hamlets. All of Charlie Company's initial casualties were due to mines, snipers, and booby traps, but because they received no advance warnings about them from the villagers, they grew to distrust and hate them.[12] Labeling people as Viet Cong "sympathizers" in effect led to their loss of noncombatant immunity.

Improper judgment and conduct were often exhibited by Charlie Company's officers. Capt. Ernest Medina apparently ordered his men to kill some fishermen, though they appeared to be unarmed. Prisoners were tortured and executed, some reportedly on the direct orders of Medina and Calley. Other patterns of brutality by the soldiers started to develop. Civilians began to suffer beatings and random killings inflicted by them. Some of the men became serial rapists of local women, without being subject to any disciplinary action.

And soldiers who were upset by these atrocities unfortunately did not openly object to them or report them externally. Immediately prior to the massacre, Lt. Col. Barker was said to have ordered My Lai to be "neutralized" without stipulating any limits on the treatment of noncombatants, and Medina was alleged by many of his men to have specifically ordered everyone in My Lai to be killed.[13]

But Bilton and Sim also insisted that none of these antecedent factors doomed any of the soldiers to carry out a massacre:

> Despite the brutalizing war, despite the horrendous experiences the men of Charlie Company had shared together, for each and every soldier there was a moral choice at My Lai. The men who refused to take part in the massacre were those who recognized the choice that they were being asked to make. But most men didn't.[14]

AGONIZED OBEDIENCE

Why did so few members of Charlie Company disobey clearly unethical and illegal orders? If we had been members of Charlie Company that day, what would we have been most likely to do? Would we have had the courage to disobey?

Most of us want to believe that we could not bring ourselves to commit such atrocities, but Stanley Milgram's book, *Obedience to Authority*, suggests that we may be wrong to assume such a thing. Milgram conducted a series of famous experiments in the 1960s in which subjects were led to believe that they were taking part in a study of the effects of punishment on learning. In fact, they were actually being tested to see how many increasingly strong electric shocks they would inflict on a total stranger, simply because a skinny man in a white coat told them, "The experiment requires that you continue."[15]

Now as you might imagine, Milgram's experimental subjects differed from Charlie Company in many ways: Most of his subjects were older. Some were women. The subjects were not encouraged to hate the person receiving the shocks and had no prior reason to resent him. They received no special training to inculcate a habit of strict obedience. The man leading the experiment seemed much less authoritative than a military officer, and there were no penalties for refusing to obey particular commands or even quitting the whole experiment, unlike soldiers who might face court-martial or summary execution for disobedience in combat. But these differences make it all the more puzzling as to why *most of Milgram's subjects obeyed completely*, inflicting what they believed to be potentially lethal shocks on a defenseless "learner."[16]

Milgram warned us not to infer from his experiments that most people deep down are really sadistic or cruel. In fact, one of his experiments showed that when people have a choice about what level of shock to administer, they overwhelmingly tend to pick very light shocks.[17] But Milgram's experiments are disturbing in showing that *most of us tend to obey authority figures even when asked to do something that deeply violates our conscience.* This is something we ought to find profound and disturbing, because it suggests any one of us might have behaved like Pfc. Paul Meadlo reportedly did at My Lai, weeping openly as he mowed down dozens of unarmed people with his M-16 in obedience to Lt. Calley's direct order.[18]

EMOTIONAL DISTANCING

One of the purposes of repetition in military training is to enable soldiers to react to deadly threats automatically, since taking time to deliberate about whether they should use their weapons can give the enemy the killing advantage.[19] Soldiers, like police, can be trained to improve their skill in assessing dangers quickly, even amid the horrendous noise and adrenaline rush they experience in combat. There is an understandable pride among members of the profession of arms in dispassionate killing with skill and technical efficiency ("one shot, one kill"). Something analogous to that occurs in such professions as medicine, where surgeons and other physicians learn to emotionally distance themselves from their patients in the interest of treating their symptoms more effectively, and society benefits from having professionals like those: We need the soldiers who protect us to be highly efficient killers of enemy soldiers, just as we need surgeons with cool nerves and steady hands. But there is an obvious ethical risk associated with this kind of professional expertise, namely reducing the killing of human beings to just another occupational task, lacking the emotional connotations that we would expect of such a morally grave act.

A young Marine named Rick Marks wrote to his family in 1966 that as a result of his training, "a human being becomes so unimportant, and the idea of killing a Viet Cong is just commonplace now—just like a job." This callousness, he said, "scares me more than being shot at."[20] Another Marine told Jonathan Shay that after killing a North Vietnamese soldier at close range, "I built up such hate, I couldn't do enough damage. I got very hard, cold, merciless. I lost all my mercy."[21] Lt. William Calley reflected in his 1971 memoir, *Body Count*, "I pictured the people of My Lai: the bodies, and they didn't bother me. . . . I thought, it couldn't be wrong or I'd have remorse about it."[22]

The experience of war itself can induce moral numbness. Col. David Hackworth, a decorated veteran of both Korea and Vietnam, wrote in 1989 that ground combat "is like working in a slaughterhouse. At first the blood, the gore, gets to you. But after a while you don't see it, you don't feel it."[23] Philosopher Nancy Sherman remarked on that experience of emotional detachment: "No doubt some desensitization is part of the psyche's survival system for facing gruesome evil up close. It is an adaptive way of coping with horror."[24]

Emotional distancing tends also to be correlated with physical distance: In other words, the farther one is from one's human targets, the less one is likely to feel an emotional aversion to killing them.[25] Dave Grossman noted:

> The link between distance and ease of aggression is not a new discovery. It has long been understood that there is a direct relationship between the empathic and physical proximity of the victim and resultant difficulty and trauma of the kill.[26]

When victims are anonymous and faceless, our emotional ties to them tend to be much lower than if we can see and hear the effects of our weapons on their bodies at close range. The prospect of firing long-range artillery or missiles or dropping bombs from high altitudes is rarely sufficient by itself to induce moral anguish.[27]

Again, there is social utility in having professionals like those who do their work in the most efficient manner possible, which sometimes entails killing the largest number of enemy soldiers with the smallest risk to U.S. civilian and military personnel, but we must be wary of losing sight of the prima facie right of people not to be killed and the gravity of any decision to kill. War must never be reduced to a merely amoral, technical, or instrumental endeavor.

AGGRESSION AND CRUELTY

The evidence and theories noted thus far help us to understand some or even most of the behaviors exhibited by Charlie Company at My Lai, but not the most aggressive and cruel of them.

Susan Brownmiller extensively documented the persistent problem of rape in war in her groundbreaking book *Against Our Will*. From the stories and data Brownmiller unearthed from ancient to modern times, she surmised a number of plausible explanations:

> War provides men with the perfect psychologic [sic] backdrop to give vent to their contempt for women. . . . Men who rape in war are ordinary Joes. . . . Victory in arms brings group power undreamed of in civilian life. . . . A certain number of soldiers must prove their newly won superiority—prove it to a woman, to themselves, to other men. . . . Stemming from the days when women were property, access to a woman's body has been considered an actual reward of war. . . .
>
> Defense of women has long been a hallmark of masculine pride, as possession of women has been a hallmark of masculine success. Rape by a conquering soldier destroys all remaining illusions of power and property for men of the defeated side. The body of the raped woman becomes a ceremonial battlefield, a parade ground for the victor's trooping of the colors. The act that is played out upon her is a message passed between men—vivid proof of victory for one and loss and defeat for the other.[28]

World War II veteran J. Glenn Gray noted other connections between destruction and pleasure:

> Anyone who has watched men on the battlefield at work with artillery,
> or looked into the eyes of veteran killers fresh from slaughter, or studied
> the descriptions of bombardiers' feelings while smashing their targets,
> finds hard to escape the conclusion that there is a delight in destruction.
> . . . Most men would never admit that they enjoy killing, and there are
> a great many who do not. On the other hand, thousands of youths who
> never suspected the presence of such an impulse in themselves have
> learned in military life the mad excitement of destroying.[29]

Joanna Bourke scoured the memoirs of U.S., British, and Aus-
tralian soldiers who participated in various 20th-century wars and
identified other disturbing ties in their experiences between acts of
killing at close range and feelings of exhilaration. Especially when
soldiers are coached to despise their enemies, take no prisoners,
and show no mercy (e.g., against Germans, Japanese, and Vietnamese), and after witnessing some of their comrades being killed or
maimed in combat, they often find themselves feeling tremendous
satisfaction after killing anyone on the opposing side, combatant or
noncombatant: "The same combatants who admitted on one page in
their diaries to feeling intense distress when killing another human
being would confess, elsewhere, to feeling immensely happy while
committing acts of murderous aggression."[30]

A World War I combat veteran wrote,

> I secured a direct [mortar] hit on an enemy encampment, saw bodies
> or parts of bodies go up in the air, and heard the desperate yelling of
> the wounded or the runaways. I had to confess to myself that it was
> one of the happiest moments of my life.[31]

Similarly, a Marine reflecting on his Vietnam War experience stated,
"I enjoyed the shooting and the killing. I was literally turned on
when I saw a gook get shot."[32]

Bourke further narrated harrowing incidents of rape, gratuitous
mutilation of bodies, and soldiers collecting enemy body parts (such

as ears, teeth, fingers, even women's breasts) as war trophies, all of which vividly reinforce the ultimate domination and humiliation of the enemy.[33]

In domestic life, we might expect to see such behaviors restricted to the minute fraction of society who become serial killers or rapists, but the conditions of combat can apparently elicit sadism from a larger percentage of the population. Of course, every era of human history contains incidents of indiscriminate slaughter, rape, and mutilation in war. So Bourke's data should by no means be taken to suggest that Anglo–American soldiers are any more prone to atrocities than are people in other cultures; indeed, theirs tend to pale in comparison with those perpetrated by Nazi Germany, Imperial Japan, Soviet Russia, the Khmer Rouge, Bosnian Serbs, Rwandan Hutus, Al Qaeda, Hamas, and Hizbollah.

OUR CONFLICTED GENETIC INHERITANCE

There is considerable evidence elsewhere that atrocities are not simply associated with culture (or military training programs), but that they have genetic roots as well, according to anthropologists and primatologists Richard Wrangham and Dale Peterson.

Picture a hunting-gathering tribe, living permanently in a region where there is no shortage of game or edible fruits and vegetables. A small group of husky males, sometimes accompanied by a female or two, regularly patrols inside the boundaries of the tribe's territory, usually in search of game. But occasionally they travel outside of their tribal boundaries, on the lookout not for food but for individuals or small groups from neighboring tribes. When they find them, if they perceive their own group to have the advantage in strength or numbers, they frequently attack those neighbors and *beat them to death*, without any provocation, and even when those individuals are former members of their own tribe.[34]

A few decades ago, such behaviors were believed to be exclusive to human beings; but they're now known to characterize tribes of *chimpanzees* as well, our close genetic relatives. When aggressive, warlike behavior among chimps was first observed in the early 1970s. It caused a tremendous stir because it suggested that our own tendencies to slaughter one another might have genetic roots and not simply be the product of an artificial culture that we might someday outgrow like a bad haircut.[35]

Wrangham and Peterson's theory about the origins of human and chimp aggression is complex and draws on data from many different scientific disciplines, but a condensed version of their argument is captured in the following train of quotes. In the prehistoric African savannah where our species evolved,

> Ecological pressures kept females from forming effective alliances. With females unable to rely on each other, they became vulnerable to males interested in guarding them. Males seized the opening, collaborated with each other to possess and defend females, and started down the road to patriarchy . . . where the males hold sway by combining into powerful, unpredictable, status-driven, and manipulative coalitions, operating in persistent rivalry with other such coalitions . . . to include unprovoked aggression. . . .
>
> Males have evolved to possess strong appetites for power because with extraordinary power males can achieve extraordinary reproduction. . . . [S]exual selection has apparently favored male temperaments that revel in high-risk/high-gain ventures. At the individual level, this temperamental quality can show relatively trivial effects. Men may sometimes drive their cars faster or gamble more intensely or perhaps play sports more recklessly than women. But the sort of relatively discountable wildness that, for example, hikes automobile insurance rates for adolescent boys and young men also produces a greater willingness to risk their own and others' lives; and that sort of risk attraction becomes very significant once men acquire weapons. And where men combine into groups—gangs or villages or tribes or nations—this driving, adventurous ethic turns quickly aggressive and lethally serious.[36]

In sum, the authors have concluded that our pride, desire to dominate others, tendency to draw arbitrary divisions between Us and Them, and related practice of waging aggressive wars against Them are deeply rooted in human evolution. Although Wrangham and Peterson don't believe that for that reason we're doomed to annihilate one another, they effectively dispel the myth that human nature is originally and fundamentally peaceful. We can't return to any Garden of Eden or Golden Age of human civilization, they claim; no human society has ever been free of aggressive violence. We need to face the "demon" in our nature and cultivate mitigating character traits, democratic political institutions, critical ethical thinking, and moral imagination to limit its destructiveness.[37]

The good news is that, along with tendencies toward aggressive violence, capacities for compassion, violence-avoidance, and reconciliation are also rooted in our genes. As William Damon has explained, emotions essential to morality, for example, empathy, shame, guilt, admiration, and outrage against injustice, begin to develop very early in children, in every culture. As their cognitive abilities increase, reason serves to refine their emotional judgments, and they develop the ability to imagine the rich and complicated thoughts and feelings of others, which is necessary to promoting their welfare appropriately. Rudimentary judgments of fairness expand beyond themselves and their immediate family and friends to encompass wider and wider realms of justice. Although all of these character traits and skills require reinforcement from others to develop properly, they're perfectly natural to people, in the sense that apart from a small number of psychopaths, the vast majority of our species are born with the potential to develop all of the moral virtues.[38] Incidentally, we also share some foundational moral capacities with our chimp relatives, including empathy and a basic sense of reciprocity and fairness, but that's another very interesting story.[39]

PREVENTING ATROCITIES

I'm convinced that U.S. military leadership, command climate, rules of engagement, and training are much better today than they were thirty or forty years ago in guarding against the risks of such atrocities as the My Lai Massacre. As a result, in the Gulf War and recent wars in Afghanistan and Iraq, our soldiers have almost always shown admirable restraint and humanity toward enemy soldiers and civilians,[40] but our contemporary military leaders at every level of command must not discount the perennial need to anticipate and prevent atrocities.

There will always be a small portion of human society that is deeply sadistic or sociopathic.[41] The military will continually need to screen out such people from its recruit pool and discharge any who get through that screen before they're deployed.[42] Perhaps we need to redouble our efforts here, to avoid sacrificing the quality of our troops to meet numerical recruiting objectives.[43] Commanders also need to be aware of the extremely aggressive violence that can emerge from otherwise gentle people and avoid inducing such hatred of the enemy in their soldiers that they are unable to regard them as having basic rights.

Sometimes even our best moral emotions can get us into serious trouble. We can vividly imagine what soldiers feel seeing close friends killed and maimed by unseen enemies day after day, but there's a fine line between legitimate moral outrage and blind, indiscriminate rage. We need to retain a valid sense of moral injustice but stop ourselves from lashing out in frustration against innocent people.[44]

Military leaders must avoid reinforcing a belief among their troops that every inhabitant of an insurgent stronghold, for example, is guilty of aiding the insurgents, that is, that no one is a noncombatant. Small children, at least, are always innocent, even if nobody else is,[45] and adults who might sympathize with our side are sometimes threatened by the insurgents with death if they assist our forces.[46] In any case, no officer or soldier is authorized to be judge, jury, and executioner of suspected insurgent sympathizers.

We also need to guard against the moral equivalent of negligent homicide of noncombatants. Commanders must take care to avoid suggesting any rules of engagement (ROE) that would permit soldiers to "clear" a dwelling with grenades or blind weapon-firing with no prior indication that combatants are present. In the wake of an infamous incident in Haditha, Iraq, in November 2005, some Marines claimed that such oral ROE existed,[47] though their printed

ROE cards stipulated otherwise: As Josh White of the *Washington Post* reported, "The Marine division's rules of engagement card in effect at the time in western Iraq instructed Marines to '*always minimize collateral damage*' and said that targets must be positively identified as threats before a Marine can open fire."[48]

Briefing troops on core values is important. They need to see their leaders take ownership of high ethical standards, that they're not simply parroting the party line.[49] Hypothetical and practical scenarios can be useful in teasing out the proper and improper applications of ethical principles and legal obligations.[50] Nancy Sherman has compellingly argued for the importance of acts of imagination in cultivating empathy and respect for the dignity, interests, and rights of others:

> Empathy may be a natural propensity. . . . But untutored, it can do no moral work. Military leaders, bound by the humanitarian laws of the Geneva Conventions, have a moral mandate to try to make it serviceable. Indeed, all soldiers, in swearing to uphold the Geneva Conventions, have indirect moral duties to cultivate the imaginative skills that underlie a capacity for the empathy necessary for dignitary respect.[51]

Realistic exercises are also important in eliciting the kinds of emotional states that can make atrocities *likely*, experiences that can then be the subject of reflection and discussion during after-action reviews. To quote a wise Army colonel who spoke at the Naval War College in 2003, ideally troops should be thoroughly trained "until they know what the right thing to do *feels* like."

Most importantly, leaders must keep a close eye on their troops' attitudes, emotional states, and stress levels before, during, and after raids and patrols. A colonel serving in Bosnia recognized his own vulnerability when he reminded a chaplain that, "the Army trains me to kill people and break things. Your job, chaplain, is to keep me from ever getting to a point where I *like* doing it."[52] Ideally, commanders should teach their soldiers to carefully monitor *their own* emotions and attitudes as well as those of their buddies, to look for warning signs of moral fatigue that can lead even decent people to commit atrocities: verbal expressions of indiscriminate rage, callous indifference to the deaths of civilians, unusually aggressive behavior, sullen withdrawal, and so forth.[53]

Finally, even the clearest code of ethics and the most thorough training programs can still be undermined by the wrong objectives, incentives, and pressures set by organizational leaders. U.S. Army general Peter Chiarelli warns, "One of the military's greatest strengths is its can-do attitude, but that attitude can be a liability when it causes us to take ethical and moral shortcuts to accomplish our mission."[54]

To illustrate, if military leaders tell their subordinates that their overriding priority is getting actionable intelligence about the enemy, and especially if they add that they don't want to hear any hand-wringing about "quaint" or "obsolete" laws or ethics, we shouldn't be surprised if those subordinates come up with very creative ways to make their commanders happy, things that even they might be embarrassed or ashamed to do in public. This is one of the lessons of the Abu Ghraib detainee-abuse scandal.

Part of being a responsible, accountable commander is providing clear guidance and monitoring how one's subordinates achieve one's objectives. This is especially important in situations that are highly complex and ambiguous, as frequently occur in the "global war on terror."

Chivalry and humanity in war conduct, even in counterinsurgency, are neither dead nor obsolete. We still need warriors who are effective killers *and* humane captors, tough soldiers who will nonetheless show mercy to the defenseless, every time.

NOTES

1. Gen. William Tecumseh Sherman, *Memoirs*, cited in Michael Walzer, *Just and Unjust Wars*, 4th ed. (New York: Basic Books, 2006), 32.

2. Cited in Joanna Bourke, *An Intimate History of Killing* (New York: Basic Books, 1999), 176. Bourke obtained that quote from a 1917 book written by two British officers, T. W. Pym and Geoffrey Gordon, *Papers from Picardy by Two Chaplains*, so I'm assuming that the unnamed colonel was British as well.

3. Quoted in Thomas Ricks, *Making the Corps* (New York: Simon & Schuster, 1997), 82.

4. Walzer, *Just and Unjust Wars*, 33.

5. Michael Bilton and Kevin Sim, *Four Hours in My Lai* (New York: Penguin, 1992). Americans were first apprised of the massacre in November 1969, through a three-part series of articles in the *St. Louis Post-Dispatch* by Seymour Hersh. The Army subsequently conducted its own thorough investigation of the incident, the events leading up to it, and the subsequent cover-up by officers at many levels; its findings were published in Lt. Gen. W. R. Peers, *Report of the Department of the Army Review of the Preliminary Investigations into the My Lai Incident*, 4 vols. (Washington, D.C.: Department of the Army, 1970).

6. A similar range of behaviors exhibited by German soldiers against Jews in occupied Poland was described by Christopher Browning in *Ordinary Men: Reserve Police Battalion 101 and the Final Solution in Poland* (New York: HarperCollins, 1992).

7. Bilton and Sim, *Four Hours in My Lai*, 16, 37.

8. Bilton and Sim, *Four Hours in My Lai*, 14–15, 31–32, 39–40.

9. Bilton and Sim, *Four Hours in My Lai*, 39, 53–55.

10. Bilton and Sim, *Four Hours in My Lai*, 13–18, 33, 36, 38, 44, 58–60.

11. Walzer, *Just and Unjust Wars*, 188–96.

12. Bilton and Sim, *Four Hours in My Lai*, 66–74, 83–85.

13. Bilton and Sim, *Four Hours in My Lai*, 21, 64, 76–83, 92–101.

14. Bilton and Sim, *Four Hours in My Lai*, 19.

15. Stanley Milgram, *Obedience to Authority: An Experimental View* (New York: Harper & Row, 1974).

16. Milgram, *Obedience to Authority*, 3–6, 14–16, 33, 41, 57, 60, 62–63.

17. Milgram, *Obedience to Authority*, 61, 70–72.

18. Milgram, *Obedience to Authority*, 179–89, where Milgram interpreted the My Lai Massacre in light of his experimental results. Milgram's insights in turn were employed in Browning, *Ordinary Men*, and Dave Grossman, *On Killing: The Psychological Cost of Learning to Kill in War and Society* (Boston: Little, Brown, 1995), 141–46, 187–91.

19. Ricks, *Making the Corps*, 81–83, 111–14. Marine recruits who successfully learn killing techniques are encouraged by their instructors with such compliments as "Good violence" and "Nice kill." See also Grossman, *On Killing*, 253-54.

20. Cited in Bourke, *An Intimate History of Killing*, 58–59.

21. Jonathan Shay, *Achilles in Vietnam: Combat Trauma and the Undoing of Character* (New York: Atheneum, 1994), 78–79.

22. Quoted in Shay, *Achilles in Vietnam*, 159.

23. David Hackworth and Julie Sharman, *About Face*, quoted in Shay, *Achilles in Vietnam*, 344.

24. Nancy Sherman, *Stoic Warriors: The Ancient Philosophy behind the Military Mind* (New York: Oxford University Press, 2005), 92.

25. Milgram, *Obedience to Authority*, 33–40, confirmed that insight in permutations of his experiments that varied the distance between "teachers" and "learners."

26. Grossman, *On Killing*, 97.

27. Grossman, *On Killing*, 102.

28. Susan Brownmiller, *Against Our Will: Men, Women, and Rape* (New York: Fawcett Columbine, 1975), 32, 33, 35, 38. See also Dorothy Thomas and Regan Ralph, "Rape in War: Challenging the Tradition of Impunity," *SAIS Review*, Winter–Spring 1994, 82–99, and Thom Shanker, "Sexual Violence," in *Crimes of War: What the Public Should Know*, ed. Roy Gutman and David Rieff (New York: W. W. Norton, 1999), 323–26. Rape as a terror tactic in war occurred frequently during World War II, Vietnam, Bangladesh, and Bosnia, and continues today in such places as Darfur (Sudan) and the Democratic Republic of the Congo.

29. J. Glenn Gray, *The Warriors: Reflections on Men in Battle* (New York: Harcourt, Brace, 1959; Lincoln: University of Nebraska Press, 1998), 51–52.

30. Bourke, *An Intimate History of Killing*, 362; see also xiv–xv, 1–3, 18–21, 171–80, 205, 211, 215–20.

31. Quoted in Bourke, *An Intimate History of Killing*, 19. Compare Grossman, *On Killing*, 234–36.

32. Quoted in Bourke, *An Intimate History of Killing*, 20.

33. Bourke, *An Intimate History of Killing*, 25–31.

34. Richard Wrangham and Dale Peterson, *Demonic Males: Apes and the Origins of Human Violence* (Boston: Houghton Mifflin, 1996), 12–21, describe many violent raids by chimps.

35. Wrangham and Peterson, *Demonic Males*, 21–26.

36. Wrangham and Peterson, *Demonic Males*, 232–35.

37. Wrangham and Peterson, *Demonic Males*, 242–47.

38. William Damon, *The Moral Child: Nurturing Children's Natural Moral Growth* (New York: Free Press, 1988).

39. Frans De Waal, *Peacemaking among Primates* (Cambridge, Mass.: Harvard University Press, 1989), and *Good Natured: The Origins of Right*

and Wrong in Humans and Other Animals (Cambridge, Mass.: Harvard University Press, 1996).

40. Colin Kahl, "How We Fight," *Foreign Affairs* 85, no. 6 (November–December 2006): 83–101.

41. Benedict Carey, "For the Worst of Us, the Diagnosis May Be 'Evil,'" *New York Times*, 8 February 2005, F1.

42. Benedict Carey, "When the Personality Disorder Wears Camouflage," *New York Times*, 9 July 2006, D3; Jim Dwyer and Robert Worth, "Accused G.I. Was Troubled Long before Iraq," *New York Times*, 14 July 2006, A1; Andrew Tilghman, "'I Came over Here Because I Wanted to Kill People,'" *Washington Post*, 30 July 2006, B1; Ryan Lenz, "'Homicidal' Soldier Was Returned to Duty," *Houston Chronicle*, 10 January 2007, A1.

43. Errol Louis, "Thugs Have No Place in the Military," *New York Daily News*, 11 July 2006, www.nydailynews.com/archives/opinions/2006/07/11/2006-07-11_thugs_have_no_place_in_the_m.html (23 November 2008).

44. For rich reflections on "warrior anger," drawing on insights from Aristotle and Seneca, see Sherman, *Stoic Warriors*, ch. 4.

45. Walzer, *Just and Unjust Wars*, 193.

46. U.S. Army colonel Doug Mulbury, who served more than a year in Iraq as a battalion commander, wrote in an unpublished paper ("The Ethical Challenges of Counterinsurgency Operations," for my ethics and warfare class in May 2008) that although he could "personally attest to the courage, composure, and restraint of our soldiers on countless contacts with the enemy," nonetheless he "had to remind the soldiers that the enemy often threatened, intimidated, injured, or even murdered any Iraqi who was seen to be collaborating with us" (quoted with the permission of the author).

47. John Broder, "Contradictions Cloud Inquiry into 24 Iraqi Deaths," *New York Times*, 17 June 2006, A1; "The Killings in Haditha," CBS News, *60 Minutes*, segment aired 18 March 2007, www.cbsnews.com/stories/2007/03/15/60minutes/main2574973.shtml (23 November 2008).

48. Josh White, "Death in Haditha," *Washington Post*, 6 January 2007, A1; Paul Von Zielbauer, "The Erosion of a Murder Case against Marines in the Killing of 24 Iraqi Civilians," *New York Times*, 6 October 2007, A8. On 27 December 2007, Staff Sgt. Frank Wuterich of the Marines was charged with dereliction, voluntary manslaughter, aggravated assault, reckless endangerment, and obstructing justice in connection with the Haditha killings. A previous charge of murder was dismissed.

CHAPTER 4

49. The need for military leaders to do that is recognized in *U.S. Army/ Marine Corps Counterinsurgency Manual*, that is, *Field Manual 3-24/Warfighting Publication 3-33.5* (Chicago: University of Chicago Press, 2007), ch. 7, "Leadership and Ethics in Counterinsurgency."

50. A fine set of fourteen cases with commentary is provided in Anthony Hartle, *Moral Issues in Military Decision Making*, 2nd ed. (Lawrence: University Press of Kansas, 2004), 181–227. A more extensive collection of cases, though mostly lacking commentary, is W. R. Rubel and George Lucas, eds., *Case Studies in Military Ethics* (Boston: Pearson Education, 2004.)

51. Sherman, *Stoic Warriors*, 177.

52. Sherman, *Stoic Warriors*, 119, emphasis added.

53. *U.S. Army/Marine Corps Counterinsurgency Manual*, 240.

54. Lt. Gen. Peter Chiarelli and Maj. Stephen Smith, "Learning from Our Modern Wars: The Imperatives of Preparing for a Dangerous Future," *Military Review* 87, no. 5 (September–October 2007): 14.

5

THE CIA'S ORIGINAL "SOCIAL CONTRACT"

Only those deceptive practices [that] can be openly de-
bated and consented to in advance are justifiable in a
democracy.

—Sissela Bok[1]

SECRET INTELLIGENCE AND AMERICAN DEMOCRACY

Few today would dispute the idea that the consent of the governed is a necessary condition for legitimate government, if not
a sufficient condition. Even illegitimate rulers pay lip service to the
concept of popular consent in designating their regimes "people's
republics" and the like. Yet if consent is clearly fundamental to the
constitution of legitimate political authority, it is less obvious how it
ought to impinge upon the day-to-day functioning of a democratic
republic. Of course, freedoms of speech and the press, free elections of representatives, and the separation of governmental powers
together ensure that the consent of the governed is not completely
taken for granted in governmental decisions and actions. Consent
must be more than tacit to be authentic. The deontological force of
the idea of consent undergirds perennial efforts to make democracy

more participatory, but this form of moral logic is not without challenges arising from teleological considerations.

For example, the sheer volume of information that must be absorbed daily by the U.S. government if it is to function with any competence or efficiency demands a highly diversified, bureaucratic division of labor. No single government representative can possibly keep abreast of the amount of information required to make a fully informed decision about every piece of legislation demanding his or her vote. This is doubly true for the citizen constituent far removed from those decisions—but conveniently so in an important sense, since if citizens could not delegate government to their representatives, many other important matters (e.g., science, the arts, private enterprise) would suffer from neglect.

We are also mindful that in all but the smallest and most homogeneous communities, consent must be filtered, distilled, and often compromised through various representatives within competing governmental branches to prevent manipulation of officials or policy by powerful factions, even majority ones. (That idea is at least as old in this country as *Federalist* essays #10 and #51.)

In short, a subtle but inevitable tension exists between the ideal of public participation in decision-making and the values of professional/bureaucratic expertise and efficiency. This problem was helpfully summarized by Elizabeth Gunn:

> Although the United States is not unique in its concern over the appropriate role for ethics in the administrative structure of government, our constitutional democracy is based on principles which, when juxtaposed with the authority and responsibility invested in the bureaucracy, produce conflicts and tensions yet to be fully resolved. The most fundamental issue seems to be whether . . . such democratic ideals as individual liberty, social equality, and public participation in decision making can be reconciled with such bureaucratic principles as expertise, discipline, hierarchy, and efficiency.[2]

This tension cannot finally be resolved.[3] The challenge of balancing the deontological principle of popular participation with the consequentialist principle of efficiency is always present in a democratic republic.

More difficult questions emerge, though, in consideration of the duties and powers of intelligence agencies. Here the overarching problem for a democracy is not information overload as much as information secrecy. The professional activities of intelligence officers are removed from our purview, not simply because as ordinary citizens we don't have the time, training, or expertise to carry them out ourselves, but rather because many intelligence activities, if they are to be carried out at all, must be carried out in secret, unlike the activities of most other government officials. The goals and tactics of covert action, the sources and methods of espionage, the conduct of intelligence officers—these are matters deliberately hidden from public scrutiny. Yet how could they not also be matters worthy of public debate and philosophical attention?

In a study of political propaganda, Murray Dyer argued:

> In a free society it is the right of a people to know on what terms its government may undertake, in the national interest, to trick, distort, suppress, arouse fear, or, at times, simply convey straight facts, but in a manner that keeps their significance from being realized by the general public.[4]

Unfortunately, many studies of intelligence that have had any intentional bearing on ethics or political philosophy have focused all too often on procedural questions about the proper degree of congressional oversight of U.S. intelligence.[5] Those are perfectly valid questions, of course: One is obviously justified in asking what the right of consent means in terms of institutional checks on executive branch abuses of power, but what has often been missed in such examinations is substantive ethical analysis of intelligence operations themselves.

One of the more influential misconceptions to have arisen in Western political philosophy is the idea that ethical principles are not appropriate to apply to "statecraft" or international politics, as if in doing so one makes a kind of "category mistake." Now it is clearly important to make conceptual distinctions between transactions involving states and those involving individuals, but those distinctions do not necessarily mean that ethical considerations are irrelevant to international relations. An international treaty, for example, is different in many respects from a promise made between individual persons. A treaty that ceases to be beneficial to a country is not necessarily accorded the same legitimacy as a promise that ceases to be convenient to an individual promisor, yet a treaty is a kind of promise, in that it demands of those who would annul it that they provide sound, convincing justification for doing so. Even the idea of a state's "national interest"—which might in fact serve as justification for breaking a treaty—itself bears moral weight, that is, an implicit appeal to the rights and well-being of the state's domestic citizens, though whether a state's action is indeed in its national interest and whether that conclusively justifies that action are frequently controversial.[6]

Similarly, although society grants to the state the use of deadly force in its behalf, it does not thereby accede to all possible uses of that force. The proscription of cruelty and excessive violence is as relevant to the relations between states as it is to the interactions between persons; moreover, although U.S. government employees—including intelligence officials—are bound to defend a particular Constitution, that Constitution is based upon certain universal principles—including the right of consent affirmed by the Declaration of Independence—which as such apply not only to U.S. domestic citizens but also to the citizens of foreign countries, especially as the latter are affected by U.S. government actions. Respect for the autonomy and consent of persons, whatever their nationality, implies that they not be coerced or deceived absent thoroughgoing ethical justification. The proper question, then, is not whether ethical principles apply to statecraft but rather how they should be validly applied to statecraft.

JUST-WAR CRITERIA

Among the many types of normative ethical theory that bear on international relations,[7] the tradition of "just-war" thinking may be seen to inform the approach taken in subsequent chapters on espionage and covert action.[8] In other words, I'm attempting to provide a structure for moral thinking about those matters analogous to just-war theory. I hope to achieve something similar to what that tradition achieved: a working synthesis of the strengths of both deontological and teleological principles in a manner that enhances public debate on foreign intelligence operations. Such operations, I suggest, can be justified under certain conditions resembling *jus ad bellum* criteria but are further subject to ethical constraints on its means, analogous to those of *jus in bello.*

The criterion of *legitimate authority* is implicit in my conception of government-by-consent. In this chapter, I argue that loyalty to a state should be contingent upon the legitimacy of that state, therefore treason against illegitimate states—and, by extension, espionage and covert action carried out against them by other states—can be morally justified. In the next chapter, I examine the origins, functions, and tactics of the Soviet KGB (Committee for State Security), illustrating the kind of regime against which covert action can be justified, in part due to its illegitimacy.

The criterion of legitimate authority is also closely related here to that of *just cause.* One of my intentions is to show that the nature of the Soviet Union and the activities of the KGB provided just cause for the United States to create and maintain the CIA's espionage and covert action capabilities. By contrast, a later chapter indicates how certain historical cases of U.S.-sponsored covert action were unjust, because they exhibited either insufficient consideration for the rights and well-being of the citizens of the target country or situations where U.S. national objectives were corrupted by narrow interests.

The *jus ad bellum* criterion of *proportionality* (including its requirement that war be the *last resort*) is also illuminating in this context. Both war and covert action are species of coercion, though obviously to differing degrees. The gravity of their effects upon a society demands that they not be employed until less problematic options have been tried or at least carefully considered. Thus, where it's possible to achieve a desired objective in a foreign country by other means, the criterion of proportionality would preclude engaging in covert action unnecessarily.

But espionage and covert action are usually not perceived to be as damaging and provocative as acts of military aggression and partly for that reason are not kept in reserve by states as measures of last resort. In fact, the cautious vetting[9] that ideally goes into the recruitment and handling of foreign agents demands that if such agents are to be had at all, they must be in place well before a crisis arises. Furthermore, in the case of a nation that poses a significant military threat to the United States or its allies, to forgo knowledge about its leaders' intentions that may only be available from human agents would be both foolish and irresponsible. In this case there is "just cause" for *not* keeping espionage as a "last resort." The use of espionage and covert action to reduce or eliminate the need for military force implicitly upholds the just-war principle of using violence only as a last resort.

Finally, the just-war criterion of *noncombatant immunity* is relevant to the need to calculate the consequences of espionage and covert action for affected persons and societies beyond the specific targets of intelligence operations and the agents ("combatants") involved, especially in the practice of interrogation when it may be unclear whether the detainee is guilty or innocent of plotting terrorist attacks, and so forth.

CIA COVERT ACTION

What is covert action? How did it come to be used by the U.S. government? What kinds of ethical arguments have been made for and against it? What strengths and weaknesses can be identified in those arguments?

The term *covert action* denotes the attempt by government agents to secretly influence the political climate of a foreign country. Discreet financial support of foreign political leaders, planting deceptive rumors or news stories to malign or confuse political adversaries, hidden sponsorship of coups d'état, "unattributable" assassinations—all are forms of covert action. (A later chapter examines illustrations of these types of covert action.)

Covert action has played a part in nations' foreign affairs for many centuries. Such ancient political manuals as the Persian *Book of Kings*, the Indian *Arthasastra*, and Sun Tzu's *Art of War* prescribe ruthless intrigue in the interest of their respective realms' stability and power. In the West, the usefulness of covert action in the service of political ends was affirmed in Machiavelli's recommendations of princely duplicity, the *arcana imperii* and *raison d'état* of absolute monarchs, and the conspiracy, propaganda, and repression of Nazis and Bolsheviks.[10]

However, covert action has not been only the prerogative of despotic regimes: Even in the early days of the United States, when fear of a tyrannical executive branch caused powerful legislative and judicial checks to be constituted, the occasional necessity of "perfect secrecy and immediate despatch" in protecting U.S. interests was nonetheless recognized.[11] Prior to Pearl Harbor, though, U.S. foreign intelligence operations were rather modest by Old World standards.[12]

Much of the credit for the conception and creation of an agency to coordinate U.S. intelligence goes to William Donovan, a hero of World War I, a successful Wall Street lawyer, and an energetic opponent of U.S. isolationism. In 1940, Donovan pushed hard for U.S. liaison with the British Secret Intelligence Service. President Franklin D. Roosevelt appointed him coordinator of information in July 1941, and then director of the Office of Strategic Services (OSS) in June 1942. The OSS served as the "unconventional" arm of the U.S. military during the war, primarily in Europe.[13]

Although Donovan employed many communists and former communists—"I'd put Stalin on the OSS payroll if I thought it would help us defeat Hitler," he said—he was also one of the first high-level officials to recognize the threat to U.S. interests that the Soviet Union was likely to pose in the postwar world.[14]

The Central Intelligence Agency (CIA) was created by an act of Congress on 26 July 1947. The CIA's covert action capabilities were born of the merger of OSS-developed guerrilla and propaganda tactics with the postwar aims of communist containment and rollback.

Historian John Ranelagh has suggested that initial U.S. trepidation about creating a peacetime foreign intelligence organization was off-set by growing concern over Soviet actions: refusal to conduct demo-cratic elections in the territories it controlled; refusal to contribute to reconstruction in Europe; maintenance of large occupation forces; obstructionism in the UN and other international organizations; evidence of its concerted efforts to subvert democratic processes in Western Europe; and guerrilla campaigns in the Balkans, Greece, and China.[15] In early 1948, a Soviet-backed coup in Czechoslovakia and the attempt to blockade Berlin convinced the White House that war with the Soviet Union was imminent.[16]

U.S. reaction to these ominous events was further reflected in National Security Council Directive 10/2 of 18 June 1948, which es-tablished an office of "special projects" within the CIA, arguing that "the overt foreign activities of the U.S. government must be supple-mented by covert operations."[17] The CIA's role in such projects was reinforced by a special report to President Dwight D. Eisenhower dated 30 September 1954.[18] Focusing on the threats presented by Soviet capabilities, actions, and intentions, the report concluded that the United States faced "an implacable enemy whose avowed objective is world domination by whatever means and at whatever cost." In a passage that has become virtually notorious among analysts of the history of U.S. intelligence, the report strenuously argued the need for the United States to "learn to subvert, sabo-tage, and destroy [its] enemies by more clever" and "more ruthless" methods than those of its opponents. The report conceded that this entailed a "fundamentally repugnant philosophy" and contradicted "long-standing American concepts of 'fair play,'" but it insisted that such an approach was necessary given the grave international situ-ation that existed.[19]

During the past six decades, the CIA has engaged in a number of covert operations that have provoked great controversy: an-ticommunist political parties and labor unions were financed in Italy, France, and throughout Latin America; governments were overthrown in Syria, Iran, and Guatemala; assassinations were plot-ted against the political leaders of Cuba, the Congo, Iraq, and the

Dominican Republic; counterinsurgency was fostered in Southeast Asia and Latin America; and insurgents were supported in at least 23 countries. In each of these cases, the action was originally taken with the intention of hiding U.S. involvement.[20]

Revelations of such activities have spawned myriad government investigations, legislative reforms, independent exposés, and memoirs of former intelligence officers, but this literary explosion has unfortunately not engendered popular or scholarly debate of sufficient conceptual precision or comprehensiveness regarding the morally acceptable ends and means of U.S. covert action. In some respects, the public debate over covert action has been hampered by the lumping of highly diverse activities under its heading. For example, the CIA maintains liaison relationships with many overseas intelligence agencies, even in countries that are not particularly supportive of the United States in public fora but that nonetheless find it prudent to share information on terrorist cells, for example, in exchange for U.S. aid in combating them. Significant ethical issues can arise in liaison work, for example, when the foreign counterpart is known to use physical torture and summary executions against its real or perceived opponents. One former CIA officer revealed that his efforts to file internal reports criticizing the local military's use of torture were repeatedly downplayed by other CIA officers and the U.S. military attaché serving in the same embassy, apparently so as not to risk losing the liaison relationship itself.[21] Today, there are concerns that the United States has avoided forcing Sudan to end its genocidal practices in the Darfur region to permit the CIA to continue receiving Sudanese intelligence on terrorist groups.[22] But despite the fact that intelligence liaison relationships are sometimes termed *covert action*,[23] they would rather seem to fit more reasonably within the category of "quiet diplomacy," since deception of the liaison partner is not necessarily present.

Conversely, support for paramilitary operations is extremely difficult to keep secret over any great length of time, and for that reason, it usually should not be termed covert action either. Even two former high-ranking CIA officials, Richard Helms and Lyman Kirkpatrick, were sufficiently concerned about the risk of U.S. exposure in paramilitary operations that they frequently opposed attempts to conduct them covertly.[24] Clear illustrations of that risk would include the Bay of Pigs fiasco in 1961 and the mining of Nicaraguan harbors in 1984.

Covert action is best seen as an attempt to deceive both the target government and the general public as to the sponsor and, by extension, the full intent of an activity, and not just for the sake of temporary, tactical surprise, but over the long haul.[25] This is the essential meaning of the intended "plausible deniability" of covert action:

> Covert operations may be described . . . as involving activities [that] are observable by those immediately at hand, [that] have an identifiable instigator, but [that] conceal the identity of, or permit plausible deniability by, the actual sponsor.[26]

The lack of a consistent and stable definition of covert action among its critics and advocates has undoubtedly hindered substantive debate. Both sides, however, have brought important moral values and principles to bear on the subject. In general, critics of the practice have primarily appealed to nonconsequentialist principles, while advocates of covert action have largely relied on consequentialist warrants.

Critics of covert action, first of all, have raised a number of claims against its use by officers and agents of the U.S. government.[27] Covert action, its foes argue, raises acute questions of public consent and legitimate political authority, seemingly undermining fundamental principles of representative government. It usually violates international law and diplomatic courtesy. If successfully covert, it unjustly dupes foreign (and sometimes domestic) citizens; if exposed, it alienates allies and encourages reprisals. It sometimes resembles war's means yet goes undeclared. And it threatens to corrupt the agents and officers who carry it out.[28]

Notwithstanding the credibility of these claims, as well as their resonance with central themes in U.S. political philosophy, the moral issues pertaining to covert action are more complex than its critics make them out to be. For example, if the United States contemplates an overseas intervention based on knowledge gained from foreign agents, an overt response, though more subject to public examination and critique, may reveal traces of espionage to the target organization's counterintelligence personnel, to the risk of agents' lives. Of course, this begs the question of the moral justification for employing those espionage agents in the first place, but the point against prohibiting covert action in support of such agents in justified cases is nonetheless plausible.

Some critics of CIA covert action have written as if hostile powers' covert maneuvers did not exist or were irrelevant to the question of the justification of U.S. secret operations.[29] For example, the practice of numerous right-wing dictators of cynically labeling their political opponents "communist" to justify their own antidemocratic agendas—a sadly frequent occurrence in such countries as Argentina and Chile in the 1970s and Guatemala and El Salvador during the 1980s—apparently led many critics of U.S. covert action to conclude that it was not worth the time to investigate whether the KGB or other hostile intelligence agencies, or terrorist groups, were in fact active abroad. Such critics undermine their case in debates surrounding U.S. covert action because they have not grasped its full strategic and moral context. Other opponents of covert action have revealed or simply restated facts about various operations, assuming that to expose is to condemn conclusively, while neglecting to put forth a solid ethical framework within which those revelations might validly be interpreted and evaluated. Moreover, those who would entirely prohibit U.S. covert action have not shown that legitimate foreign policy goals could always be achieved via overt or diplomatic measures, since even benevolent intervention risks censure in the international diplomatic community as "imperialistic."[30] Even philosopher Sissela Bok, who is normally a strong critic of government deception, allows that there are times when it is justifiable:

> Even though appeals to retribution and fairness do not excuse lies to enemies . . . appeals to self-defense and to the prevention of harm may well do so. Honesty ought not to allow the creation of an emergency by the enemy, when deception can forestall or avert it. . . .

CHAPTER 5

Whenever it is right to resist an assault or a threat by force, it must then be allowable to do so by guile.[31]

In sum, covert action suggests elements of prudence and morality too rarely examined by its foes.

Covert action advocates, in contrast to its critics, have tended to stress the foreign threats in response to which covert U.S. measures have been enacted and focus primarily on the strategies and methods they deem essential to meeting those threats.[32] In many essays by former CIA officers, one finds a further suggestion that the peculiar nature of the knowledge and expertise of intelligence professionals relative to grave external threats requires extraordinary or specialized morality.[33] Some covert operators have thus implied that, like politicians who compromise their personal moral scruples for the sake of the public interest, or like soldiers in a just war, their vital if esoteric role warrants excusing them in that capacity from certain ordinary moral constraints. This type of argument has been described in the literature on professional ethics as implying "strong moral role differentiation"[34] or a "separatist thesis,"[35] and in the literature on political ethics as claiming the necessity of "dirty hands."[36]

That perspective at least recognizes that some professional roles credibly appear to require special obligations at odds with other important ethical considerations that would normally apply to all people. Investigative journalists may be permitted to misrepresent their identity to gain the confidence of a government official they suspect of corruption. Or defense lawyers may be expected to try to undermine the credibility of a prosecution witness in cross-examination, even if they know the witness is telling the truth about the defendant. Some of the virtues required for military and intelligence work, for example, discretion, loyalty, and tenacity, are also instrumental to such professions as diplomacy, law, business, and journalism. But many of the skills and character traits drawn upon and reinforced by the professions of intelligence and the military are very different from those expected of the average citizen or other professionals.

The argument for a sharply distinct professional ethic may at least be said to represent an improvement over fallacious Realist and Marxist claims to the effect that moral concerns when applied to international affairs are necessarily either naïve or smoke screens for power or class interests.[37] But advocates of covert action have too often not adequately divided just from dubious policy ends or appropriate from inappropriate covert means to just ends. It is not enough, for example, to justify covert influence by proving that an adversary engages in it: such an argument is open to the criticism that we ought to perhaps forgo even palpably benevolent and just ends if they can only be achieved by unethical means.[38] One might also question whether in the conflict of values and loyalties inherent in espionage, and among the diverse effects of covert action, avoidable tragedy is sometimes incurred. Moreover, covert action as deceptive influence[39] would appear to infringe the right of autonomous, rational adults to consent to governmental interventions into their lives—even benevolently paternalistic interventions[40]—yet its advocates have yet to argue convincingly for ethical criteria by which that right may justifiably be infringed.

Even a representative democracy, defending itself with "secrecy and dispatch" against totalitarian enemies, risks taking on ominous characteristics of its foes. This point is perhaps the most telling one made by critics of covert action against the "repugnant philosophy" of some of its advocates. As David Wise and Thomas Ross noted in *The Invisible Government* more than forty years ago:

> Special operations pose dangers not only to the nations against which they are directed, but to ourselves. They raise the question of how far a free society, in attempting to preserve itself, can emulate a closed society without becoming indistinguishable from it. . . . A free society has difficulty in adopting such practices because of its moral tradition that the end does not justify the means. It must proceed with caution, alert to the danger of succumbing to the enemy's morality by too eagerly embracing his methods.[41]

We do have a sense, though, that a consequentialist argument can be constructed in support of a foreign intelligence organization in the service of a constitutional democracy. Given the real threats to U.S. security since the late 1930s, if the CIA did not exist, it would have been morally acceptable—perhaps morally obligatory in the interest of national defense[42]—to invent something like it. Stated differently, a community constructing a "social contract," and having knowledge of the subversive techniques and/or devastating weapons of various foreign regimes, would be prudent to devise an organization like the CIA with at least the capability of collecting secret intelligence. The fact that we can sensibly speak of an underlying "social contract" for U.S. foreign intelligence is why we can then distinguish ethically among the CIA's strategies and tactics. Of course, the CIA was established as a result of federal legislation in 1947, so its "social contract" is considerably more solid than a merely hypothetical one would be.

The previously noted temptation to see professionals as having "separate" moralities[43] is perhaps connected with the fact that professional roles and practices sometimes cause us to question the validity of our "normal" ethical principles. It is possible, of course, that certain professional practices are indeed immoral and should be prohibited. It is also possible, though, that professional practices can show how and why some of our "normal" ethical principles and rules are in fact erroneous, or at least erroneously applied under certain circumstances, in effect necessitating the creation of new moral principles or rules that are based on better premises, are more comprehensive, and so forth. (Recall the discussion in chapter 1.)

To illustrate, espionage conflicts with our normal condemnation of *treason*, since if treason is immoral, it can hardly be ethical to induce someone to commit treason by spying on their own government. Treason is considered morally suspect for both deontological and teleological reasons: It involves a betrayal of public trust or a basic obligation of citizenship, and it can expose the nation to subversion or military defeat by hostile states. In addition, covert action conflicts with our moral sensibility that rational adults and their government representatives ought not to be deceived or manipulated, that people generally deserve to be told the truth and allowed to manage their own affairs without paternalistic interferences.

These normal ethical assumptions are challenged in some respects, however, when we explore the question, Are there certain states, regimes, or organizations that do not deserve the loyalty or honesty of their citizens or members? Consider organized crime, which often requires rigid loyalty of its members but clearly does not actually deserve such loyalty—hence the justification for the FBI and other law enforcement agencies to penetrate and subvert such organizations by means of informers and undercover agents.

States and regimes are also subject to the question of deserved loyalty. One can readily point to principles of ethics and political philosophy found in numerous documents in the Western tradition, including Thomas Aquinas's *On Kingship* (1266), Algernon Sidney's *Discourses Concerning Government* (1698), and the U.S. Declaration of Independence,[44] which in effect justify treason against regimes that constitutionally and regularly violate "natural" or "unalienable" human rights.

But if treason and other dishonest acts against certain states can be justified, then we can begin also to see the potential justification of espionage and covert action carried out against those same states by *other* states, assuming that the latter are themselves legitimate and are pursuing just goals.[45] This is a highly "loaded" assumption, however, since legitimate intelligence goals cannot justify any and all means. Many espionage and covert action techniques remain morally problematic despite their employment in the service of a worthy cause by a justified profession. It is apparent that to manipulate persons into becoming espionage agents, to employ coercive interrogation techniques, or to deceive foreign citizens via covert action, may infringe rights that cannot legitimately be infringed without rigorous appeal to more fundamental ethical principles. Although the concept of "national interest" implies the tacit consent of domestic citizens, it cannot unequivocally warrant coercive intelligence methods, in part because it cannot be assumed to satisfy the tacit or even hypothetical consent of foreign citizens.

This is not to argue that, in a "zero-sum" conflict[46] between the vital interests of domestic and foreign citizens, one cannot justify pursuing the former at the expense of the latter. On the contrary: Duties to defend one's country—so long as that country can plausibly be described as a constitutional democracy—can be justified on the basis of a theory of universal human rights.[47] The point, however, is that the moral justification of coercive intelligence methods requires either a true "zero-sum" conflict—a situation that cannot simply be assumed to exist in every relation between enemies—or a credible appeal to foreign citizens' *hypothetical consent* (in the absence of their expressed consent), meaning that one has good reason to believe that they would concur if they had relevant knowledge and deliberated in an unbiased fashion.[48]

Chapter 5 argues that both of these moral requirements—zero-sum conflict plus hypothetical consent—were met in many of the intelligence operations carried out by the United States against the former Soviet Union. This case study also serves as a fruitful point of comparison to contemporary analogues like Al Qaeda.

NOTES

1. Sissela Bok, *Lying: Moral Choice in Public and Private Life* (New York: Pantheon, 1978; Random House, 1979), 191. Note that Bok advocated public debate on general practices and policies, not on each and every actual implementation of such policies. See also Bok, *Secrets: On the Ethics of Concealment and Revelation* (New York: Pantheon, 1983; Random House, 1984), chs. 12–13.

2. Elizabeth Gunn, "Ethics and the Public Service: An Annotated Bibliography and Overview Essay," *Public Personnel Management* 10, no. 1 (1981): 172.

3. I owe this point to Edwin Delattre.

4. Murray Dyer, *The Weapon on the Wall: Rethinking Psychological Warfare* (Baltimore: Johns Hopkins University Press, 1959), 176.

5. Intelligence oversight was addressed in Daniel Hoffman, *Governmental Secrecy and the Founding Fathers: A Study in Constitutional Controls* (Westport, Conn.: Greenwood, 1981); John Oseth, *Regulating U.S. Intelligence Operations: A Study in Definition of the National Interest* (Lexington: University Press of Kentucky, 1985); Loch Johnson, *America's Secret Power: The CIA in a Democratic Society* (New York: Oxford University Press, 1989); and Frank Smist Jr., *Congress Oversees the United States Intelligence Community, 1947–1989* (Knoxville: University of Tennessee Press, 1990). Interesting

comparisons between the oversight powers of the U.S. Congress and the British Parliament were made in *Secrecy and Foreign Policy*, ed. Thomas Franck and Edward Weisband (New York: Oxford University Press, 1974).

6. Similar points were made by John Langan in "National Interest, Morality, and Intelligence," *Studies in Intelligence* 27, no. 3 (Fall 1983): 57–69.

7. A fine collection of scholarly essays spanning the range of these theories is Terry Nardin and David Mapel, eds., *Traditions of International Ethics* (New York: Cambridge University Press, 1992).

8. Prior to my 1993 doctoral dissertation (*Covert Action*), from which this chapter was largely derived, other essays that applied just-war criteria to covert action included Anne Rudolph, "The Ethical Dimension of Covert Action," *Governance*, Spring 1984, 40–44; William Colby, "Public Policy, Secret Action," *Ethics and International Affairs* 3 (April 1989): 61–71; and Arthur Hulnick and Daniel Mattausch, "Ethics and Morality in U.S. Secret Intelligence," *Harvard Journal of Law and Public Policy* 12, no. 2 (Spring 1989): 509–22.

9. To "vet" an agent means to investigate and establish his or her authenticity, to determine that the agent is not already in the employ of an opposing intelligence service, a terrorist organization, and so forth.

10. See Adda Bozeman, "Covert Action and Foreign Policy," in *Intelligence Requirements for the 1980s: Covert Action*, ed. Roy Godson (Washington, D.C.: National Strategy Information Center, 1981), 15–78, and Bok, *Secrets*.

11. Secrecy and "despatch" were commonly joined in discussions of executive "energy" at the time. See *Federalist* essays #64 and #70.

12. Ray Cline, *The CIA under Reagan, Bush, and Casey* (Washington, D.C.: Acropolis, 1981), ch. 1.

13. John Ranelagh, *The Agency: The Rise and Decline of the CIA*, Rev. ed. (New York: Simon & Schuster, 1987), chs. 1–2.

14. Ranelagh, *The Agency*, 65, 70–71.

15. Ranelagh, *The Agency*, 124–25.

16. Harry Rositzke, *The CIA's Secret Operations: Espionage, Counterespionage, and Covert Action* (Boulder, Colo.: Westview, 1988), ch. 1. Rositzke was the first chief of the Special Projects Division/Soviet of the Strategic Services Unit, a forerunner to the CIA and a successor to the OSS.

17. Cited in William Leary, ed., *The Central Intelligence Agency: History and Documents* (Tuscaloosa: University of Alabama Press, 1984), 131.

18. James Doolittle, "Report on the Covert Activities of the Central Intelligence Agency," cited in Leary, ed., *The Central Intelligence Agency*, 143–45.

19. Leary, ed., *The Central Intelligence Agency*, 143–44.

20. Many of these activities were described in John Prados, *Presidents' Secret Wars: CIA and Pentagon Covert Operations since World War II* (New York: William Morrow, 1986). See also Loch Johnson, "Covert Action and Accountability: Decision Making for America's Secret Foreign Policy," *International Studies Quarterly* 33 (1989): 86.

21. This officer also claimed that he used information gleaned from the ongoing liaison arrangement to warn and protect persons who appeared on death squad hit lists and was proud to say that "people are alive and doing good, constructive things for their country today" because of his actions. Confidential interview, Fall 1991.

22. Ken Silverstein, "Official Pariah Sudan Valuable to America's War on Terrorism: Despite Once Harboring Bin Laden, Khartoum Regime Has Supplied Key Intelligence, Officials Say," *Los Angeles Times*, 29 April 2005, A1, and "Sudanese Visitor Split U.S. Officials," *Los Angeles Times*, 17 June 2005, A1.

23. For example, by Shultz, "Covert Action and Executive-Legislative Relations: The Iran–Contra Crisis and Its Aftermath." *Harvard Journal of Law and Public Policy* 12, no. 2 (Spring 1989)," 705–6.

24. Thomas Powers, *The Man Who Kept the Secrets: Richard Helms and the CIA* (New York: Knopf, 1979; New York: Simon & Schuster, 1981), 129–33.

25. On these distinctions among diplomacy, paramilitary operations, and covert action, see Christopher Felix [James McCargar], *A Short Course in the Secret War* (New York: Dutton, 1963; New York: Dell, 1988), ch. 9; David Atlee Phillips, *The Night Watch* (New York: Ballantine, 1982), 353–54; Hans Moses, *The Clandestine Service of the Central Intelligence Agency* (McLean, Va.: Association of Former Intelligence Officers, 1983), 2, 10–13; Rositzke, *The CIA's Secret Operations*, xxxii–xxxv, 264–67.

26. Maurice Tugwell and David Charters, "Special Operations and the Threats to United States Interests in the 1980s," in *Special Operations in U.S. Strategy*, ed. Frank Barnett, B. Hugh Tovar, and Richard H. Shultz (Washington, D.C.: National Defense University Press and National Strategy Information Center, 1984), 42, note 7. See also Rositzke, *The CIA's Secret Operations*, 153–54.

27. Note that in CIA parlance, an intelligence "officer" is almost always a U.S. citizen, whereas an "agent" is a foreign citizen. In contrast, in FBI jargon, the counterpart to a CIA officer is an FBI "agent," while the analogue to a CIA agent is an FBI "informer."

28. Cogent articulations of these concerns were presented in Paul Blackstock, *The Strategy of Subversion* (Chicago: Quadrangle, 1964); Bok, *Secrets*, chs. 8, 12, 13, 17; Congress, Senate, Select Committee to Study Governmental Operations with Respect to Intelligence Activities, *Alleged Assassination Plots Involving Foreign Leaders*, Interim Report #94-465, 94th Congress, 1st session, 1975; E. Drexel Godfrey Jr., "Ethics and Intelligence," *Foreign Affairs* 56, no. 4 (April 1978): 624–42; Powers, *The Man Who Kept the Secrets*; Jonathan Kwitny, *Endless Enemies: The Making of an Unfriendly World* (New York: Congdon & Weed, 1984; New York: Penguin, 1986).

29. Roy Godson was highly critical of what he terms "the antiintelligence lobby" on this point. See Ernest Lefever and Roy Godson, *The CIA and the American Ethic: An Unfinished Debate* (Washington, D.C.: Ethics and Public Policy Center, 1979), ch. 3.

30. The shortsighted approaches described in this paragraph are exhibited in Victor Marchetti and John Marks, *The CIA and the Cult of Intelligence* (New York: Knopf, 1974; New York: Dell, 1983); Philip Agee, *Inside the Company: CIA Diary* (New York: Bantam, 1976); Morton Halperin, Jerry Berman, Robert Borosage, and Christine Marwick, *The Lawless State: The Crimes of the U.S. Intelligence Agencies* (New York: Penguin and the Center for National Security Studies, 1976); John Stockwell, *In Search of Enemies: A CIA Story* (New York: Norton, 1978).

31. Bok, *Lying*, 149, 151.

32. Felix, *A Short Course in the Secret War*; Rositzke, *The CIA's Secret Operations*; Peer de Silva, *Sub Rosa: The CIA and the Uses of Intelligence* (New York: Times Books, 1978); B. Hugh Tovar, "Covert Action," in *Intelligence Requirements for the 1980s: Elements of Intelligence*, ed. Roy Godson (Washington, D.C.: National Strategy Information Center, 1979), 67–79; Cord Meyer, *Facing Reality: From World Federalism to the CIA* (Lanham, Md.: University Press of America, 1980); Donald Jameson, "The Clandestine Battlefield: Trenches and Trends," *Strategic Review*, Winter 1983, 19–28; and the essays in Bozeman, *Intelligence Requirements for the 1980s*, ed. Godson.

33. Arthur Jacobs, Letter to the Editor, *Foreign Affairs* 56, no. 5 (July 1978): 867–75; Miles Copeland, *The Real Spy World* (London: Sphere, 1978), 282–83; Hulnick and Mattausch, "Ethics and Morality in U.S. Secret Intelligence," 520–22.

34. Alan Goldman, *The Moral Foundations of Professional Ethics* (Totowa, N.J.: Rowman & Littlefield, 1980).

35. Alan Gewirth, "Professional Ethics: The Separatist Thesis," *Ethics* 96, no. 2 (January 1986): 282–300.

36. The scholarly literature on this topic is rich and includes most notably Michael Walzer, "Political Action: The Problem of Dirty Hands," *Philosophy and Public Affairs* 2, no. 2 (Winter 1973): 160–80; W. Kenneth Howard, "Must Public Hands Be Dirty?" *Journal of Value Enquiry* 11, no. 1 (Spring 1977): 29–40; Stuart Hampshire, ed., *Public and Private Morality* (New York: Cambridge University Press, 1978); Donald Jones, ed., *Private and Public Ethics* (New York: Edwin Mellen, 1978); Martin Hollis, "Dirty Hands," *British Journal of Political Science* 12, no. 4 (October 1982): 385–98; Dennis Thompson, *Political Ethics and Public Office* (Cambridge, Mass.: Harvard University Press, 1987), ch. 1; Peter Johnson, *Politics, Innocence, and the Limits of Goodness* (New York: Routledge, 1988); Leslie Griffin, "The Problem of Dirty Hands," *Journal of Religious Ethics* 17, no. 1 (Spring 1989): 31–61; C. A. J. Coady, "Dirty Hands," in *A Companion to Contemporary Political Philosophy*, ed. Robert Goodin and Philip Pettit (Cambridge, Mass.: Blackwell, 1993), 422–30.

37. Excellent critiques of Realist assumptions of a Hobbesian "state of nature" between nations are Charles Beitz, *Political Theory and International Relations* (Princeton, N.J.: Princeton University Press, 1979), and Marshall Cohen, "Moral Skepticism and International Relations," *Philosophy and Public Affairs* 13, no. 4 (Fall 1984): 299–346. A trenchant refutation of Marxist theories of imperialism is Benjamin Cohen, *The Question of Imperialism: The Political Economy of Dominance and Dependence* (New York: Basic, 1973).

38. John Howard Yoder, *The Politics of Jesus* (Grand Rapids, Mich.: Eerdmans, 1972), 244, stated this criticism (though not of covert action explicitly) in particularly forceful fashion, but similar questions have been raised by many other writers in arguments against utilitarianism.

39. The element of manipulation in covert action was briefly but insightfully examined in Charles Beitz, "Covert Intervention as a Moral Problem," *Ethics and International Affairs* 3 (April 1989): 54–57. Robert Goodin, *Manipulatory Politics* (New Haven, Conn.: Yale University Press, 1980), 9–26, argued that even well-intentioned manipulation should be presumed to be "prima facie evil."

40. The conditions for the justification of various deceptive practices were examined in Gewirth, "Professional Ethics," and especially in Donald VanDeVeer, *Paternalistic Intervention: The Moral Bounds on Benevolence* (Princeton, N.J.: Princeton University Press, 1986). Compare Thompson, *Political Ethics and Public Office*, 160: "Because citizens legitimately disagree about the ends of paternalistic intervention, they should have the

chance, regularly and openly, to choose and review the ends that paternalistic policies and practices impute to them and their fellow citizens."

41. David Wise and Thomas Ross, *The Invisible Government* (New York: Random House, 1964), 352–53.

42. Hulnick and Mattausch, "Ethics and Morality in U.S. Secret Intelligence," 511: "In a world in which many societies are closed, or in which information does not circulate completely freely, the state must engage in clandestine information gathering to protect against foreign threats to its security." Note, though, that since this statement does not distinguish between just and unjust states, it could just as easily have served to warrant the existence of the KGB as that of the CIA.

43. Gewirth, "Professional Ethics," conclusively argued that no such normative separation can be defended credibly.

44. Cf. Paul Conkin, *Self-Evident Truths* (Bloomington: Indiana University Press, 1974), ch. 1. A number of writers have pointed out that the American revolutionaries sought and received covert financial assistance from France to prosecute the war with Britain.

45. Michael Walzer similarly argued in *Just and Unjust Wars*, 4th ed. (New York: Basic Books, 2006), 82, that "a state (or government) established against the will of its own people, ruling violently, may well forfeit its right to defend itself against a foreign invasion."

46. I assume a "zero-sum" conflict to be one in which one side's gain unavoidably results in the other side's loss.

47. Alan Gewirth, "Ethical Universalism and Particularism," *Journal of Philosophy* 85, no. 6 (June 1988): 283–302. See also Philip Pettit, "The Paradox of Loyalty," *American Philosophical Quarterly* 25 (April 1988): 163–71, and Stephen Nathanson, "In Defense of 'Moderate Patriotism,'" *Ethics* 99, no. 3 (April 1989): 535–52.

48. Similar distinctions among types of consent were made in Gewirth, "Professional Ethics," VanDeVeer, *Paternalistic Intervention*, and Jean Hampton, "Contract and Consent," in *A Companion to Contemporary Political Philosophy*, ed. Robert E. Goodin and Philip Pettit (Oxford, U.K.: Blackwell, 1993), 379–93.

6

THE KGB: THE CIA'S TRADITIONAL ADVERSARY

As long as a country has no civil liberty, no freedom of information, and no independent press, then there exists no effective body of public opinion to control the conduct of the government and its functionaries. Such a situation is not just a misfortune for citizens unprotected against tyranny and lawlessness, it is a menace to international security.

—Andrei Sakharov[1]

At the conclusion of John Ranelagh's history of the CIA, he opined that the CIA was no longer viewed by Americans as the world's savior or corruptor, but rather "as a reminder of how old and corrupt and incorrigible the rest of the world is."[2] An outline of the history of the Soviet KGB reminds us of the incorrigibility (as well as inscrutability) of at least a sizeable part of the world, thereby suggesting consequentialist elements of prudence and just cause underlying the creation of the CIA and its covert action capabilities.

This chapter supports the following points. 1) The Bolshevik government was from the beginning illegitimate and unjust, and therefore could not rightly claim the loyalty of its citizens, or deny the just cause underlying paternalistic interventions launched against it by other states on behalf of those citizens. 2) The activities of the political police against Soviet citizens and foreign countries warranted the creation of such intelligence agencies as the CIA to counteract them. Overt means were insufficient to achieve the legitimate objective of reducing the power of the Soviet state. 3) The Soviet political police maintained their powers, strategies, and tactics essentially unchanged until the collapse of the Soviet Union in late 1991, thus it was incorrect to assume, as many critics of the CIA have argued, that the Cold War would have ended sooner had the United States toned down its intelligence operations, for example, after the death of Stalin or during the Gorbachev era. 4) These points nevertheless did not justify the use by the CIA of methods "more ruthless" than those of the KGB, as is urged in the previously cited secret report to President Dwight D. Eisenhower in 1954. The existence of just cause does not entail that all methods undertaken to support that cause are themselves justified.

How did the KGB become such a potent force in Soviet life? What threat did the Soviet regime present to its own citizens and to other countries to justify intelligence operations conducted against it? As Ronald Hingley has shown, the KGB had deep historical roots in predecessor organizations stretching back more than four centuries: the Oprichnina under Ivan the Terrible; the Secret Office under Tsar Alexis; Peter the Great's Preobrazhensky Office and Secret Chancellery; Empress Anne's Chancellery for Secret Investigations; the Secret Bureau under Peter III, Catherine the Great, and Paul; Alexander I's Special Chancellery; the Third Section and Corps of Gendarmes under Nicholas I and Alexander II; and the Okhrana or Protective Sections under Alexander III and Nicholas II, the last Russian tsar. In most cases, these organizations operated without parliamentary or judicial checks on their jurisdiction, methods, or powers.[3]

Richard Pipes described broader factors in Russian history that not only inhibited the development of democratic institutions but also enabled the emergence of many elements of a totalitarian police state. Pipes contended that devastating invasions from Asia over many centuries contributed to a common view of political authority as arbitrary and absolute. The land and the peasants who worked it were considered to be the property of the rulers. Forced labor and torture were common. Isolation from foreigners and their ideas was enforced; even domestic news was considered a state secret. Russian subjects—even Orthodox priests—were legally obliged to denounce dissidents and suspected subversives to the authorities. The legal code also specified that families of "traitors," including their minor children, were liable to execution for failure to inform the authorities in time to prevent the crime from being committed.[4]

> Since 1845, Russian [and Soviet] criminal codes have each contained a political "omnibus" clause worded with such imprecision that under its terms the organs of state security have been able to incarcerate citizens guilty of crimes no more specific than intent to "weaken," "undermine," or "arouse doubts" or "disrespect" for existing authority.[5]

By the 1880s, Russia's Department of Police and Corps of Gendarmes had been granted sweeping authority to declare martial law and investigate crimes against the state, virtually unchecked by the judiciary. They had the power "to search, arrest, interrogate, imprison, and exile persons either guilty of political activity or suspected of it," politics being the exclusive prerogative of high officials. Moreover, with the Ministry of the Interior, they required citizens to submit for their approval myriad mundane requests for permission to start a business or charity, to travel, to sponsor newspapers or plays, and so forth.[6] Pipes affirmed the view of "a knowledgeable American observer," writing in 1888–1889 that, in regard especially to Russian peasant villages, "the police [were] omnipresent and omnipotent regulators of all human conduct—a sort of incompetent bureaucratic substitute for divine Providence."[7]

As Leszek Kolakowski argued, the totalitarian principle of the subordination of every social activity to the aims of the state was readily taken over from tsarist Russia by Lenin and the Bolsheviks.[8] It would be wrong to assume, though, that totalitarian rule was the only political alternative possible after the collapse of the Romanov dynasty in February 1917. A democratic republic came very close to being successfully formed.

In November of that year, Russian citizens were allowed to vote for representatives to a Constituent Assembly in Petrograd, the first Russian parliament to be freely elected on the basis of universal unrestricted franchise and secret ballot.[9] The results clearly reflected a repudiation of the Provisional Government's continuation of Russia's disastrous involvement in World War I. A solid majority of Assembly seats were won by Socialist Revolutionaries, who were most popular among peasants. The Bolsheviks won about 25 percent of the 707 deputy seats, but not intending to be challenged by any independent legislature or opposing political party, they dissolved the Assembly by armed force after its first meeting on 5 January 1918.[10] In Lenin's words,

> The dissolution of the Constituent Assembly by the Soviet government means a complete and frank liquidation of the idea of democracy by the idea of dictatorship. It will serve as a good lesson.[11]

The Bolshevik government was from the beginning, then, illegitimate. To defend and expand its power, it relied heavily on its own secret police. One month prior to the ominous demise of the Assembly, the Bolsheviks had established a political police organization called the All-Russian Extraordinary Commission for Combating Counter-Revolution and Sabotage. Commonly called Vecheka (VChK) or Cheka (ChK), after the initial letters of its abbreviated Russian title, this commission was to be the precursor of the GPU, OGPU, NKVD, MGB, and (from 1954 to 1991) the KGB.[12]

At first, the Cheka had only the authority to investigate "counterrevolution" and "sabotage" (which, however, included workers' strikes and "profiteering"), but within weeks it was granted not only the power to arrest but moreover to judge guilt and impose punishment, including the death penalty. Hostage taking, concentration camps, forced labor, and summary executions very soon became standard Cheka practices.[13]

George Leggett noted the important influence on Lenin of certain Russian "Jacobin" theorists, who had preached the application of ruthless terror to consolidate the dictatorship of a revolutionary party after it had seized power by means of a violent insurrection. Lenin's own letters and telegrams after the Bolshevik coup frequently urged mass searches, imprisonment, deportations, and executions of perceived opponents, whom he conveniently referred to as "enemies of the people." Such measures were commonly approved by other Bolshevik leaders like I. K. Peters, G. I. Petrovsky, M. I. Latsis, Joseph Stalin, and the head of the Cheka from 1918 to 1926, Felix Dzerzhinsky.[14] Trotsky's 1920 pamphlet *Terrorism and Communism* is illustrative of their ethical assumptions: "As for us, we were never concerned with the Kantian-priestly and vegetarian-Quaker prattle about the 'sacredness of human life.'"[15]

Latsis frankly stated in a 1918 Cheka periodical the important relation between terror and "class" in Bolshevik ideology:

> We are not waging war against individual persons. We are exterminating the bourgeoisie as a class. During the investigation, do not look for evidence that the accused acted in deed or word against Soviet power. The first questions that you ought to put are: To what class does he belong? What is his origin? What is his education or profession? And it is these questions that ought to determine the fate of the accused. In this lies the significance and essence of the Red Terror.[16]

This way of thinking sealed the fate of millions of people, not only under direct Soviet rule but wherever Leninist parties subsequently came to power: Eastern Europe, China, North Korea, Vietnam, Cambodia, and so forth.[17]

During Russia's Red Terror and Civil War period, circa 1918–1921, the use of torture, summary executions, and wholesale reprisals by the Cheka reached truly appalling proportions. We know this from the unavoidably "public" nature of many mass executions near or in towns and villages, from the testimony of witnesses and former Cheka prisoners, and also from the Cheka habit of publishing lists of its victims as a warning to the populace.[18] Stalin (like Hitler, whose Gestapo imitated many Cheka methods) later learned the prudence of being more discreet about summary executions.[19]

As Hingley suggested, Cheka practices repudiated any lingering Russian respect for due process of law:

> From the beginning, arbitrariness was the hallmark of the Cheka's operations. Punishment was meted out according to the whim of

the local police chief, and the nature of the victim's offense might remain a mystery to all concerned, not necessarily deriving even from anything as solid as an anonymous denunciation. It frequently happened that an individual was shot because his surname happened to coincide with that of someone else who figured on a list of condemned persons.[20]

That Soviet terror was to be more than simply a temporary expedient was indicated in the treatment of peasants under policies of grain seizures and forced collectivization. Throughout Bolshevik-controlled territory beginning in 1918, Party and Cheka officials set quotas of grain to be requisitioned from regions and villages, quotas that were typically grossly unrealistic. This practice was accompanied by an ideological crusade against the "kulak," a term that meant village moneylender and mortgager[21] or, more negatively, rural speculator,[22] but that came to be applied to any peasant who resisted collectivization or hid grain from the official requisitioners.

From 1918 to 1921, peasant rebellions against Bolshevik grain extortion were suppressed locally by Cheka and Red Army troops,[23] but beginning in 1928, comprehensive "emergency" measures were enacted to combat what Stalin termed the kulaks' economic "sabotage" of the Party's grain collection.[24] Members of the Cheka (by then renamed the United State Political Directorate [OGPU][25]), assisted by Party activists, began mass arrests, deportations, and executions of purported kulaks. In the Ukraine, Caucasus, and Kazakh regions, those methods were coupled with such extreme grain quotas that devastating famine ensued. Robert Conquest estimated that 14.5 million peasants died as a direct result of these measures from 1930 to 1937.[26] A ridiculously unproductive and inefficient effort when viewed from a strictly economic perspective, Stalin's extortion of grain and forced collectivization were quite effective as methods of imposing total political control, which in fact was his primary intention.

John Dziak argued that Soviet attacks against the peasantry set the stage for Stalin's bloody purges of the Party, military, and NKVD (successor to OGPU) from 1936–1938:

Those military commanders who collaborated with OGPU counter-parts in shooting starving peasants later had no moral alternative than to collaborate in the denunciation of their comrades-in-arms, and then themselves, in the purges. As for the state security cadres themselves, their bestial enforcement of the famine was but another step in the sequenced psychological and moral degradation of these men and women.[27]

By 1920, the Cheka had become in Pipes's estimation the most powerful institution in Soviet Russia, reaching into every aspect of the society.[28] In December 1920, Dzerzhinsky expanded its scope of operations, issuing a secret directive authorizing the creation of false opposition groups to provoke real internal dissenters into re-vealing themselves, to penetrate émigré organizations, and to lure émigré and foreign government agents and money into the hands of the Cheka. This directive also proposed an increase in the number of hostages taken from among the relatives in Russia of prominent émigrés, as well as the formation of special detachments to carry out acts of terrorism against enemies of the Soviet state living on foreign soil (precursors of OGPU, NKVD, and KGB kidnap and assassination squads).[29]

In 1921, Dzerzhinsky launched what Dziak regarded as "the prototypical strategic deception and provocation operation in the Soviet repertoire."[30] Soviet agents pretending to oppose Bolshevik rule made quiet contact with influential Russian émigrés and Brit-ish, French, Polish, and U.S. officials. These Soviet agents claimed to represent a powerful and well-organized monarchist group oper-ating secretly within Russia. Called the Monarchist Association for Central Russia and commonly referred to as "the Trust," the group's ostensible purpose was to collaborate with Western powers and émi-gré organizations to overthrow the Soviet regime.[31]

Trust operatives soon convinced their contacts of their authen-ticity, passing on information carefully crafted by Soviet intel-ligence and, in return, ironically receiving substantial monetary support from the West. In time, the role of the Trust was altered slightly to persuade the West that the Soviet Union was turning toward capitalism, that communist ideology was waning there, and that Stalin had no aggressive international ambitions.[32]

In 1926, after Polish and other Western leaders began to suspect the veracity and value of the information obtained from Trust sources, Stalin folded the operation and publicly celebrated its achievements by announcing that it had been a clever fiction from the beginning. This revelation humiliated Western diplomats and demoralized Russian émigré groups, creating an image of Soviet intelligence as omniscient and omnipotent within Russia.[33] Unfortunately, this experience did not prevent the West from being fooled again after World War II by a similar provocation in the form of a fake Polish underground army, which like the Trust absorbed Western funds and agents before being announced as a glorious fraud by Stalin.[34]

Stalin was perhaps the most highly skilled Soviet practitioner of the game of provocation and scapegoat creation, inventing enemies at every turn with ever more incredible claims of subversion and conspiracy to rationalize countless orders of imprisonment and execution. The secret police played a vital role in his attainment and maintenance of absolute power.[35]

It is important to recognize that the pattern of terror tactics employed by Soviet security police was known in the West many years prior to the creation of the CIA in 1947. Numerous articles and books were published beginning in the early 1920s in Germany, France, England, Italy, and the United States, testifying to the brutality of the Cheka and its successors.[36] Furthermore, despite the alliance between the United States and the Soviet Union in the war against Hitler, there were plenty of indications that Stalin's postwar intentions were neither conciliatory nor reformist. The creation of the CIA thus occurred not in a vacuum but in the face of increasingly ominous Soviet activities in Eastern Europe and elsewhere.[37]

However, Stalin's conspiratorial expertise and obsession made it impossible for Western powers to accurately predict his—and thus, the Soviet government's—full intentions apart from the development of their own intelligence operations targeted against the Kremlin. One indication of this was revealed in a recently declassified OSS cable from November 1944, which reported the existence

of no less than 1,200 NKVD agents operating at that time in Bu-
charest in the wake of Romania's "liberation" by the Red Army.[38]
From what Moscow subsequently accomplished throughout Eastern
Europe, this must have only been the tip of the iceberg. Soviet spies
were even able to penetrate the top-secret Manhattan Project in
the United States, which produced the first atomic weapons. Soviet
agents in the Unites States began to be exposed by defectors in late
1945, while others were identified from Soviet cables decoded by
U.S. Army cryptanalysts.[39]

In contrast to the revolutionary rhetoric of the Bolsheviks and
the open brutality of the Cheka, by 1945 Stalin showed that he had
learned the tactical value of propaganda and camouflage when he
set about creating communist regimes in Soviet areas of influence.
In Eastern Europe, the formation of broad political coalitions and
the use of "salami" tactics to slowly eliminate rivals successfully
masked the true intentions of communist cadres until their absolute
power was fait accompli.[40] With the assistance of the NKVD, each
new government quickly constructed its own potent intelligence
service and began rounding up actual and potential opponents to be
incarcerated, shot, or exiled to Soviet or internal labor camps.[41]

Among revisionist historians, it has been intellectually fashion-
able to accuse the United States of inventing the Cold War ex nihilo
and maintaining it artificially to support its own power projection
throughout the world. A typical view of this school of thought was
expressed by Joyce and Gabriel Kolko: "Washington often assigned
the Kremlin powers in the world that must have surprised the quite
circumspect rulers of that war-devastated country. . . . [I]t was often politically convenient for America's leaders to fix the blame for
capitalism's failures on the cautious men in the Kremlin."[42]

It is important, therefore, to recall that the threat to other states
from communist countries was for many years all too real. The Soviet-dominated Comintern and Cominform (the shortened names
for the Communist International) had standard policies of creating
illegal (covert) communist parties along with legal (overt) parties
throughout the world, and both types were overwhelmingly infiltrated and dominated by Soviet state security officers.[43] Moreover,

prior to Gorbachev's "new thinking" in foreign policy, the Soviet Union and its allies had scored during the previous four decades an alarming number of successes in Europe, Asia, Africa, and even Latin America. Communist parties had come to power in diverse cultures using combinations of camouflage and terror very similar to those employed in postwar Eastern Europe.[44]

CIA officers and agents were often on the "front lines" observing such developments. It should not be surprising, then, that they often discerned global patterns in these developments, or that they often prescribed drastic and forceful methods of countering them, or even that they considered themselves to be waging a just (if shadowy) war against an enemy that had no respect for liberal democracy. This does not mean that the CIA was justified in employing methods "more ruthless" than those of the KGB (recalling the famous report written for President Eisenhower in 1954), but an understanding of the nature of the Soviet regime and the tactics of the KGB does suggest that the United States was justified in creating the CIA and employing it to engage in operations proportional to the threat.

After Stalin's death in 1953, the Party hierarchy instituted a number of domestic legal reforms ostensibly reducing the authority of the KGB to engage in summary executions. At the same time, it revived media campaigns to portray Chekists as courageous, dedicated, self-less, and humane.[45] Amy Knight quoted a typical expression of this public relations effort from a book published in 1981 in Azerbaijan:

> All good Chekists are infinitely kind people. A Chekist is not a punisher; he is more like a doctor. Sometimes he is compelled to use painful surgical intervention. But this is only when necessary and on the basis of an exact diagnosis.[46]

Vladimir Kryuchkov, head of the KGB from 1988 to 1991, asserted in a 1989 interview, "Violence, inhumanity, and violation of human rights have always been alien to the work of our secret services." He also claimed that the KGB did not even keep files on Soviet citizens.[47] In reality, the KGB retained from Khrushchev to Gorbachev the same extralegal prerogatives it had held under Lenin and Stalin.[48] It is noteworthy, for example, that Khrushchev's famous 1956 speech denouncing Stalin criticized the NKVD's repression of only Communist Party members, leaving the terrorization and slaughter of millions outside the party unmentioned.[49] The reason for this "oversight," of course, is that the Party had no intention of democratizing after Stalin's death and needed the secret police to maintain its grip on power unchallenged. Knight concluded in 1988:

> Changes in the [Soviet] republic codes of criminal procedure from 1961 to the present have extended the purview of the KGB's investigatory apparatus, while revisions in the criminal codes have broadened definitions of political crimes, making it easier to prosecute Soviet citizens on criminal charges [e.g., "hooliganism"].[50]

The KGB continued well into the Gorbachev era to punish "anti-Soviet agitation"—protests against political trials, the 1968 invasion of Czechoslovakia, and the 1980 invasion of Afghanistan, for example—by means of termination of employment and blacklisting, internal exile, incarceration in remote labor camps, and beatings. Ludmilla Alexeyeva was one of many dedicated Soviet citizens who thoroughly documented the persecution of religious and nationalist demonstrators, publishers of *samizdat* (especially the *Chronicle of Current Events*), the Initiative Group for the Defense of Human Rights in the USSR, Helsinki Watch groups, and other expressions of nonviolent opposition.[51]

Until quite recently, the KGB regularly committed dissidents to "psychiatric" institutions—often to face debilitating drug treatments in addition to less "scientific" brutalities—cynically reasoning that people who criticize the Soviet state or the wisdom of its rulers must therefore be mentally ill.[52]

Dissidents were sometimes accused of having more devious motives. Viktor Chebrikov, KGB chairman from 1982 to 1988, was inclined to label Soviet dissidents as serving "the interests of foreign intelligence."[53] A similar view aired on official Soviet television in February 1985: "All dissidence—no matter what noble phrases it may cover itself with—ends up as the same thing, subservience to the CIA and therefore alliance with Nazis, Zionists, former members of the

Polizei, and other human rabble."[54] On 14 April 1989, *Pravda* accused the dissident Democratic Union of direct connection to "Western special services' activities,"[55] and in December 1990, a Soviet legislator accused the Interregional Group of accepting CIA funds.[56]

Beginning in 1988, however, the Soviet press, emboldened by Gorbachev's policy of *glasnost,* or "publicity," began publishing articles and letters critical of the KGB and its predecessor organizations. Citizens wrote of their experiences under Stalin's NKVD, many demanding punishment of NKVD officials who were still alive and, by implication, perhaps still at work in the KGB. A reader of *Ogonek* magazine suggested in an August 1988 letter that the KGB should be subject to Western-style public oversight.[57] In October 1989, some 1,500 Soviet citizens held an unprecedented candlelit vigil outside KGB headquarters in Moscow in memory of the millions of victims murdered by its personnel.[58] In Warsaw, a similar vigil by 2,000 mourners memorialized the 43,000 Poles believed to have been killed in prison from 1945 to 1956.[59]

The KGB was also embarrassed by the testimony of former high-ranking KGB officer Oleg Kalugin, who became somewhat of a media sensation in 1989 and 1990 with such bold public statements as the following: "The new image of the KGB is cosmetic and just consists of applying rouge over the quite flabby face of the old Stalin-Brezhnev system."[60]

The KGB no doubt suffered a serious setback following the revolutionary events in Eastern Europe in 1989 and 1990, with the subsequent loss there of its satellite intelligence services and agent networks, especially in East Germany.[61] KGB officials must have observed with regret and foreboding the slow dismantling of the Eastern European intelligence agencies they had created and sustained,[62] but within the Soviet Union itself, reform of the KGB was only marginal prior to the August 1991 coup attempt. For example, the wording of laws on dissent ("anti-Soviet agitation and propaganda") was changed repeatedly during 1989, but they remained ambiguous and subject to broad interpretation.[63] Boris Yeltsin stated in July 1989 that during the previous four years (i.e., under Gorbachev), there had been "no radical restructuring" of the KGB.[64]

In August 1989, KGB chief Vladimir Kryuchkov announced the abolition of the KGB's notorious Fifth Directorate, which had been responsible for suppressing political and religious dissent. But in its place a new Directorate for the Protection of the Soviet Constitution was created, having as its purpose suppressing "organized antisocialist groups aimed at destabilizing the internal political situation."[65] And although a law on the KGB adopted by the USSR Supreme Soviet in May 1991 formally separated the KGB from the Communist Party, it did not reduce the formidable powers the KGB wielded up to that point.[66]

On 18 August 1991, in a desperate attempt to halt the impending disintegration of the Soviet Union and the authority of the Kremlin, a "palace coup" was launched against Soviet president Mikhail Gorbachev by senior officials of the KGB, defense and interior ministries, and the Communist Party.[67] For a few tense days, the possibility of a bloody repression like the June 1989 crackdown in China seemed all too likely. Given the enormous number of armed troops under KGB control at the time of the coup, the outcome could easily have been very different, but the coup faltered and collapsed in the face of divisions within the military and KGB forces, not to mention the unprecedented numbers of Soviet citizens who rallied in support of Boris Yeltsin's defiant rejection of the coup's legitimacy.[68] The dismantling and wholesale reorganization of party and state structures that began to unfold in the wake of the coup's defeat may prove to be the most important development in world history since the end of World War II.

Under pressure from Yeltsin following the failed coup, Gorbachev quickly appointed Vadim Bakatin to head the KGB, replacing Vladimir Kryuchkov, who was imprisoned for his role in the putsch, and Leonid Shebarshin, whom Gorbachev had initially named to replace Kryuchkov.[69] Bakatin soon announced a massive purge of "reactionaries" throughout the KGB; promised an end to internal surveillance of politicians, journalists, and foreign business people; and vowed to establish the first effective civil oversight panel in the history of Soviet intelligence.[70]

The abortive coup attempt was hoped by many Russians to signal the beginning of the end of the old KGB. Unfortunately, the

KGB's successor organizations in Russia, the Foreign Intelligence Service and the Federal Security Service, have proven to be very resilient and resistant to reform. J. Michael Waller concluded in his 1994 book that the Yeltsin government had utterly failed to change the KGB:

> Russia inherited a KGB that was reorganized and renamed but not reformed. Instead of starting anew and ridding itself of the Chekist legacy or shunning it as a threat to democratization, the Russian government chose to embrace it and rely upon it as a pillar of stability and a starting point for future society. . . . Neither the internal security nor foreign intelligence services attempted to expose or denounce past KGB crimes and transgressions. . . . Russia's security and intelligence organs today are merely extensions of the Soviet KGB.[71]

Not surprisingly, Russia's intelligence agencies maintained their immunity to reform during the subsequent presidency of former KGB officer Vladimir Putin. Under his rule, moreover, censorship of the press increased dramatically, political rivals were prosecuted and jailed, and investigative journalists were mysteriously murdered, reviving many old KGB tactics.

Having outlined some of the patterns in the history of the KGB, we are now better able to evaluate various intelligence capabilities and operations that the United States developed after World War II in large measure to oppose the Soviet Union and its allies and "proxies." If the existence and activities of the KGB provided just cause for the *creation* of the CIA, what ethical considerations bear on the *conduct* of the CIA?

Chapter 7 analyzes CIA methods of recruiting and handling agents in foreign countries, drawing upon memoirs and interviews of former intelligence officers in a manner unprecedented in the literature on ethics and intelligence.

NOTES

1. Quoted by Efrem Yankelevich, "Helsinki, Ottawa, and the London Sakharov Hearing," in *Fifth International Sakharov Hearing*, ed. Allan Wynn (London: Andre Deutsch, 1986), 9.

2. John Ranelagh, *The Agency: The Rise and Decline of the CIA*, Rev. ed. (New York: Simon & Schuster, 1987), 732.

3. Ronald Hingley, *The Russian Secret Police: Muscovite, Imperial Russian, and Soviet Political Security Operations, 1565–1970* (London: Hutchinson, 1970), chs. 1–6.

4. Richard Pipes, *Russia under the Old Regime* (New York: Charles Scribner's Sons, 1974), chs. 1, 2, 4, 9, 11.

5. Pipes, *Russia under the Old Regime*, 294.

6. Pipes, *Russia under the Old Regime*, 305–12.

7. Quoted in Pipes, *Russia under the Old Regime*, 309.

8. Leszek Kolakowski, *Main Currents of Marxism: Vol. 2, The Golden Age*, trans. P. S. Falla (New York: Oxford University Press, 1978), 306, 514.

9. On the election and dissolution of the Constituent Assembly, consult Richard Pipes, *The Russian Revolution* (New York: Knopf, 1990), 537–58.

10. George Leggett, *The Cheka: Lenin's Political Police* (New York: Oxford University Press, 1981), 41ff.

11. Quoted in Leggett, *The Cheka*, 45.

12. Leggett, *The Cheka*, xxi. The diverse nomenclature should not be allowed to obscure the greatly similar powers held by these successive organizations. Until August 1991, KGB employees proudly referred to themselves as *Chekisty* ("Chekists"). A useful diagram outlining the complicated organization of Soviet state security from the Vecheka to the KGB appears in Boris Levytsky, *The Uses of Terror: The Soviet Secret Police, 1917–1970* (New York: Coward, McCann & Geoghegan, 1972), 321.

13. Leggett, *The Cheka*, 18, 31–32.

14. Leggett, *The Cheka*, xxxiv, 54, and ch. 6.

15. Quoted in Kolakowski, *The Golden Age*, 510.

16. Quoted in Leggett, *The Cheka*, 114.

17. Alexander Dallin and George Breslauer, *Political Terror in Communist Systems* (Stanford, Calif.: Stanford University Press, 1970), is an important comparative study.

18. See the detailed and vivid account by Sergey Melgounov (a respected Russian historian and politician exiled in 1923), *The Red Terror in Russia*, trans. C. J. Hogarth, (London: J. M. Dent & Sons, 1925).

19. Alexander Orlov (an NKVD official who defected to the United States), *The Secret History of Stalin's Crimes* (New York: Random House, 1953).

20. Hingley, *The Russian Secret Police*, 128.

21. Robert Conquest, *The Harvest of Sorrow: Soviet Collectivization and the Terror-Famine* (New York: Oxford University Press, 1986), 23.

22. Pipes, *Russia under the Old Regime*, 159.

23. Leggett, *The Cheka*, 330–34.

24. Conquest, *The Harvest of Sorrow*, ch. 5.

25. John Dziak, *Chekisty: A History of the KGB* (New York: Ballantine, 1988), 200–201.

26. Conquest, *The Harvest of Sorrow*, 306.

27. Dziak, *Chekisty*, 65.

28. Pipes, *The Russian Revolution*, 816–42.

29. Leggett, *The Cheka*, 294–95. On provocation, see also Peter Deriabin and T. H. Bagley, *KGB: Masters of the Soviet Union* (New York: Hippocrene, 1990), ch. 19.

30. Dziak, *Chekisty*, 52.

31. Natalie Grant, "Deception on a Grand Scale," *International Journal of Intelligence and Counterintelligence* 1, no. 4 (1986): 51–77.

32. Grant, "Deception on a Grand Scale," 61.

33. Dziak, *Chekisty*, 54.

34. Dziak, *Chekisty*, 136–38; Ranelagh, *The Agency*, 227.

35. Hingley, *The Russian Secret Police*, chs. 8–9.

36. These early sources included Melgounov, *Red Terror in Russia*, also published as *Krasni Terror v Rossi* (Berlin: Vataga, 1924); George Popoff, *The Tcheka: The Red Inquisition* (London: A. M. Philpot, 1925); Boris Cederholm, *In the Clutches of the Tcheka*, trans. F. H. Lyon (Boston: Houghton Mifflin, 1929); E. V. Dumbadze, *Na sluzhbe Cheka i Kominterna* (Paris: n.p., 1930); A. Denikin, *The White Army*, trans. Catherine Zvegintzov (London: J. Cape, 1930); Vladimir Brunovsky, *The Methods of the OGPU* (London: Harper & Brothers, 1931); George Agabekov, *OGPU: The Russian Secret Terror* (New York: Brentano's, 1931), also published as *La GPU: Memorie di un Membro della Ceca* (Milan: Fratelli Treves, 1932); Bey Essad, *OGPU: The Plot against the World* (New York: Viking, 1933), also published as *Histoire du Guépéou: La Police Secrète de l'U.R.S.* (Paris: Payot, 1934); George Kitchin, *Prisoner of the OGPU* (New York: Longmans, Green, 1935); V. V. Tchernavin, *I Speak for the Silent Prisoners of the Soviets* (Boston: Hale, Cushman & Flint, 1935); Roman Gul, *Dzerzhinskii–Menzhinskii–Peters–Latsis–Iagoda* (Paris: n.p., 1936), also published as *Los Años de la Cheka* (Santiago, Chile: Ercilla, 1940); Maurice Edelman, *GPU Justice* (London: Allen & Unwin, 1938); Simon Liberman, *Building Lenin's Russia* (Chicago: University of Chicago Press, 1945).

37. Ranelagh, *The Agency*, 70–72. See also a recently declassified assessment by the Central Intelligence Group on "Soviet Foreign and Military

Policy," dated 23 July 1946, in *The CIA under Harry Truman: CIA Cold War Records*, ed. Michael Warner (Washington, D.C.: Central Intelligence Agency Center for the Study of Intelligence, 1994), 65–76, and the famous State Department telegram written by George Kennan ("X"), "The Sources of Soviet Conduct," *Foreign Affairs* 25, no. 4 (July 1947): 566–82, which both reflected and reinforced the apprehension in Washington at the time regarding Soviet intentions.

38. OSS cable dated 3 November 1944, in "General William J. Donovan, Selected OSS Documents, 1941–1945," record group 226, National Archives, Washington, D.C.

39. Robert Louis Benson and Michael Warner, eds., *Venona: Soviet Espionage and the American Response, 1939–1957* (Washington, D.C.: National Security Agency and Central Intelligence Agency, 1996).

40. Thomas Hammond, "The History of Communist Takeovers," in *The Anatomy of Communist Takeovers*, ed. Thomas Hammond (New Haven, Conn.: Yale University Press, 1975), 22–27.

41. Hélène Carrère d'Encausse, *Big Brother: The Soviet Union and Soviet Europe*, trans. George Holoch (New York: Holmes & Meier, 1987), chs. 2–3; Jonathan Adelman, ed., *Terror and Communist Politics: The Role of the Secret Police in Communist States* (Boulder, Colo.: Westview, 1984).

42. Joyce Kolko and Gabriel Kolko, *The Limits of Power: The World and United States Foreign Policy, 1945–1954* (New York: Harper & Row, 1972), 4–5. See also William Appleman Williams, *The Tragedy of American Diplomacy*, Rev. ed. (New York: Dell, 1962), and Walter LaFeber, *America, Russia, and the Cold War, 1945–1990* (New York: McGraw-Hill, 1991).

43. Günther Nollau, *International Communism and World Revolution* (Westport, Conn.: Greenwood, 1975), 162–63, 177–83, 231.

44. See Walter Laqueur, ed., *The Pattern of Soviet Conduct in the Third World* (New York: Praeger, 1983); Stephen Hosmer and Thomas Wolfe, *Soviet Policy and Practice toward Third World Conflicts* (Lexington, Mass.: Lexington Books and Rand Corporation, 1983); Richard Shultz Jr., *The Soviet Union and Revolutionary Warfare* (Stanford, Calif.: Hoover Institution Press, 1988).

45. Amy Knight, *The KGB: Police and Politics in the Soviet Union* (Boston: Allen & Unwin, 1988), ch. 2.

46. Knight, *The KGB*, 106, note 24.

47. David Remnick, "KGB Adopting a Revised, Friendlier Image," *Washington Post*, 8 September 1989, A1, A27.

48. Dziak, *Chekisty*, 156.

49. Hingley, *The Russian Secret Police*, 229.

50. Knight, *The KGB*, 185.

51. Ludmilla Alexeyeva, *Soviet Dissent: Contemporary Movements for National, Religious, and Human Rights*, trans. Carol Pearce and John Glad (Middletown, Conn.: Wesleyan University Press, 1987).

52. See John Barron, *KGB: The Secret Work of Soviet Secret Agents* (New York: Bantam, 1974), 148–57; Sidney Bloch and Peter Reddaway, *Psychiatric Terror* (New York: Basic, 1977); Alexeyeva, *Soviet Dissent*, 291, 310–11, 315–16, 347–49.

53. Knight, *The KGB*, 208.

54. *Conspiracy against the Land of the Soviets*, Soviet documentary television program, cited in Knight, *The KGB*, 209.

55. Don Ritter, "Cloud over Glasnost," *Washington Post*, 26 May 1989, A23.

56. David Remnick, "New Soviet Hard-Liners Display Hatred for the West: Reformers Attacked as Pro-American," *Washington Post*, 28 December 1990, A1, A23.

57. Amy Knight, "The KGB and Soviet Reform," *Problems of Communism* 37, no. 5 (September–October 1988): 64–65.

58. David Remnick, "Stalin's Victims Honored," *Washington Post*, 31 October 1989, A17.

59. Blaine Harden, "Warsaw Rite Recalls Terrors of Stalin Era," *Washington Post*, 31 October 1989, A1, A17. This figure does not include the thousands of Poles who died in Soviet labor camps.

60. Amy Knight, "The Future of the KGB," *Problems of Communism* 39, no. 6 (November–December 1990): 26–28. See also David Remnick, "KGB Ex-General Assails Infiltration of Soviet Society," *Washington Post*, 17 June 1990, A29, A30.

61. Knight, "The Future of the KGB," 23, 29.

62. On the efforts of officials in Poland, Hungary, and Czechoslovakia to reform their secret police, see Vladimir Kusin, "The Secret Police: Disliked and Weakened, But Not Beaten Yet," *Report on Eastern Europe*, 9 February 1990, 36–39; Mary Battiata, "A Nostalgia for Terror: Dissolving E. Bloc's Secret Services Difficult," *Washington Post*, 18 February 1990, A1, A42; Edith Oltay, "Intelligence Services Burdened by Communist Legacy," *Report on Eastern Europe*, 10 May 1991, 11–14; Jan Obrman, "The New Intelligence Services," *Report on Eastern Europe*, 28 June 1991, 6–11. Kjell Engelbrekt, "The Lasting Influence of the Secret Services," *Report on Eastern Europe*, 19 July 1991, 5–9, indicated that Bulgarians encountered considerable dif-

ficulty in persuading the KGB to leave their country. Romania's Securitate initially underwent only superficial reform consistent with the ambiguous nature of that country's 1989 "revolution."

63. Ritter, "Cloud over Glasnost."

64. Alexander Rahr, "Gorbachev and the Post-Chebrikov KGB," *Report on the USSR*, 22 December 1989, 16, note 1.

65. Knight, "The Future of the KGB," 22.

66. Victor Yasmann, "Law on the KGB Published," *Report on the USSR*, 2 August 1991, 12–18.

67. As historian Martin Malia reminded us, all of the main players in the coup had been appointed by Gorbachev himself, and the August events were foreshadowed by a number of ominous actions taken by them (with Gorbachev's acquiescence) during the previous year. Martin Malia, "The August Revolution," *New York Review of Books* 38, no. 15 (26 September 1991): 22–28.

68. On the coup and its immediate aftermath, see *Washington Post*, 19–31 August 1991.

69. David Remnick, "Yeltsin Asserts Power in Shake-Up," *Washington Post*, 24 August 1991, A1, A18, Fred Hiatt, "New Security Chiefs Viewed as Reformists," *Washington Post*, 24 August 1991, A1, A20.

70. David Remnick, "KGB Chief Vows Purge: Vicious 'State within State' Denounced," *Washington Post*, 31 August 1991, A1, A20. Bakatin's image as a reformer was clouded by the fact that under his leadership between 1988 and 1990, the Ministry of Internal Affairs created the notorious OMON ("Black Beret") detachments and used them to suppress nationalistic demonstrations in the Caucasus and Baltic Republics. See Victor Yasmann, "Law on the KGB Published," *Report on the USSR*, 2 August 1991, 15.

71. Michael Waller, *Secret Empire: The KGB in Russia Today* (Boulder, Colo.: Westview, 1994), 148, 276. Victor Yasmann, "The KGB and Internal Security," *RFE/RL Research Report* 1, no. 1 (3 January 1992): 19, surmised that the Russian Federation remained "the home base of the entire KGB foreign intelligence apparatus." Bakatin was forced to resign as KGB head in December 1991, complaining that the organization was resistant to reform. "Former KGB Chief Speaks Out," *RFE/RL Research Report* 1, no. 5 (31 January 1992): 68. Alexander Rahr, "Old KGB Remains Alive and Well in Post-Soviet Russia," *Post-Soviet/East European Report* 9, no. 17 (10 March 1992): 3, argued that Bakatin wanted to cut KGB personnel from 486,000 to 39,000, but said that he was opposed by Russian KGB leaders Viktor Ivanenko and Viktor Barannikov.

7

ESPIONAGE

This is such a dishonest business that only honest people can be in it.

—Unidentified CIA officer[1]

DO WE STILL NEED SPIES?

The Central Intelligence Agency (CIA) contributes to the formidable task of ascertaining the capabilities and intentions of foreign regimes and significant substate actors like terrorist cells. Much of the work of its analysts involves sifting through and evaluating public sources of information as well as data obtained by satellites and monitors of electronic transmissions. Such sources can by themselves elicit tremendously valuable intelligence, all the more so when disparate bits of information can be cross-referenced and pieced together by means of powerful computer systems.

During the 1970s, many people in the United States came to believe that technical and overt means of gathering intelligence might eliminate the need for human agents or spies. Victor Marchetti and John Marks, for instance, argued in their 1974 work:

The Clandestine Services' espionage operations using human agents have already been made obsolete by the technical collection systems which, along with open sources, supply the U.S. government with almost all the information it needs on the military strength and deployments of the Soviet Union and China.[2]

John Ranelagh has shown that similar views were held by President Jimmy Carter and the man he appointed director of Central Intelligence, Admiral Stansfield Turner.[3]

Belief in the sufficiency of technical methods and overt sources has since been discounted, though: Although they can provide myriad data on military capabilities, for example, they are less useful in gauging how and when an enemy intends to use them.[4] Experience has reinforced this point:

> Over the years, the United States has become superb at spying from space. But the Gulf War [1990–1991] made clear that those methods mainly yield information on a foe's capabilities, not its plans and intentions. That requires more spies on the ground—human intelligence, or "humint" in CIA parlance.[5]

Espionage using human agents (HUMINT) thus remains an intelligence tool that nations would not gladly do without, and it is frequently the only way to gain secret access to an enemy's (or ally's) sensitive documents and conversations.

In the efforts of a state's intelligence service to recruit agents in foreign countries, the service may have very specific offensive or defensive goals, or it may wish simply to build "assets"—human sources of information and influence—for future use. Richard Bissell, the CIA's deputy director for plans (1958–1962), testified before Congress in 1975:

> It was the normal practice in the agency and an important part of its mission to create various kinds of capability long before there was any reason to be certain whether those would be used or where or how or for what purpose. The whole ongoing job of . . . a secret intelligence service of recruiting agents is of that character.[6]

Covert action also frequently depends upon foreign citizens serving as secret agents, though in a different mode from intelligence gathering. The moral texture of covert action is greatly conditioned by the prior moral context of espionage, and it is useful to examine certain morally relevant techniques of agent recruitment and handling as much as they can be inferred from open sources.

The literature suggests overall that foreign citizens become agents of the U.S. government for a wide variety of personal reasons. Former clandestine service officer Joseph Smith indicated in his memoirs that his trainers boiled down the categories of agents' motivations to three: financial considerations, ideological convictions, and coercion.[7] Other writers suggest a broader range of motives and situations enabling the recruiting and handling of agents: the lure of adventure, excitement, and secrecy; ideology or sense of duty; desire for money; sexual and other blackmail; agents' resentment and frustration regarding their overt careers; or some combination of these.[8] A more instructive approach for our purposes is to distinguish among techniques of agent recruitment and handling according to various degrees of freedom of action, although I also explore ethical issues common to all uses of human agents.

VOLUNTARY AGENTS

Some agents require little or no persuasion on the part of intelligence officials to engage in espionage on behalf of the United States, although in the interest of "compartmentation" (the restriction of information to only those who can justify their "need to know"), they may never be told how the information they provide is actually used. Some voluntary agents are motivated by the sheer excitement of spying and the promise of steady extra income, but many commit espionage out of a deep-seated antagonism toward their native regimes.[9] This was true, for example, of a number of high-ranking Soviet military and KGB officials who either passed sensitive documents to the CIA or defected when they no longer in good conscience could serve the Soviet regime.

One such agent, Pyotr Popov, a Soviet military intelligence officer, supplied valuable information to the CIA during the 1950s, largely out of repugnance toward the KGB's treatment of Russian peasants.[10] Another Soviet defector-in-place, Oleg Penkovskiy, fearing that Nikita Khrushchev intended to launch a preemptive nuclear strike, provided U.S. intelligence with thousands of pages of Soviet military documents, including information on Soviet nuclear weapon capabilities, which proved vital to President John F. Kennedy's actions during the 1962 Cuban missile crisis.[11]

One of the more interesting viewpoints to emerge fairly consistently from the memoirs and other writings of former CIA personnel is that intelligence officers and their intermediaries occasionally develop close emotional ties to the agents they supervise,[12] especially those agents who engage in espionage out of a sense of duty. For instance, Frank Wisner, the CIA's deputy director for operations 1951–1958), reportedly suffered a nervous breakdown chiefly as a result of his being ordered *not* to aid rebels resisting the Soviet crackdown in Hungary in 1956.[13] It is not too far-fetched to believe that, in a state characterized by an oppressive political system, espionage intended to undermine that system's power and prestige can actually provide authentic hope to agents and dissident groups, and in this way can be ennobling rather than exploitative. Former CIA officer Harry Rositzke argued that although agents sent on missions against the Soviet Union in the late 1940s and early 1950s "knew from the beginning that the cards were stacked against them," they were nonetheless "highly motivated," having witnessed the effects of Soviet power in Eastern Europe, the Ukraine, and the Baltic States.[14]

However, espionage against one's government is considered treason in every part of the world and, if exposed, frequently entails severe punishment for the agent. Both Popov and Penkovskiy, for example, were reportedly executed after their capture and interrogation by the KGB. Thus the fact that an agent is a volunteer does not thereby purge his or her CIA case officer of moral responsibility or liability.

Although witting agents usually have no illusions about the consequences of capture, their covert sponsors may ask them to accomplish tasks entailing greater risk than those of which they are aware or which they would agree to accept. Rositzke described how a nervous double agent was emboldened to meet with his KGB handler: The CIA polygraphed the agent but then showed him a different graph than his own to convince him that he could successfully withstand a KGB debriefing.[15]

In contrast, Popov reportedly refused a request by over-eager U.S. officials to organize "a small, tightly knit resistance group" of his military colleagues out of fear of the KGB's wholesale infiltration of society. In fact, Popov wouldn't even provide the CIA with the names of anyone who might be a Soviet dissident, fearing that a failed attempt by the CIA to recruit any of them could easily "blow back" on him.[16]

The desire to ensure the safety of agents can occasionally conflict with wider diplomatic objectives. Witness these excerpts from a *New York Times* article:

> Two or three undercover agents believed to be working for Israel in a Syrian-based terrorist group were unmasked and killed . . . not long after the United States gave the Damascus government information about terrorist activities in the country.
>
> Officials said the administration argued that Mr. Assad should be given an unusually detailed briefing about the actions of Syrian-based terrorists to impress upon him the weight of the evidence against his government. Intelligence officials are said to have warned that such a briefing would put undercover agents and methods of gathering information at risk.
>
> "It was quite an argument," said one official who has been informed of the debate. "The intelligence guys finally told them, 'Okay, but the blood will be on your hands if something happens.'"
>
> Undercover penetrations of terrorist groups are among the most difficult tasks in all espionage, and so the losses of agents are viewed as especially grave.[17]

Agents working against tyrannical organizations have a compelling ethical claim to have their clandestine activities very closely guarded by their CIA handlers.

Some voluntary agents, though, have been regarded as "expendable" in the interest of maintaining plausible deniability and the secrecy of intelligence operations and methods.[18] James McCargar, a former operations officer, asserted that many U.S. agents have been gratuitously slandered by the CIA upon their termination or "disposal" as agents, presumably to render them less credible should they attempt to publicize their former espionage work.[19]

British journalist Tom Mangold learned through extensive research into the long tenure of James Angleton as the CIA's head of counterintelligence that a number of bona fide Soviet defectors and other CIA agents were grossly mistreated—some even betrayed to the KGB—due to Angleton's sloppy homework, paranoia, and damaging reliance on the bizarre, self-serving opinions of one particular Soviet defector, Anatoliy Golitsyn. To the agency's credit, following Angleton's forced retirement, it made efforts to compensate some of the agents and CIA officers who had unjustly suffered as a result of Angleton's and Golitsyn's suspicions.[20]

Other issues attending the use of voluntary agents are illustrated in the statement of a character in John le Carré's novel *The Little Drummer Girl*, regarding a request from the character's supervisor to penetrate a terrorist organization:

> I'll find you an agent. I'll train him, help him trail his coat, gain attention in the right places, feed him to the opposition. . . . And you know the first thing they'll do? . . . They'll invite him to authenticate himself. To go shoot a bank guard or an American soldier. Or bomb a restaurant. . . . Terrorist organizations don't carry passengers. . . . They don't have secretaries, typists, coding clerks, or any of the people who would normally make natural agents without being on the front line. They require a special kind of penetration. You want to crack the terror target these days . . . you practically have to build yourself your own terrorist first.[21]

This suggests the risk of demanding or allowing the moral corruption and liability of the agent to occur in the interest of exposing the members and sponsors of the target organization, an issue also faced domestically by the Federal Bureau of Investigation (FBI) in the use of its undercover agents and informers.

The CIA has also been criticized for building up the hopes of agents beyond what the U.S. government really intended to support. McCargar stated that U.S. intelligence developed a cooperative relationship with an unnamed Eastern European monarchist group, deceiving them into believing that the restoration of the monarchy was intended by the United States (it was not) to benefit from the "considerable intelligence" the group provided.[22] Ranelagh accused the United States of a "cold ruthlessness" in supporting partisans in postwar Ukraine and elsewhere when it had no intention to commit its military forces to save them from being annihilated.[23]

U.S. culpability has been mitigated, however, in regard to certain covert operations in Poland, Albania, and Cuba, where long-term U.S. objectives were defeated by the compromise of its operations and communications by enemy intelligence. U.S. officials were unaware, for example, that British intelligence officers Kim Philby and George Blake were actually Soviet agents who would succeed in betraying numerous espionage and covert action projects and cause the deaths of hundreds of Western agents.[24]

The temptation to exploit voluntary agents for Realpolitik purposes must be considered as a plausible moral risk, though. The Kurds of Iraq and Iran, for example, are quite mindful of the ways in which various powers have repeatedly inflated Kurdish nationalist hopes solely to place temporary pressure on one or the other government, only to abandon them out of expediency.

Other espionage agents are not voluntary, raising a number of additional ethical issues.

DECEPTION AND COERCION IN AGENT RECRUITMENT

When the CIA is unable to obtain voluntary agents, it sometimes "recruits" them, so to speak, through *deception*. In some cases, people who wouldn't willingly work for the CIA are made unwittingly to do exactly that by passing information to a trusted friend or associate who happens to be in the CIA employ but who presents himself as one with loyalties more congenial to the person being duped.[25] This method is sometimes called "false-flag" recruitment,[26] since the recruiter claimed to be someone he's not. It's essentially a con game, wherein one first ascertains the potential agent's basic loyalties and core values to concoct a scheme to persuade him to provide sensitive information without upsetting his conscience or arousing his suspicions.

In his book published during the Cold War, Miles Copeland suggested that "[i]f the prospective agent hates Americans," for example, the recruiter "can tell him he is acting on behalf of the French—or the British, the Soviets, or some senator or crusading newspaperman," whatever his conscience is assessed as most likely to tolerate.[27] David Phillips, another former CIA officer, attested that, "there are unsuspecting zealots around the world who are managed and paid as spies; they sell their countries' secrets believing all the while they are helping 'the good guys.'"[28] Note that one's opponent can also play this game; Phillips continued:

A Soviet KGB officer . . . might pose as a right-wing American in approaching a conservative U.S. government employee. He would attempt to persuade the American to report on the inner workings of his agency or department "to help my patriotic organization to be sure the Commies aren't infiltrating our institutions."[29]

Former CIA counterintelligence officer William Johnson described another example of deceptive recruitment:

Once . . . we found the KGB using a false Israeli flag; that is, pretending to represent the Israeli Service in recruiting Jewish refugees who had access to Allied secrets. At first, the recruited agents were asked to provide information from Allied files on Nazi war criminals, and then they were blackmailed to give Allied military information.[30]

A false-flag recruitment is odd from a moral perspective, since in one respect the agents willingly provide sensitive information, probably knowing that they would be punished if their activities were exposed, but of course the voluntary nature of such an action is only superficial, since if the agents knew to whom the information was actually being passed, they would most likely not provide it.

Copeland asserted that agented recruited under false-flag premises may be treated more leniently than fully witting agents if caught
by their own country's police or counterintelligence agency, if they
sincerely believe that they've only provided information to an investigative journalist, for example.[31] One doubts, though, whether
such a story would be believed. But Copeland also related a more
plausible illustration of how a false-flag scenario can be attractive to
an intelligence agency. In 1956, a CIA official in Prague used one of
his agents, a Soviet colonel, to organize a network of agents in Czech
industries. These agents were told that they were to monitor Czech
scientific establishments to detect instances in which the Czechs
were concealing their inventions and progress from the Soviets and
that this information would be forwarded to "a special section of the
KGB." In reality, what they unwittingly provided—to the CIA—were
details of Czech–Soviet exchanges of secret scientific information.[32]
Note that amid the somewhat comic tone to this case is an element
of coercion: The Czech agents would have taken as deadly serious
the fiction that the *KGB* was demanding their cooperation!

Two other general types of coercive recruitment have been cited
in the literature.[33] In some cases, knowledge of an agent's potentially
embarrassing or patently illegal activities is used to extort espionage
service. Prospective agents may be confronted with proof of their past
crimes and blackmailed into working as spies in exchange for their covert employer keeping such evidence from their own country's police.
As another former CIA officer indicated, in many cases the local police
would already be aware of such crimes but would cooperate with the
CIA in not referring them for prosecution.[34] Since this method closely
resembles that of the FBI in coercing criminals into becoming informers, it may be seen as less objectionable than some other methods of
agent recruitment (although, as I argue later, there are ethical concerns
regarding the agent's society that should not be ignored).

In other cases, though, embarrassing situations can be created
for previously innocent potential agents and the threat of exposure
used to extort their compliance. One technique regarded by some
writers as the most effective and which can be used in combination with a false-flag approach is where an agent's conscience is

"stretched" by the recruiter's careful counseling to gradually allow actions he or she would previously have found unacceptable. The recruiter typically develops a friendship or another ostensibly trustworthy relationship with someone who has access to sensitive information. Casual requests for seemingly innocuous data subtly evolve to more obviously illegal assignments, until the agent either makes a conscious decision to remain an informant or continues out of fear of exposure.[35]

> Those cultivating the spy will press favors upon him, without, in the initial stages, asking for anything in return. This is clearly a matter in which sensibilities must be catered to in order to avoid giving offense or having one's motives suspect. Reciprocity obliges most people to respond in kind; the trick is to escalate the exchange to the point where a more compromising engagement can be undertaken.[36]

Espionage activity that is initiated in a deceptive manner can thus at some point take on more obviously coercive characteristics. James Angleton reportedly described this method as "incremental entrapment in a subtle web of irresistible compromises."[37]

The degree to which the CIA employs blatantly coercive methods in its agent recruitment and handling[38] has actually been a topic of contention among former CIA officers. Arthur Jacobs argued that, "there is rarely to be found any effective means of exercising absolute control [over an agent], even by such lurid devices as blackmail or exposure of offensive relationships or personal habits of the source."[39] James McCargar agreed, stressing that since the case officer is dependent upon the actions of the agent, this naturally inhibits the degree to which an agent can be dominated: "To this extent every agent is a free agent." He also argued that, "compulsion is a very limited technique," since the agent thus "is in no frame of mind to exploit his own skills or possibilities to the fullest."[40] Note that neither Jacobs nor McCargar implied that coercive methods would be morally objectionable *if* they were *effective*.

But if CIA officials actually concluded that absolute control over an agent was impossible, this was not for lack of trying. For at least two decades, the agency funded extensive experiments using mind-altering drugs, electroshock, hypnosis, sensory deprivation, and other techniques in an elusive quest to find foolproof ways to manipulate agents. Some of the motivation behind these efforts lay in fears that the Soviet Union and China had developed technical "brainwashing" methods that needed to be understood and countered by U.S. intelligence, but sadly little consideration was given to the rights of the largely unwitting human subjects of CIA mind-control experiments.[41]

Even if agents cannot be completely controlled by their covert supervisors, it may be inferred that espionage agents are almost by definition regarded by their sponsors first as means to the end of collecting intelligence. The full range of habits, beliefs, virtues, and vices making up the character of an individual agent are to the prudent espionage officer merely helps or hindrances to the production of useful intelligence for his or her superiors.[42] Of course, instrumentalist relationships are common to a wide variety of human endeavors, business negotiations being perhaps the most obvious. We have come to expect and tolerate such relationships (though perhaps not without regret) as a necessary concomitant of modern society.[43] It is therefore the element of crude manipulation that can apparently be present in espionage that elicits our heightened ethical scrutiny.

William Hood has written that an element of control is not simply desirable but imperative in agent recruitment:

> No espionage service can tolerate the merest whiff of independence or reserve on the part of an agent. . . . With a new agent, the case officer's first task is to maneuver him into a position where there is nothing that he can hold back—not the slightest scrap of information [or] the most intimate detail of his personal life. Until this level of control has been achieved, the spy cannot be said to have been fully recruited.[44]

James Angleton, Hood's former boss in counterintelligence, apparently held a similar view, according to Edward Epstein:

> Whereas money, sex, ideology, and ambition provide the means for compromising targets, the lever used to convert a man into a mole

tends to be blackmail. . . . Whatever lure is used, the point of the sting is to make it impossible for the recruit to explain his activities to his superiors. He is compromised, not so much by his original indiscretion, but for failing to report it.[45]

E. Drexel Godfrey Jr., a former CIA analyst, has strongly criticized CIA methods of recruiting agents, stating that CIA officers are "painstakingly trained in techniques that will convert an acquaintance into a submissive tool . . . shred away his resistance and deflate his sense of self-worth."[46]

Miles Copeland, expressing a more sanguine view, asserted that the CIA uses coercion in agent recruitment "only when there is a good chance of converting it into positive motivation":

As quickly as possible, the principal [an intermediary between officer and agent] must enable the agent to deceive himself into believing that he would have become an agent even had he not been caught with his pants down and that what he is doing is justifiable on its own merits.[47]

Moreover, Copeland says, the agent must be persuaded that the government employing him in espionage regards his safety as more important than any particular piece of information he might forward:

Maintaining such an attitude might occasionally mean passing up some item of tremendous importance, but in the long run it pays off because it keeps the agent feeling safe and happy and maintains his productivity over a long period of years.[48]

Another former CIA official, Howard Stone, acknowledged that the CIA often recruits agents by bribery or blackmail, but believing that such methods often produce unreliable agents who only pretend to have access to important information, he hoped that the CIA would try instead "to win over prominent foreign officials of sound moral character."[49]

One former CIA officer, who served many years in Latin America, told me that none of his agent relations were based on blackmail or other coercion. Like Stone, he believed that such methods invariably produced "servile" and unreliable agents who "don't exercise good judgment." In contrast, this officer said that his agents "produced for me because they knew I was reliable and they could count on me in a pinch. They would and did risk their lives for me." He added, though, that different methods might be necessary in other countries where the stakes and pressures were greater, such as the Soviet Union or Cuba.[50] It seems likely that a CIA officer having qualms about deceptive or coercive recruiting methods would simply not be assigned to such countries or would not remain there very long at least in a recruiting capacity.

The disparate opinions expressed in the literature, supplemented by interviews with former intelligence officers, lead me to believe that the degree of deception or coercion employed in agent recruitment and handling is a function of three factors: 1) the individual officer's personality and scruples; 2) the pressure on the officer to obtain information (i.e., faster and more of it in a crisis); and 3) the frequency of "walk-in" or voluntary agents, which if plentiful reduce the need for deception or coercion to obtain needed information.

Of course, deception and coercion are morally suspect ways of treating rational adults, since they infringe their prima facie rights to privacy and freedom. On the face of it, it would seem ludicrous to think that a person could rationally will to be coerced into performing espionage, especially since there is theoretically no escape from the threat of blackmail. This recognition could lead people to condemn coercive recruitment methods out of hand.

In cases where prospective agents' prior perpetration of crimes mitigates their right to be free from *retributive* coercion, the issue of their consent loses some of its force, but this cannot be said to provide a "blank check" to a secret recruiter to coerce a criminal to engage in espionage. However, if we imagine a prospective agent who works in a sensitive capacity for the government of a manifestly *tyrannical* state, there is another sense in which, since that government itself is not and cannot be rationally willed by its oppressed citizens, neither can service to that government in ways that maintain its tyrannical nature be justified. But given the fact that opportunities to persuade citizens and government officials in tyrannical states that they ought to commit treason are sometimes quite limited, one can see that the potential justification of coerced recruitment of agents to achieve this becomes clearer, in spite of the fact that unless the tyranny poses a dire threat to other countries, coercive recruitment would appear to be a form of paternalistic intervention.

Coercive recruitment of agents within a tyrannical state becomes even more acceptable as that state's threat to other countries becomes more grave or imminent. Remembering Sissela Bok's assertion that "whenever it is right to resist an assault by force, it must then be allowable to do so by guile,"[51] espionage can serve as an effective way to prevent a tyranny from launching an aggressive war or intimidating its neighbors. By extension, the same would hold for espionage against terrorist organizations. And especially since the 9-11 attacks, Americans are likely to support vigorous CIA efforts to penetrate such organizations with spies.[52] We need to be aware, though, of other moral implications of the relationship between an intelligence officer, his or her intermediary, and the agent. Consider the following scenario.

Using both overt and covert sources of information, an intelligence officer identifies a particular foreign citizen as one who probably has access or could obtain access to sensitive information desired by the U.S. government.[53] The prospective agent's movements are then monitored to discern any personal habits or foibles (like a gambling addiction) that could be exploited in the future.

Already, an issue of the prospective agent's right to privacy is raised. Law-abiding citizens of a democratic country would likely be outraged to find themselves being surveilled in this manner. Citizens of a police state might be less surprised and more apathetic, having experienced their rights violated on a regular basis, but this fact would not be enough in itself to justify an additional infringement: The burden of moral justification would rest with the intelligence agency conducting the surveillance.

The next step in the hypothetical scenario would be for the intelligence officer to arrange for an intermediary to meet the prospective agent in a familiar setting. The intermediary himself would have been selected to be similar to the agent in terms of ethnicity and class, so that their meeting would seem perfectly natural to the agent and others.[54]

From this point, the intermediary (guided by the intelligence officer) would take one or more of a variety of approaches, many of which were noted earlier in this chapter. If the prospect voices opinions critical of his government or sympathetic to the United States, a straightforward "pitch" might be made to work for U.S. intelligence, though precautions would need to be taken to ensure that the individual was not "planted" by an opposing intelligence service. At least this approach entails little deception of the agent by the intermediary.

If the prospect is deemed unlikely to voluntarily become a spy but has a history of criminal activity or simply a personal habit that if exposed would be objectionable to his superiors or family, a "sting" could be set up to coerce his cooperation. We can even imagine a second intermediary telling the prospect that the first intermediary had been detained for questioning on suspicious activities, possibly involving the prospect himself, and that the latter would be prudent to cooperate with the second intermediary. This variation on a "good cop/bad cop" routine would of course be entirely fictional, but it might be enough to induce the prospect to steal sensitive data or plant bugging devices, activities that would generate their own grounds for blackmail.

If the prospective agent is perceived to be immune to blackmail yet unlikely to volunteer to serve U.S. intelligence, the intermediary might create a false-flag scenario, requesting increasingly sensitive information in return for seemingly innocuous favors or in the interest of serving some cause agreeable to the prospect. A false-flag approach in theory might be maintained indefinitely, but once the agent begins to provide secret data, the intermediary is able to suggest unpleasant consequences at any sign of the agent's reluctance or resistance.

Even if we acknowledge that these travesties of friendship might be justified under certain conditions, such as the tyrannical or threatening nature of the target state or terrorist organization, two additional concerns arise. First, we can imagine how the ability to "recruit" an agent coercively could easily generate its own imperative apart from the perceived value or gravity of the data he or she could credibly provide. In other words, the fact that the pool of prospective agents is theoretically very large could lead to coercive manipulation as a practice unconstrained by any consideration of proportionality. Recall Richard Bissell's statement that the CIA typically recruits agents "long before there [is] any reason to be certain whether [they] would be used or where or how or for what purpose."[55]

The second concern arising out of this discussion has to do with the fact that intelligence officers and their intermediaries must be trained to manipulate people in calculated ways (though some likely have greater native ability in this skill than others). This recognition is shocking and disturbing to citizens in democracies, even though we are aware that other vital professions, for example, the police and military, must by necessity train their recruits in other unpleasant skills to be effective against criminals and enemy soldiers. The concern is that such training may reinforce or result in the moral corruption of the trainee; this warrants more detailed attention in a later chapter on interrogation.

COMPARISONS WITH COVERT ACTION

Some writers have raised interesting questions regarding the moral similarities and differences between espionage and covert action. Harry Rositzke argued that the kind of agent manipulation that frequently occurs in espionage and counterespionage operations may not apply to some types of covert action. Covert financial support for a political leader or dissident, for example, need not entail his or her coercion since it serves his or her interests.[56] James McCargar expressed a similar opinion:

> In a political operation, the case officer must have arrived at a clear and workable accommodation of interests with the agent. Control

by the case officer there must be, but not duplicity. The purposes of case officer and agent must have been presented with the maximum permissible clarity and then a reconciliation of conflicts and limitations negotiated. In brief, the outstanding characteristic of the political case officer-agent relationship is that it must be an alliance, not a utilization of the agent by the case officer, as often occurs in intelligence.[57]

But the fact that this state of affairs applied for a time to CIA relations with Panamanian dictator Manuel Noriega,[58] among others, indicates that Rositzke's and McCargar's points do not dispel moral concern for the wider context of covert action. In other words, knowing that a covert action coincides with the interests of particular foreign nationals is not sufficient to justify it ethically, since covert action may involve the violation of rights that ought to override those interests. It is also likely that an intelligence officer would seek to "vet" (test the authenticity of) an agent of covert influence against the evidence supplied by informers or espionage agents, hence the need to use some method of agent recruitment and handling having one or more of the attendant moral concerns previously identified.

Since the "product" of a covert action agent is in some respects public (unlike the product of an espionage agent), it is perhaps more difficult to *deceive* a covert action agent than an espionage agent as to the real intentions of his or her secret employers. One can more easily imagine, though, a potential agent (e.g., a newspaper reporter or editorialist) being *coerced* through blackmail or other threats into engaging in covert action. Such considerations provide further qualification, then, to Rositzke's and McCargar's assertions of the voluntary participation of those agents.

WIDER SOCIETAL CONCERNS

Another set of moral issues has to do with the subtle effects upon a society in which duplicity is engendered by espionage. The logical and practical extension of the relentless nurture of duplicity is either a Hobbesian state of nature or a totalitarian system where basic reciprocal trust between persons is utterly subverted. A dark vision of such a crippled society was imagined eight centuries ago by German poet Walther von der Vogelweide:

> The sun no longer shows
> His face; and treason sows
> His secret seeds that no man can detect;
> Fathers by their children are undone;
> The brother would the brother cheat;
> And the cowled monk is a deceit. . . .
> Might is right, and justice there is none.[59]

Although it is rather unlikely that an intelligence agency by itself could produce this result in a foreign country (without an army of occupation or police powers to support it, that is), the fact remains that espionage has morally significant effects beyond those experienced by the agent alone. For example, feeding or exploiting an agent's biases, fears, or ideology to enhance his or her espionage productivity may contribute in some small way to wider social, ethnic, or even international conflicts—to a greater extent if the agent is or becomes an influential leader. Undoubtedly, many conflicts that have old roots will continue to exist for generations. Arabs and Jews, Hindus and Moslems, Sunni and Shi'a, Croats and Serbs—the animosities among groups like these will remain with or without the added variable of U.S. espionage, but intentionally contributing additional fuel to old hatreds is irresponsible.

Of course, CIA agents can no doubt sometimes be recruited among persons with broader vision who seek to counteract violent hatred and those who would inflame it. The infiltrators of terrorist groups would ideally do so out of repugnance toward their violence and not because of blackmail or other coercion. Many infiltrators, though, would never be able to bring themselves to knowingly work for the CIA, hence the tactical advantage of a false-flag approach.

In penetrating a terrorist organization, though, a tension can arise between preserving innocent lives and maintaining intelligence sources. U.S. intelligence reportedly had curious liaison contacts with Palestine

Liberation Organization (PLO) officials Abu Hassan (Ali Hassan Salameh) and Abu Iyad (Salah Khalaf), both of whom had planned Black
September's massacre of Israeli athletes at the 1972 Olympic Games in
Munich, but who apparently made a deal to protect Americans overseas from terrorist attacks to enhance PLO prestige with the United
States.[60] The implication here is that PLO attacks on *non*-Americans
would not encounter direct opposition by U.S. intelligence.

West German intelligence apparently had as an agent a Jordanian
explosives expert who belonged to the group later blamed for the
December 1988 bombing of a Pan Am jet over Lockerbie, Scotland,
in which 270 people died.[61] It's possible that the Germans did not
exercise sufficient control over the agent, or that they waited too
long to prevent the bombing, or that the agent simply didn't inform
them of that particular plan.

These examples suggest that in developing potentially productive
intelligence relationships with members of terrorist organizations,
a coldly utilitarian calculus would entail insufficient consideration
of the rights and well-being of innocent third parties. In this connection, mention should also be made of the obstruction of justice
involved in sheltering criminals who agree to become agents. An
extreme example of the questionable moral nature of such relationships was the recruitment by U.S. intelligence of a number of Nazi
war criminals to engage in espionage and covert operations against
the Soviet Union.[62] Christopher Simpson quoted Harry Rositzke as
telling him in a 1985 interview: "It was a visceral business of using
any bastard as long as he was anti-Communist . . . [and] the eager-
ness or desire to enlist collaborators meant that sure, you didn't look
at their credentials too closely."[63]

Simpson argued, however, that U.S. intelligence did indeed know
about the war-crimes "credentials" of many of its postwar recruits,
as did the British, French, and Soviets, who also employed suspected
and proven war criminals in intelligence roles.[64] Simpson also
showed that this practice became risky to U.S. intelligence as well,
when ex-Nazis threatened to publicize U.S. covert operations in
which they had participated unless the United States helped them
to escape abroad to avoid prosecution for their wartime atrocities.[65]

In hindsight at least, it seems obvious that espionage and covert actions relying upon criminals as intelligence assets[66] bear a strong burden of moral justification, chiefly since the victims of their crimes cannot be assumed to give tacit consent to their shelter from prosecution, but also because they can pose a threat to the societies in which they are secretly sheltered.[67] Furthermore, in cases where perpetrators of mass murder (or even ordinary murder) have sought refuge in intelligence work, it is difficult to see how the practice could be justified at all, even under the pressures that CIA officers felt in the early postwar years to quickly develop an underground network in the event of war with the Soviet Union.[68]

SUMMING UP

Let us now review the main ethical strengths and weaknesses of the espionage methods that this chapter describes. The use of human agents—voluntary and nonvoluntary—is intended to provide information believed to be unobtainable through other methods. The risks inherent in all espionage activities suggest, though, that for the sake of the agent alone, efforts should be made to determine before the agent is recruited that the information needed cannot be ascertained by less problematic methods. In addition, since after an agent is recruited the agent–officer relationship takes on a life and momentum of its own, care must be taken to avoid situations where innocent third parties would be harmed or justice obstructed in the interest of preserving the agent's identity and continued service.

Recruiting voluntary agents has the advantage of involving no deception about the identity and general motives of the recruiter. Furthermore, a just cause can be served by intelligence officers and voluntary agents working together to undermine an unjust regime, but such agents usually deserve not to be deceived about the risks involved in the operations they are asked to carry out, nor should the fact that their work is secret tempt their handlers to treat them as expendable, to allow them to be callously sacrificed to Realpolitik or the shifting winds of diplomacy.

The chief advantage of employing a false-flag approach or black-mail in certain situations is that intelligence gathering objectives can be pursued even where foreign citizens are highly unlikely to voluntarily serve as CIA agents, but such methods raise very difficult ethical questions. False-flag methods by definition deceive the agent as to the identity of the recruiter, and thus hide from the agent the full risks inherent in his or her tasks as well as their true purposes. Blackmail is blatant coercion. It is difficult enough to justify its use against known criminals; all the more so when it arises out of the calculated entrapment of a previously innocent person who merely happens to have probable access to sensitive information desired by the CIA. Finally, to the extent that false-flag and blackmail tactics seek to "stretch" the agent's conscience, they can result in the corruption of the agent in addition to his or her victimization.

The primarily deontological concerns about espionage are challenged, though, by the consequentialist reply that if one rules out an espionage source or method, one may thereby eliminate the possibility of knowing certain kinds of vital information. It's not difficult to construct hypothetical cases in which having particular information about the intentions of a tyrannical regime or a terrorist cell could mean the difference between life and death for many people, cases that would therefore question the validity of strict prohibitions on deceptive and coercive intelligence methods or the use of criminals as agents.

The examination of Soviet tactics in chapter 6, for example, suggests the broad outline of an argument for a just cause undergirding U.S. espionage capabilities. Even if the role of state security in Soviet history and external affairs is downplayed, the military threat posed by the Soviet Union after World War II would have been enough by itself to warrant the development of a global U.S. clandestine intelligence collection capability, supplemented by intelligence liaison with allied governments to expose and expel Soviet spies.

The Soviet case is admittedly anomalous in the sense that no other country has posed the same sort of threat to the United States in degree or scope, but a generalization can legitimately be made from the Soviet case to justify U.S. espionage efforts against other countries and organizations similarly antagonistic toward liberal democracy. Clandestine collection of intelligence using human agents will remain vital in penetrating hostile intelligence agencies (counterespionage); in monitoring the existence, movements, proliferation, and elimination of weapons of mass destruction; and in monitoring and subverting international terrorism and narcotics trafficking.

An additional point needs to be made, however, concerning the meaning of moral justification in the present context. To say that a decision or action is morally justified does mean that is the right or best decision or action all things considered, but it does not necessarily mean that the outcome from such a decision is unequivocally good. It may be, for example, that coercive recruitment of an agent can be morally justified in a particular situation (given the dire consequences of not having the information that he or she can provide, say, plus a lack of morally acceptable alternatives), but since coercion involves an infringement of the agent's freedom (and conceivably other basic rights), the external good that may result from the recruitment cannot do away with the fact that the agent—an autonomous human being with values, emotions, hopes, and dreams, who is not merely an abstract "source," "asset," or "penetration"—suffers real harm in the process. This recognition at least ought to have a sobering effect on the consideration of the ends of U.S. espionage and covert action. If national security can justify the coercive recruitment of agents, it is not clear that lesser ends can.

SPYING FOR CORPORATIONS?

Soon after the end of the Cold War, some U.S. officials and business leaders called for the CIA to spy on behalf of American corporations, much as France and Japan were said to already be doing for their native companies.[69] One CIA officer also suggested that the agency sometimes does provide intelligence to U.S. corporations operating overseas, in exchange for their providing nonofficial cover for some of its officers.[70] But the moral justification of espionage (let alone covert action) is highly dubious in the service of preserving or enhancing the global competitiveness of U.S. corporations. The reasons that American companies might offer to persuade the CIA to spy for them almost certainly could not be weighty enough to override the rights of foreign citizens duped or coerced into committing espionage, nor would voluntary agents incurring great risks to deliver secret intelligence to the CIA be amused to learn that their reports were being forwarded to U.S. corporations to enable them to tap previously untouched consumer markets or gain an edge over their foreign competitors.

A similar point was stressed by former CIA director Robert Gates in an April 1992 speech:

> [U.S. intelligence] does not, should not, and will not engage in industrial espionage. . . . Plainly put, it is the role of U.S. business to size up their foreign competitors' trade secrets, marketing strategies, and bid proposals. Some years ago, one of our clandestine service officers said to me, "You know, I'm prepared to give my life for my country, but not for a company." That case officer was absolutely right.[71]

Even if it were possible to "sanitize" corporate intelligence in ways that did not jeopardize intelligence sources and methods, questions of fairness would still arise. For example, which American companies would be given that information?[72] Should it be free (i.e., subsidized by taxpayers) or should companies pay for it? By contrast, the longstanding practice of the U.S. government of providing *counterintelligence* advice to U.S. companies overseas (e.g., how to prevent company phones from being tapped) is perfectly ethical. Such assistance has been provided for many years through the State Department's Overseas Security Advisory Council.

NOTES

1. Testimony of "Michael Mulroney," in Congress, Senate, Select Committee to Study Governmental Operations with Respect to Intelligence

Activities, *Alleged Assassination Plots Involving Foreign Leaders*, Interim Report #94-465, 94th Congress, 1st session, 1975, 436, note 27.

2. Victor Marchetti and John Marks, *The CIA and the Cult of Intelligence* (New York: Knopf, 1974; New York: Dell, 1983), 323.

3. John Ranelagh, *The Agency: The Rise and Decline of the CIA*, Rev. ed. (New York: Simon & Schuster, 1987), 632–45.

4. President Carter realized this himself as a result of the humiliation of the United States in Iran in 1979. See Ranelagh, *The Agency*, 648–55.

5. Walter Mossberg and Gerald Seib, "Delay in Naming New CIA Chief Leaves Spy Agencies Unable to Start Overhaul," *Wall Street Journal*, 23 July 1991, A24.

6. Richard Bissell, cited in *Alleged Assassination Plots*, 186, ellipsis in the original. Bissell's statement has some rather alarming ethical implications that this chapter later discusses.

7. Joseph Burkholder Smith, *Portrait of a Cold Warrior* (New York: Ballantine, 1981), 114.

8. Christopher Felix [James McCargar], *A Short Course in the Secret War* (New York: Dutton, 1963; New York: Dell, 1988), 54ff.; Morton Grodzins, *The Loyal and the Disloyal: Social Boundaries of Patriotism and Treason* (Chicago: University of Chicago Press, 1956); Richard Blum, *Deceivers and Deceived: Observations on Confidence Men and Their Victims, Informants and Their Quarry, Political and Industrial Spies and Ordinary Citizens* (Springfield, Ill.: Charles C. Thomas, 1972), chs. 5–6; H. H. A. Cooper and Lawrence Redlinger, *Making Spies: A Talent Spotter's Handbook* (Boulder, Colo.: Paladin, 1986), ch. 2; Chapman Pincher, *Traitors* (New York: St. Martin's, 1987; New York: Penguin, 1988). Felix, *A Short Course in the Secret War*, 61, asserts that in the vast majority of cases, the motives of agents are mixed.

9. Arthur Jacobs, Letter to the Editor, *Foreign Affairs*, 56, no. 5 (July 1978): 870; Smith, *Portrait of a Cold Warrior*, 114–15. See also Blum, *Deceivers and Deceived*, ch. 6, for support of the contention that defectors to (as opposed to defectors from) the United States tend to be motivated more by ideological factors than financial inducements.

10. William Hood, *Mole* (New York: Random House, 1982; New York: Ballantine, 1983); Harry Rositzke, *The CIA's Secret Operations: Espionage, Counterespionage, and Covert Action* (Boulder, Colo.: Westview, 1988), 67–69.

11. Oleg Penkovskiy, *The Penkovskiy Papers*, trans. Peter Deriabin (New York: Doubleday, 1965). See also Rositzke, *The CIA's Secret Operations*, 69–71; Thomas Powers, *The Man Who Kept the Secrets: Richard Helms and*

the CIA (New York: Knopf, 1979; New York: Simon & Schuster, 1981), 127, 205; Ranelagh, *The Agency*, 400–402.

12. Cf. Felix, *A Short Course in the Secret War*, part II; Phillips, *The Night Watch* (New York: Ballantine, 1982), ch. 4; Smith, *Portrait of a Cold Warrior*, 258ff.; Miles Copeland, *The Real Spy World* (London: Sphere, 1978), 129–30; Hood, *Mole*; Orrin DeForest and David Chanoff, *Slow Burn: The Rise and Bitter Fall of American Intelligence in Vietnam* (New York: Simon & Schuster, 1990).

13. Powers, *The Man Who Kept the Secrets*, 91ff., and Ranelagh, *The Agency*, 306–7.

14. Rositzke, *The CIA's Secret Operations*, 26–28.

15. Rositzke, *The CIA's Secret Operations*, 123–24.

16. Hood, *Mole*, 96–97.

17. Michael Wines, "Two or Three Agents Are Believed Killed after Rare U.S.–Syrian Contacts," *New York Times*, 7 February 1991, A1, A18.

18. DeForest and Chanoff, *Slow Burn*; Felix, *A Short Course in the Secret War*, 107.

19. Felix, *A Short Course in the Secret War*, 62–63. McCargar regarded that practice as "inept" but didn't specifically call it unethical.

20. Tom Mangold, *Cold Warrior: James Jesus Angleton: The CIA's Master Spy Hunter* (New York: Simon & Schuster, 1991).

21. John le Carré [David Cornwell], *The Little Drummer Girl* (New York: Bantam, 1984), 242. That such a situation arises in real life as well as fiction was indicated by Phillips, *The Night Watch*, 331–32; Gary Marx, *Undercover: Police Surveillance in America* (Berkeley: University of California Press, 1988), 144; and a former CIA officer in a Fall 1991 confidential interview.

22. Felix, *A Short Course in the Secret War*, 112–13.

23. Ranelagh, *The Agency*, 137, 226–28, 287, 302–9. See also John Prados, *Presidents' Secret Wars: CIA and Pentagon Covert Operations since World War II* (New York: William Morrow, 1986), chs. 2–3, and Powers, *The Man Who Kept the Secrets*, 44, 403 note 4. On the Hungarian uprising of 1956, see Stephen Ambrose, *Ike's Spies: Eisenhower and the Espionage Establishment* (New York: Doubleday, 1981), 235–40.

24. Pincher, *Traitors*, 24. On Albania, see Nicholas Bethell, *The Great Betrayal: The Untold Story of Kim Philby's Biggest Coup* (London: Hodder and Stoughton, 1984).

25. Copeland, *The Real Spy World*, 125–29; Felix, *A Short Course in the Secret War*, 112.

26. Phillips, *The Night Watch*, 263–64; Philip Agee, *Inside the Company: CIA Diary* (New York: Bantam, 1976), 86; Edward J. Epstein, *Deception: The Invisible War between the KGB and the CIA* (New York: Simon & Schuster, 1989), 89, 182–83. Phillips preceded his description of false-flag recruitment with this interesting comment (263): "Most intelligence officers who set out to persuade someone to become a traitor have to reach an accommodation of some sort with the code of ethics and morality they have inherited or adopted. Sometimes dirty tricks are involved in the recruiting of spies."

27. Copeland, *The Real Spy World*, 128–29. Copeland also asserted (129) that "*most* spies really don't know which espionage service they are working for," but that claim was judged to be ridiculous by three former CIA officers in separate confidential interviews.

28. Phillips, *The Night Watch*, 264.

29. Phillips, *The Night Watch*.

30. William R. Johnson, "The Ambivalent Polygraph," *International Journal of Intelligence and Counterintelligence* 1, no. 3 (1986): 81.

31. Copeland, *The Real Spy World*, 106–7.

32. Copeland, *The Real Spy World*, 68–69. Copeland didn't actually use the term false-flag, preferring to call unwitting agents "Willies" (24). Another former CIA officer reported in a confidential interview that Copeland could not have had knowledge of the story of the Soviet colonel in Prague.

33. I have seen no evidence to suggest that the CIA has ever imitated the tactic of the Mafia, KGB, or Viet Cong of threatening to kill people or their families if they do not agree to cooperate. Former CIA officer B. Hugh Tovar, in a letter to me dated 25 February 1992, said (5–6) that any CIA officer who made such a threat "would have been fired outright."

34. Smith, *Portrait of a Cold Warrior*, 115.

35. Copeland, *The Real Spy World*, 127–28.

36. Cooper and Redlinger, *Making Spies*, 108.

37. Epstein, *Deception*, 180. It is not actually clear whether those were Angleton's words or only Epstein's. Epstein conducted numerous interviews with Angleton before the latter's death in 1987.

38. Examples of coercion applied on informers by U.S. federal and local law enforcement agencies are provided in Gary Marx, "Thoughts on a Neglected Category of Social Movement Participant: The Agent Provocateur and the Informant," *American Journal of Sociology* 80, no. 2 (1974): 414–15.

39. Jacobs, letter to *Foreign Affairs*, 871. The ineffectiveness of black-mail in agent recruiting was also suggested by former CIA director William Colby in an interview on 14 September 1991.

40. Felix, *A Short Course in the Secret War*, 51, 56.

41. John Marks, *The Search for the "Manchurian Candidate": The CIA and Mind Control* (New York: W. W. Norton, 1979, 1991).

42. Cooper and Redlinger, *Making Spies*, 10, 19.

43. Further, we show disdain for *gemeinschaftliche* relations inappropri-ately influencing *gesellschaftliche* decisions by labeling them as favoritism and nepotism.

44. Hood, *Mole*, 29.

45. Epstein, *Deception*, 183. Note that here Angleton was referring to a special type of agent, the "mole" or penetration agent, within an enemy's intelligence service. Not all espionage agents would be necessarily com-promised by failing to report certain activities to their employer, but an intelligence officer would.

46. E. Drexel Godfrey Jr., "Ethics and Intelligence," *Foreign Affairs* 56, no. 4 (April 1978): 631.

47. Copeland, *The Real Spy World*, 150–51.

48. Copeland, *The Real Spy World*, 130. Cf. Hans Moses, *The Clandestine Service of the Central Intelligence Agency* (McLean, Va.: Association. of For-mer Intelligence Officers, 1983), 8.

49. David Ignatius, "In from the Cold: A Former Master Spy Spins In-triguing Yarns of His Past Intrigues," *Wall Street Journal*, 19 October 1979, 1, 41. The author offered his own opinion that agents recruited by the CIA "can be a rather scurvy lot."

50. Confidential interview, Fall 1991.

51. Sissela Bok, *Lying: Moral Choice in Public and Private Life* (New York: Pantheon, 1978; Random House, 1979), 151.

52. Craig Whitlock, "After a Decade at War with West, Al Qaeda Still Impervious to Spies," *Washington Post*, 20 March 2008, A1, indicated that the CIA and its allied intelligence services have had virtually no success in infiltrating human agents into Al Qaeda or recruiting existing members to be informers.

53. A CIA process of identifying potentially valuable agents by carefully compiling and cross-checking information files was described in DeForest and Chanoff, *Slow Burn*.

54. I have seen no evidence to suggest that the CIA ever kidnaps pro-spective agents, even in a false-flag scenario where its intermediaries could

pretend to be the secret police of the agent's own country. That of course would be a highly "unnatural" way to contact a prospect. Note that this is distinct from cases of secret kidnappings or renditions of terrorist suspects for interrogation and incarceration.

55. *Alleged Assassination Plots*, 186.

56. Rositzke, *The CIA's Secret Operations*, 185–86.

57. Felix, *A Short Course in the Secret War*, 144–45.

58. Frederick Kempe, "Ties That Blind: U.S. Taught Noriega to Spy, but the Pupil Had His Own Agenda," *Wall Street Journal*, 18 October 1989, A1, A20.

59. Walther von der Vogelweide (ca. 1170–1230), *Millennium*, trans. Jethro Bithell, cited in *John Bartlett's Familiar Quotations*, 15th ed., ed. Emily Morison Beck (Boston: Little, Brown, 1980), 138. On the all-too-real "mass atomization" of Soviet society, see Hannah Arendt, *The Origins of Totalitarianism* (San Diego, Calif.: Harcourt Brace Jovanovich, 1973), ch. 10.

60. David Ignatius, "Mideast Intrigue: PLO Operative, Slain Reputedly by Israelis, Had Been Helping U.S.," *Wall Street Journal*, 10 February 1983, 1, 10; Bob Woodward, *Veil: The Secret Wars of the CIA, 1981–1987* (New York: Simon & Schuster, 1987), 244–45; Jonathan Randal, "Document Suggests Abu Nidal Was Behind Slaying of Arafat Aide," *Washington Post*, 23 July 1991, A17. Both men were assassinated, Salameh in 1979 by Israeli intelligence, and Khalaf in 1991 by Abu Nidal's rival Palestinian group.

61. Stephen Engelberg, "Bonn Had Informant in the Group Suspected in the Pan Am Bombing," *New York Times*, 23 May 1989, A6. Dan Raviv and Yossi Melman, *Every Spy a Prince: The Complete History of Israel's Intelligence Community* (Boston: Houghton Mifflin, 1990), 424–27, suggested that the Israelis had actually infiltrated the group implicated in the bombing and warned the West Germans in advance. The Germans arrested sixteen suspects but released fourteen of them within two weeks. The bombing occurred six weeks after that.

62. See Christopher Simpson, *Blowback: America's Recruitment of Nazis and Its Effects on the Cold War* (New York: Weidenfeld & Nicolson, 1988), chs. 8–12, on "Operation Bloodstone." The only major drawback in Simpson's analysis is his sanguine view of postwar Soviet capabilities and intentions. Perhaps this resulted in part from his inordinate reliance (evident in many of his footnotes) upon the opinions of disaffected former CIA analyst Victor Marchetti, but Simpson also exhibited a more general affection for revisionist views of the Cold War.

63. Simpson, *Blowback*, 159, ellipsis and brackets in the original.

64. Simpson, *Blowback*, 73. Rositzke mentioned in *The CIA's Secret Operations*, 27–28, 166–73, that ethnic Russians, Balts, Ukrainians, Armenians, and Georgians were recruited as agents for missions against the Soviet Union. He stressed their justified resentment against Soviet oppression but didn't discuss how Nazi collaborators identified among them were handled.

65. Simpson, *Blowback*, 175. On 251–52, Simpson noted Miles Copeland's role in arranging for ex-Nazis to be brought to Cairo to serve as advisers to President Gamal Abdul Nasser's intelligence service. In Copeland's memoirs, *The Game Player* (London: Aurum, 1989), 181, he justified that project by claiming that the smuggled Germans were all bumbling and stupid—that is, it was really a joke on Nasser—and that Mossad (Israeli foreign intelligence) used Nazis, too—implying that if the victims of Nazi crimes can justify such action, why should the United States deny itself useful assets? (Both are highly questionable and self-serving claims.)

66. For allegations of CIA uses of organized crime figures, see Alfred McCoy, *The Politics of Heroin in Southeast Asia* (New York: Harper & Row, 1972), and *Alleged Assassination Plots*.

67. A notable case in which these concerns were implicitly affirmed was the U.S. Drug Enforcement Agency's rejection of a Colombian drug cartel's offer to spy on leftist guerrillas in exchange for amnesty. Michael Isikoff, "Medellin Cartel Leaders Offered United States a Deal," *Washington Post*, 20 July 1988, A4.

68. Simpson, *Blowback*, 159–60, quoted Franklin Lindsay, who apparently in the early 1950s oversaw CIA paramilitary operations in Eastern Europe that involved some former Nazi collaborators, as saying, "You have to remember that in those days even men such as George Kennan believed that there was a fifty-fifty chance of war with the Soviets within six months. . . . We were under tremendous pressure to do something, do anything to prepare for war." Rositzke, *The CIA's Secret Operations*, 21, reported that during a heated meeting at the Pentagon in 1949 an army colonel banged his fist on the table and shouted, "I want an agent with a radio on every goddamn airfield between Berlin and the Urals." That was, of course, a few years before the advent of U-2 and satellite reconnaissance.

69. Amy Borrus, "Should the CIA Start Spying for Corporate America?" *Business Week*, 14 October 1991, 96–100; Thomas McCarroll, "Next for the CIA: Business Spying?" *Time*, 22 February 1993, 60–61.

70. An unnamed official interviewed by Kristian Gustafson, *Hostile Intent: U.S. Covert Operations in Chile, 1964–1974* (Washington, D.C.: Potomac, 2007), 191.

71. George Lardner Jr., "U.S. Demands for Economic Intelligence Up Sharply, Gates Says," *Washington Post*, 14 April 1992, A5.

72. Loch Johnson, *Secret Agencies: U.S. Intelligence in a Hostile World* (New Haven, Conn.: Yale University Press, 1996), ch. 6.

8

COVERT ACTION

A real diplomat is one who can cut his neighbor's throat
without having his neighbor notice it.

—Trygve Lie[1]

There is a sense in which espionage or clandestine intelligence
collection by itself represents a kind of intervention into another country's political affairs, since it can result in foreign officials
assuming that certain important secrets are safe when they are in
fact not safe, and in their ignorance making plans they might not
otherwise make, and so forth. It's also true that an espionage agent
will sometimes be capable of carrying out covert action if, for example, the agent happens to be a newspaper editorialist, a speechwriter
for a public official, or a military officer able to sway his colleagues
for or against a coup d'état. Espionage and covert action are often
closely related in practice, but there is another sense in which covert
action represents a wider intervention than espionage: its "audience" is usually larger, its deception more extensive. Espionage and
covert action are conceptually and morally distinct, as this chapter
demonstrates.

This chapter analyzes documented cases of three types of covert
action: 1) political operations, primarily meaning propaganda and
financial support of foreign political leaders, groups, and dissidents;

2) coups d'état; and 3) assassination. Technically, the second and third categories are themselves forms of political action, since they are employed to achieve some political objective—in this sense, all covert action is political action—but they are treated separately since they involve more direct forms of coercion. In evaluating the ends and means of selected U.S. covert operations, three questions are paramount. 1) In the planning of those operations, was sufficient consideration given to the rights and well-being of the citizens of the target country? 2) Were the objectives of the covert action just or were they corrupted by narrow interests? 3) In cases where its objectives were just, were covert means really necessary to achieve them or would other methods that are less ethically problematic have sufficed?

POLITICAL OPERATIONS

Angelo Codevilla, a former staff member of the Senate Intelligence Committee, suggested some reasons why covert agents of influence are seen to be politically valuable:

> What political operator from the precinct level to the international level does not dream of having a friend strategically located in the opposition's camp? That friend does not have to engage in espionage to be useful. His influence can help lead the opposition away from effective tactics, can oppose the rise of effective leaders, can occupy the opposition with wasteful pursuits, or [can] sow division in its ranks. Of course, any such "friend" or agent must hide the true purpose of his actions in order to function or even to survive.[2]

One conclusion drawn from the earlier discussion of the Soviet KGB is that there are regimes against which open internal dissent and diplomatic appeals from outside are virtually always ineffectual and futile. Although overt persuasion is usually morally preferable, it is sometimes impossible. If such regimes are to be changed, their would-be reformers must frequently act in secret, and if those reformers are to be supported by foreign powers, that support must also be secret. In spite of the obvious risk posed to its recipients if exposed, nonviolent covert aid to dissident groups in tyrannical states can be morally justified.

Jeff McMahan argued that despite familiar proscriptions against international intervention, if a state behaves in an extremely aggressive and threatening manner toward its neighbors, if it systematically brutalizes a minority group, or if it simply possesses no legitimacy whatsoever, the normal (deontological) presumption of state autonomy can be overridden.[3] Although

> communities rightly fear that surrendering control of important aspects of their collective lives to outsiders, even ones who are benevolently motivated, would mean that the community's affairs would then be determined by [people] with a less than complete understanding of and sympathy for the community's values, aims, and traditions and thus that the community's interests would be likely to suffer,[4]

nevertheless,

> [t]here are many cases in which external observers can know *more* about what is happening within a country than its inhabitants, if the government is particularly efficient at controlling the information that reaches its citizens.[5]

But as Charles Beitz cautioned, the justification of covert action is a complex issue even when conducted against totalitarian states:

> [P]aternalistic considerations could justify intervention, if at all, only if there were good reasons to believe that its consequences really would be in the interests of the target population. This is no small matter. One needs to know enough about the culture and values of the target society to make informed judgments about its welfare, and enough about its politics and history to calculate the likely consequences of the kinds of intervention contemplated.[6]

Presumably Beitz's cautionary points would apply to overt infringements on a state's sovereignty as well, for example, regarding humanitarian military interventions.

The matter of covert political action is even more problematic when its target is an open or democratic society. On 27 October 1941, President Franklin D. Roosevelt announced in a radio broadcast that an alarming Nazi plan had been discovered:

> I have in my possession a secret map, made in Germany by Hitler's government—by planners of the new world order. It is a map of South America and part of Central America as Hitler proposes to reorganize it. The geographical experts of Berlin have ruthlessly obliterated all the existing boundary lines, bringing the whole continent under their domination. . . . This map makes clear the Nazi design not only against South America but against the United States as well.[7]

The Nazi plan clearly challenged the Monroe Doctrine, potentially putting German aircraft within striking range of the Panama Canal. John Ranelagh noted that this revelation produced outrage in the U.S. Congress and the American public, helped quash any lingering isolationist sentiments, and resulted in the U.S. Congress giving President Roosevelt the authority to assist Britain for more than a month before the Japanese attacked Pearl Harbor.[8] However, the map given to Roosevelt wasn't real. It was actually a brilliant forgery concocted by British intelligence, a classic example of "black" propaganda passed on to U.S. officials to inspire greater American support for British opposition to Hitler.[9]

That is a very interesting case from an ethical perspective. On the one hand, the objective of the British to engage U.S. aid in countering Nazi Germany was certainly a just one. Perhaps the British reasoned that previous attempts to persuade Americans by nondeceptive means to abandon their isolationism had not been effective enough, and that once Americans truly understood the Nazi threat, they wouldn't mind if they learned that they had been fooled into taking action sooner than they had been inclined. But on the other hand, it is galling for a democracy to be duped by an ally, even for a good cause. Being on the receiving end of a deception has a way in turn of persuading against the U.S. engaging in covert action against another democracy.

One of the CIA's first covert action assignments after its creation in 1947 was to lend discreet assistance to anticommunist political parties and labor unions in *France* and *Italy*. Having observed Eastern European governments fall one by one under the control of Soviet-dominated communist parties and being alarmed at the growing postwar influence of communist groups in Western Europe, U.S. officials decided to supplement Marshall Plan economic assistance with covert activities. But despite the fact that these covert efforts have been viewed by many U.S. officials as highly successful, their ethical justification is not entirely clear, as the following discussion shows.

The leaders of the French and Italian communist parties at the time, Maurice Thorez and Palmiro Togliatti, respectively, were well-known officials in the Soviet-controlled Comintern and Cominform (the shortened names for the Communist International), and both had lived in Russia during the war.[10] Togliatti had also served during the 1930s with two NKVD agents on the Comintern's "Spanish Commission," which oversaw a brutal purge among leftist supporters of the Spanish republic.[11] Togliatti later denied being financially supported by Moscow, but this was not widely believed in Italy.[12] Secret contacts between Italian communist labor activists and the Russian Labor Delegation were documented in an Office of Strategic Services (OSS) report dated 6 November 1944 and a CIA report dated 10 February 1950,[13] but such reports were not made available to the Italian public at the time, probably in an effort to preserve the secrecy of intelligence sources and methods.

In response to Cominform directives, communist-controlled labor unions throughout Italy and France fomented a series of violent strikes during the late 1940s in key industries and ports where ships loaded with Marshall Plan goods docked.[14] In September 1947, Togliatti threatened to use "30,000 well-armed partisans" to overthrow the government of Christian Democrat Alcide de Gasperi if communists were not allowed to share power (although one week later he denied that his supporters were armed).[15]

Italian and French voters' concerns regarding these events were heightened by the February 1948 communist coup in Czechoslovakia and fears that similar coups might well occur in their countries as well, factors that undoubtedly contributed to the victory of non-communist politicians in elections that year.[16] But by 1953, despite earlier electoral defeats, the communists in Italy had increased in strength to the point where they clearly challenged the ruling Christian Democrats once more. U.S. ambassador Clare Boothe Luce sent a secret "Estimate of the Italian Situation" to President Dwight D. Eisenhower in November of that year, stressing that if "vigorous political action" were not taken, within two years, Italy would be the first Western democratic nation to get a communist government by legal means. Washington sent the CIA's William Colby to renew covert support of Italian noncommunist groups, armed with a $25 million annual budget (which, however, was apparently only half of what the Soviets were spending to support the communists) and marching orders to prevent a communist victory in the 1958 elections.[17]

In his memoirs, Colby indicated that a wide range of activities in Italy were secretly supported by the CIA. Payments were made to political parties to subsidize propaganda in the form of newsletters, leaflets, and posters; congresses and public rallies; membership drives; voter-registration campaigns; research and study groups; and training for cadres to be able to argue successfully with their communist opponents. In addition to political parties, many other groups received CIA assistance, including Catholic lay associations, fishermen, farmers, and veterans of the wartime resistance. News reports ("fundamentally true," Colby wrote) about life in communist countries and communist activities around the world were also forwarded to Italian journalists for publication.[18]

Colby argued that there were many reasons why the CIA's covert program in Italy was, in his words, "a moral act." Two of those reasons make implicit appeal to the just-war criteria of just cause and proportionality:[19] "It was clearly for the defense of the United States and its NATO [North Atlantic Treaty Organization] allies against the danger of Soviet expansion, and the financial and political support given was plainly a low-key and nonviolent means of acting for that end."[20]

Given what was known about the background and intentions of French and Italian communist leaders, combined with the grim results of communist takeovers in Eastern Europe, the U.S. objective of aiding noncommunist parties and labor unions appears to have been a just one. The question remains, however, whether covert U.S. assistance was called for or whether other more open methods would have sufficed.

In 1967, when the CIA's involvement in political and labor activities in postwar France and Italy was first publicly acknowledged, one question that arose was whether it had been necessary for the United States to support such groups secretly. Why, some critics asked, could they not have been openly supported by the U.S. government, thus upholding the democratic principle of public disclosure and at the same time avoiding the risk of embarrassment to both giver and recipient if and when covert funding were exposed?[21] Or why did the United States not simply assist French and Italian counterintelligence agencies in exposing and expelling Soviet spies? (In fact, the French, at least, did exercise that option in November 1947, expelling a number of Russians implicated in riots and labor disorders, but any U.S. assistance in exposing them was not mentioned in the press.)[22]

The examination in a previous chapter of ethical issues in recruiting and handling espionage agents indicated that covert action might be warranted in the interest of not exposing such agents. It is possible, therefore, that one reason why the U.S. government decided to engage in covert funding in France and Italy was to protect OSS/CIA agents who might have been revealed if overt measures were adopted instead.

There is some evidence to support this hypothesis. Ronald Filippelli claimed that the CIA's efforts in Italy were aided by the existence of prewar ties between social democratic trade unions and the American Federation of Labor (AFL), ties that had been exploited by the OSS during the war. AFL networks were thus available to the CIA after the war to serve as conduits for covert U.S. government funds,[23] and it may have been morally appropriate to avoid exposing these networks. But Senator Henry Jackson said in 1967 that the political climate in the United States after World War II would not have permitted open U.S. assistance to any European groups even remotely friendly toward democratic socialism, hence the necessity to maintain secrecy if U.S. aid to noncommunist foreign labor organizations were to occur.[24]

By contrast, other writers have asserted that the United States chose covert action because the right-wing tendencies of many secret American contacts would have proven embarrassing if revealed. Miles Copeland and Alfred McCoy stated that the CIA (like the OSS before it) used the Mafia in Italy and the Corsican underground in France to intimidate communist labor activists.[25] Roy Godson, though downplaying any U.S. connections to organized crime, described the work of the AFL's Mediterranean Committee to create paramilitary cells on ships carrying Marshall Plan and NATO-related goods to counter communist groups on those ships and defend dock workers against communist assaults and intimidation by hiring "strong-arm men." Most of those men, Godson said, "were not professional thugs, but they were not, of necessity, *enfants des choeur* (choirboys) either."[26] A 1967 article by Thomas Braden, who was the CIA's main contact with U.S. and foreign labor leaders prior to 1954,[27] stated that some CIA money went to the AFL's Irving Brown, who "needed it to pay off his strong-arm squads in Mediterranean ports, so that American supplies could be unloaded against the opposition of Communist dock workers."[28]

These accounts add substance to the theory that covert action was employed to preserve already existing human assets, but the Mafia/Corsican underground allegation tends to detract from its ethical justification. In addition, Braden's account provides no indication that overt U.S. funding efforts were carefully considered prior to implementation of his covert projects or that the reason for using covert action was that overt funding simply would not work or because it was necessary to preserve espionage sources and methods.

In contrast, Colby argued that the United States did pursue open channels of support but that they became impractical for various reasons:

Washington did in fact try to support Italy's center democratic forces by other means—through the Marshall Plan, for example. But we discovered that our government aid must go to or through the receiving government, and that the receiving government's legislature must know how the funds were disbursed. This made it impossible to funnel the funds only to democratic forces, for, obviously, the Communist deputies in the chamber would block it or demand a share. If we tried to pass such government aid directly to our friends in the open, the Italian government itself, no matter with how much sympathy it might view what we were doing, would have to stop it, because it was illegal. And, finally, the recipients of such open aid would be accused by the Communists of being in the pay and control of Washington. Thus it became quickly apparent that for an operation of this sort to succeed, the fact that the American government was the source had to remain a secret.[29]

It is important to recognize that AFL support of French and Italian unions was not much of a secret at the time.[30] Only the CIA connection was. In other words, French and Italian union members knew in a broad sense that Americans were funding their organizations, although this was publicly denied.[31] Colby added that Italians who received CIA funds but who only "had an inkling that they were in touch with the United States government in some way, though not knowing exactly in which way, were discreet enough not to ask."[32] That reflects a different situation, for example, from one that arose many years later when the CIA allegedly funneled money to the Portuguese Socialist Party through other European parties and labor unions, thus using a kind of false-flag distribution system.[33]

In hindsight, though, it would appear that U.S. officials did not adequately consider ways to openly support noncommunist groups in Western Europe through, for example, some sort of public-private organization directed by a combination of public officials and private citizens.[34] This in fact was the sort of recommendation made in the wake of the 1967 CIA revelations by a panel appointed by President Lyndon B. Johnson and headed by Nicholas Katzenbach.[35] If European noncommunist political parties and labor unions had openly received funding from a public-private organization of this type, they would not have been easy targets of communist claims that they were "in the pay and control of Washington"—an accusation that moreover is much more difficult to deny when covert support is exposed.

Colby contended that covert CIA funding at least did not corrupt its recipients: "The program in Italy gave aid to the democratic forces to obtain *their* goals. It did not 'bribe' them to follow American direction."[36] But Colby exhibited a very different view when asked by journalist Oriana Fallaci, "If I came [to the United States], as a foreigner, and financed an American party, and 21 of your politicians, and some of your journalists, what would you do?" Colby responded that he would report her to the FBI.[37] So a subtle point that Colby may have missed in his memoirs is that Italian or French citizens had reason to object to payments being made to their leaders without their knowledge, even if those leaders did not consider themselves to be accepting bribes, and even if their constituents were anticommunist and pro-U.S.

Similar concerns could be applied to covert U.S. support of the Christian Democratic Party of Chile from 1964 and 1974.[38] In an impressively well-informed and careful history of CIA activities in that country, drawing on many primary sources declassified only within the past decade, Kristian Gustafson detailed how "the CIA produced propaganda, manipulated the press, funded opposition groups, dealt with coup plotters and rebellious Army officers, [and] funded strikes," primarily with the goal of preventing Marxist leader Salvador Allende from taking and consolidating power.[39]

One reason why espionage and some forms of covert action can be morally problematic is that citizens have a prima facie right not to have their public officials (both elected and appointed) beholden to "special interests," especially ones that are not publicly disclosed. An important thread running through traditional democratic theory in general and American political theory in particular is an aversion to public officials being influenced in the conduct of their official duties by private money or favors, especially those that are secret or hidden from view. Even though Americans disagree as to whether there ought to be absolute prohibitions or maximum dollar amounts on the receipt of gifts by public officials, there has been a clear consensus that large private donations must be subject to public disclosure to allow constituents the chance to vote officials out of office if they don't like who is funding them, or especially if the officials seem to be awarding public funding to those donors as a quid pro quo. This is one of the rationales for numerous federal, state, and local "sunshine" laws.[40]

We rightly condemn corporate purchasing agents who accept or extort lavish gifts from would-be suppliers, doctors who receive kickbacks from pharmaceutical companies for prescribing certain drugs, and legislators who seek political contributions from industries they are supposed to regulate. Secret payments to foreign government leaders, even when made with good intentions, create at minimum the appearance of a conflict of interest on the part of the recipient and thus can undermine government accountability and violate public trust.

It is sometimes assumed that these are peculiarly and provincially U.S. concerns, that citizens in foreign countries and cultures do not share such sensitivity to "appearances of impropriety." Alternatively, the endemic practice of bribery in a specific country is occasionally said to prove that it is morally acceptable. Neither assertion, however, can be credibly defended,[41] nor can either serve as sufficient justification for a covert political operation.

However, since political parties at both the extreme left and right ends of the spectrum (e.g., Nazis, communists, radical Islamists) often have secret agendas to dismantle democratic structures after attaining power through them, there is at least a theoretical justification (related to citizens' hypothetical consent) for covert political action to discredit such parties and inhibit their power and influence. For instance, the CIA has frequently been criticized for its covert operations in Chile—rightly so in the case of its support (at White House urging) of a coup attempt in 1970 that led to the death of a highly admired general and violated Chile's constitutional procedures for choosing a president. But Allende did have longstanding ties to the KGB and Fidel Castro, and after becoming president, he initiated a series of unconstitutional actions, 1) to centralize control over the economy, and 2) to create a new secret security service with the advice of Cuban intelligence. In other words, Chileans might not have objected hypothetically to CIA efforts to undermine Allende's totalitarian agenda, at least if there were no effective ways of doing so overtly. Of course, the same idea would have applied to the right-wing dictatorship that emerged under Gen. Augusto Pinochet after Allende was overthrown in 1973. But Gustafson concluded from the documentary evidence that the CIA not only did not encourage that particular coup (in contrast to its backing of the abortive 1970 coup), but was ignorant of the 1973 coup plot until a couple of days before it was carried out.[42]

COUPS D'ÉTAT

The coup d'état, a form of political change in which violence is always at least an implicit threat, is not always a covert action. In other words, coup attempts need not involve the hidden hand of a foreign intelligence agency. But espionage can play a critical role in setting the stage for a coup. Although coups themselves are usually brief in duration, they are sometimes the culmination of years of work by a foreign intelligence organization secretly grooming a political or military official into a position where he is able to seize power. Since the sponsoring agency is unlikely to want its role publicly revealed, coups involving foreign intelligence are thus intended to be covert.

As coup expert Steven David has shown, the political life of many third world countries has been strongly affected by coups in recent decades. Many heads of state find it tempting to dabble in palace intrigue in other countries in part because the potential costs can be many times less than those associated with more direct forms of intervention.[43] Following the end of the Cold War, some of the variables contributing to the likelihood of coups diminished, but the continuation in many countries of rule by a corrupt elite, lack of popular participation or confidence in government, intractable ethnic conflict, lack of agreed-upon procedures for peaceful political succession, military leaders with messianic or greedy ambitions, and other conditions virtually guarantee that they will remain coup-prone—and thus susceptible to foreign intrigue—for some time to come.[44] Moreover, these factors suggest that coups may also be morally justified as a last-resort means of removing a dictatorial regime, but the ease with which covert coups can be carried out in many countries presents risks to the rights and well-being of foreign citizens as well as the potential corruption of national objectives.

In Iran in 1953 and Guatemala in 1954, the CIA was authorized to foment coups d'état whose stated objective was to prevent communist dictatorships but whose overriding purposes were less noble. In both cases, active communist parties were influential, but their potential threat was greatly exaggerated to downplay another motivation behind the coups, namely the desire of private corporations to avoid having their assets expropriated. In effect, the CIA was employed in the service of narrow corporate interests, with the result that business investments were stabilized at the cost of the rights and well-being of foreign citizens whose elected governments were replaced by dictatorships. These coups in turn greatly harmed the reputation of the United States as an ally of democracy.

*   *   *

In *Iran* in the late 1940s and early 1950s, there were legitimate reasons for concern about the country's Communist Party (known as the Tudeh) and its Soviet support. In 1945, the Red Army remained in northern Iran well after U.S. and British troops had withdrawn from the country, and the Soviets took advantage of their military occupation to supply and encourage a Tudeh uprising against Tehran in August 1945.[45] Even after the Soviet withdrawal, the Tudeh maintained obvious ties with Moscow, and if they had achieved power in Iran, there is little doubt that they would have steered the country toward the Soviet Union and away from the West. Given Iran's immense oil resources, combined with the possibility of a Soviet base emerging in the Persian Gulf, the prospect of a Tudeh-controlled Iran was not to be taken lightly. To this scenario was added in 1953 the ominous arrival in Tehran of Anatol Lavrentiev as Soviet ambassador, the man who had apparently coordinated the communist takeover of Czechoslovakia in 1948.[46]

The armed forces in Iran, however, were firmly loyal to the shah and antagonistic toward the Tudeh.[47] It is difficult to see how the Tudeh could have carried out a successful coup on their own, and any reentry of Soviet military forces into Iran (at Tudeh "invitation," say) would have been swiftly countered by U.S. and British forces. Iran was not a country like Lithuania that the Soviets could simply annex with impunity.

Mohammed Mossadegh, the charismatic Iranian politician targeted by the U.S. and British governments in the 1953 coup, had risen to power on a wave of Iranian nationalism, fueled primarily by widespread frustration with the Anglo–Iranian Oil Company's (AIOC) refusal to negotiate a fairer arrangement on its oil concessions. Mossadegh had also been an early and consistent opponent of the dictatorial abuses of Reza Shah Pahlavi.[48]

Despite the fact that he was sometimes portrayed in the West as a Tudeh sympathizer,[49] Mossadegh's traditional domestic allies were liberal democrats, and he was often bitterly criticized by the Tudeh press as a feudal landlord and stooge of the United States. For his part, Mossadegh warned the United States and Britain that a communist coup could occur if they refused to provide desperately needed economic assistance, but this ironically had the unfortunate effect of reinforcing convictions among certain U.S. and British officials that he was vulnerable to a Tudeh takeover and should be overthrown by a military leader more friendly toward the West.[50] The United States consistently overstated both the strength of the Tudeh Party and the degree to which Mossadegh cooperated with it.[51]

According to Kermit Roosevelt, the CIA officer who spearheaded the covert effort ("Operation Ajax") to oust Mossadegh, the strategy the CIA adopted (at British urging[52]) was to convince the Iranian army and masses that Mossadegh was moving dangerously close to the Soviet Union and that they must choose between Mossadegh and the shah. The CIA perceived that most Iranians mistrusted Russia and, that if forced to choose, they would be more likely to pick the shah over Mossadegh.[53]

The manipulation of Iranian opinion was achieved in part by the CIA's clever use of bribes and crowd control. At the height of the crisis in August 1953, after the Shah had unsuccessfully ordered Mossadegh's dismissal, CIA agents actually hired a large crowd to shout Tudeh slogans and denounce the Shah to provoke popular fear of a Tudeh takeover—an audacious example of "black" propaganda. Two days later, CIA agents hired a pro-shah crowd, which was soon joined by army and police units angered by the previous "Tudeh" demonstrations.[54] A fierce street battle ensued and, within a few hours, Mossadegh was defeated. Senior U.S. and British officials were elated by the coup's success. The shah was restored to power greeted by "mobs of deliriously happy citizens."[55] Mossadegh was jailed, his political career ended, and the Tudeh Party was humiliated.

Apart from CIA manipulations, the behavior of Iranians during the coup appeared to reinforce CIA assumptions that "there was still a reservoir of support for the shah among tens of thousands of Iranians either tired of the chaos of the Mossadegh regime or fearful of the Tudeh."[56] But Iranians soon came to see that they had been the dupe of British oil interests, this time supported by the United States, from whom they had hoped to obtain assistance in alleviating decades-old British and Russian intimidation.

Ambassador Averell Harriman and even many within the CIA had warned that AIOC arrogance and intransigence were unwise and ignored Iran's increasingly virulent nationalist sentiments.[57] In the end, though, despite these prescient warnings, the U.S. government chose a "quick-fix" coup to the benefit of AIOC (and U.S. oil companies as well).[58] Iranian nationalism was not eliminated, however, but merely transformed in ways that would eventually explode twenty-five years later under Ayatollah Khomeini, to the great detriment of U.S. strategic interests.[59]

*   *   *

Throughout much of the twentieth century, *Guatemala* could be described without great exaggeration as a subsidiary of the United Fruit Company (UFC). Stephen Schlesinger and Stephen Kinzer indicated the power of the company in the country's economy at mid-century:

> United Fruit controlled directly or indirectly nearly 40,000 jobs in Guatemala. Its investments in the country were valued at $60 million. It functioned as a state within a state, owning Guatemala's telephone and telegraph facilities, administrating its only important Atlantic harbor [Puerto Barrios], and monopolizing its banana export. The company's subsidiary, the International Railways of Central America,

owned 887 miles of railroad track in Guatemala, nearly every mile in the country.[60]

UFC had obtained this advantageous position aided by agreements with a series of Guatemalan dictators. In 1944, however, strongman Jorge Ubico was overthrown by a group of younger military officers, including Capt. Jacobo Arbenz Guzmán, after which the country's first democratic elections were held.

A landmark Labor Code was passed by the Guatemalan congress in 1947, the first to permit banana workers to join labor unions. In response, the UFC launched an intense public relations and lobbying campaign in the United States to convince Americans that the Guatemalan government was infiltrated by communists who intended to turn the country into a Soviet base, conquer Central America, and seize the Panama Canal. In 1948, the United States stopped selling military equipment to the country and pressured U.S. allies to do the same.[61]

Arbenz was chosen as Guatemala's second democratically elected president on 13 November 1950. In his inaugural speech, he proposed to convert the nation "from a backward country with a predominantly feudal economy into a modern capitalist state," and thereafter, he embarked on a series of projects to limit the power of foreign companies in transportation and energy and reform the country's agrarian laws.[62]

The UFC became increasingly alarmed by Guatemalan political developments, in particular a sweeping agrarian reform bill enacted on 27 June 1952. The law empowered the government to expropriate only uncultivated portions of large plantations, but the proportion of the UFC's land that was uncultivated was estimated to be 85 percent. The law also provided for compensation in the form of government bonds to owners of expropriated land, but the value of the land was to be determined from its declared taxable worth as of May 1952, and the UFC had typically undervalued its land to reduce its tax liability.[63]

Like the AIOC in Iran, the UFC made discreet overtures to the CIA to arrange a coup d'état using the company's special contacts at the top of the agency hierarchy. A key UFC lobbyist, Thomas Corcoran, was a close friend of Walter Bedell Smith, CIA director from 1950–1953, and Stewart Hadden, the CIA's inspector general. In 1952, the UFC was able to convince Bedell Smith to seek President Harry S. Truman's approval for a plan wherein CIA weapons would be transported on UFC ships to Guatemalan exiles in Nicaragua, who would then mount a coup against Arbenz. President Truman initially favored the project, code-named "Operation Fortune," but when Secretary of State Dean Acheson learned of it, he urged Truman to reconsider, and the plan was cancelled.[64]

This did not deter the UFC, however. After Eisenhower was elected in November 1952, the UFC repeated the coup concept to John Foster Dulles and Allen Dulles, who responded favorably. Both Dulles brothers had previously worked for Sullivan and Cromwell, a powerful New York law firm that had helped the UFC arrange profitable deals in Guatemala.[65] Eisenhower replaced Bedell Smith with Allen Dulles as head of the CIA, but Bedell Smith remained intimately involved in coup planning—at the same time negotiating with the UFC to obtain an executive position with the company. (He was later appointed to the UFC's board of directors. It apparently did not occur to him that his negotiations with the UFC undermined the objectivity of judgment he was morally required to uphold as a public servant.)[66]

In an extraordinary example of the lengths to which the U.S. government went to please the UFC, Allen Dulles promised the company that whoever the CIA selected as the next Guatemalan leader would not be allowed to nationalize or in any way disrupt the company's operations.[67] This is perhaps the most damning evidence that the primary motive behind the 1953 coup was not the fear of an imminent development of a Soviet military outpost in range of the Panama Canal.

It is true that the Guatemalan government took an aggressive public stand in international fora against a number of Latin American dictatorships, especially Nicaragua and the Dominican Republic, and that this position sometimes embarrassed the United States.[68] It is also true that Arbenz had allowed communists to wield heavy influence in the media, organize labor unions, and hold public office. Communists had also grown strong within the National Agrarian Department and occasionally backed illegal invasions of private lands. Like Mossadegh, Arbenz accepted the backing of communists when it served his nationalistic efforts to reform the country's economic system, but he was confident that he would be able to control them if it became necessary.[69] Even Arbenz's harshest critics in the United States admitted that his government was neither communist nor dominated by communists, but they feared that Arbenz, like Mossadegh, was naïve about the dangers of communist infiltration.[70] If the U.S. government knew that Soviet espionage or covert action agents had actually penetrated Arbenz's government, however, it apparently did not choose to inform him, and no evidence has been offered since then to prove that such infiltration existed.[71]

The plan that the CIA decided to implement to oust Arbenz in Guatemala, code-named "Operation Success," was conceived by Albert Haney, whom the CIA had chosen as the operation's field commander. Allen Dulles called the plan "brilliant,"[72] and it was indeed both ingenious and complex:

> Haney proposed that the operation begin in January 1954 with small-scale psychological harassment and escalate gradually in intensity over six months to larger and more ambitious schemes, culminating in an "invasion" before the rainy season began in July. The idea of assassinating Arbenz with a "silent bullet" was considered and discarded for fear of making him a martyr. Haney's thought, rather, was to bribe Arbenz into resigning. If that didn't work, the CIA would encourage dissension within the Guatemalan Army and help the plotters to launch a bloodless coup. Haney proposed two additional elements: a propaganda campaign by radio and leaflet to frighten the populace and foment violence . . . and the training of about 300 mercenaries and Guatemalan exiles to infiltrate Guatemala, half to commit acts of sabotage, and the other half to pose as the "spearhead" of a fictitious invasion force. In addition, the CIA would jam Guatemala's radio stations and transmit false messages on its own radio and over army channels—all to disconcert the population.[73]

The agency selected as the leader of the "invasion" force an exiled colonel named Carlos Castillo Armas. The CIA also planted caches of Soviet-marked weapons in both Nicaragua and Guatemala to serve as black propaganda against Arbenz when "discovered," reinforcing U.S. claims that the Soviets were up to no good in the region.[74]

"Operation Success" succeeded completely. Arbenz, his military chiefs, and the general populace were all fooled by the agency's clandestine radio broadcasts into believing that Castillo Armas was leading an invincible and growing rebel force toward the capital. The modest use of aircraft by CIA pilots to strafe and drop leaflets and small bombs proved Arbenz's final undoing: He had no air force to speak of with which to fight back. Finally, his military chiefs broke under the strain and forced him to resign. After a few days of confusion and continued U.S. diplomatic threats, Castillo Armas was named head of a ruling junta.[75] Castillo Armas moved quickly to outlaw the Communist Party, return all of the UFC's expropriated land, dissolve the labor unions among banana and railroad workers, and arrest and execute potential opponents.[76]

Secretary of State John Foster Dulles spoke soon after the successful coup:

> Now the future lies at the disposal of the Guatemalan people themselves. It lies at the disposal of leaders loyal to Guatemala who had not treasonably become the agents of an alien despotism [that] sought to use Guatemala for its own evil ends.[77]

But Guatemalans could perhaps be forgiven for regarding this statement with some cynicism, since out of "Operation Success" they had come to be governed by another kind of "alien despotism," one imposed not by international communism but by the CIA and UFC.

* * *

Gregory Treverton, a former staff member to the Senate Intelligence Committee, argued that U.S. goals in Iran and Guatemala were primarily strategic—that is, preventing communism—rather than commercial or economic:

> U.S. policy toward both Iran and Guatemala was widely associated with the imperialist defense of narrow economic interests. In the context of

the 1950s, however, it is fairest to conclude that U.S. officials acted because they believed strategic—not commercial—interests were at stake.[78]

Treverton's argument is challenged to some extent, though, by the evidence of inappropriate relationships between CIA officials and AIOC and UFC executives. Such ties apparently caused men like Allen Dulles to marshal CIA capabilities to aid these large companies much as Allen Dulles the attorney would garner every legal tool to serve his clients. The interests and objectives of particular corporations are not necessarily identical to those of the United States, yet this perspective was apparently lost on CIA and other U.S. officials at the time. The same men whose prescience enabled the United States to meet the many real challenges posed by the Soviet Union and its allies were nonetheless capable of rationalizing the corruption of national ends to serve a scandalously small elite.

Sadly, the coups in Iran and Guatemala were not the first cases of strong-arm U.S. regime change motivated primarily by economic advantages. As Stephen Kinzer compellingly documented, since the 1890s, the United States had exercised raw imperial force in places as diverse as Hawaii, Cuba, Puerto Rico, the Philippines, Panama, Nicaragua, and Honduras.[79] Iran and Guatemala were simply the first instances where the United States attempted to conceal its role.

However, the corruption of U.S. national objectives in these cases should not be taken to mean that no morally justifiable convergence between U.S. national interests and those of particular corporations is ever possible. The importance of Iranian oil to the economic health of the industrialized world, for example, suggests that if a Soviet-backed coup had occurred there, it might have justifiably been met with covert action or even military intervention by other powers. In such a case, the legitimate interests of many nations would have dictated many of the same goals as outside business investments. But the desire to effect the political equivalent of laser surgery, to install friends or remove enemies without leaving traces of U.S. involvement, historically spawned a number of CIA programs at least as controversial as coup d'état.

ASSASSINATIONS AND OTHER TARGETED KILLINGS

Some successful coups d'état are "bloodless," that is, they involve only the effective threat of force and not its violent use, but the fact that political leaders do not typically acquiesce in efforts to forcibly remove them from power implies that for such coups to succeed, their targets must sometimes be incapacitated or killed.

That the CIA developed the capability to disable and assassinate foreign leaders is not disputed, though precisely when that capability was conceived is unclear. The public record indicates that an internal CIA "Health Alteration Committee" existed as early as 1960, and that a CIA "executive action" capability, which included assassination, was authorized by the White House as early as 1961.[80] However, since the OSS had developed drugs during World War II for the purpose of assassinating and incapacitating Nazi leaders,[81] it is entirely possible that the CIA inherited this capability and maintained it from its inception. Some evidence suggests that in 1949 the CIA was authorized to create a special squad whose duties included kidnapping and assassination, though primarily of suspected double agents.[82]

During the Vietnam War, what we would today label as "targeted killing" of Viet Cong civilian leaders was authorized under the CIA-led "Phoenix" program, though capture of those leaders was usually preferred over killing them, since alive they could be interrogated to obtain valuable information about Viet Cong plans and personnel and sometimes even persuaded to switch sides.[83]

As John Marks detailed, CIA technicians, like their KGB counterparts, developed drugs and stockpiled bacteriological toxins that could immobilize an individual for hours, days, or months, or kill him in a manner that could not be ascertained by autopsy or that appeared to be the result of a deadly disease that the individual might plausibly have contracted naturally.[84]

Assassination of foreign officials (except during wartime) has been overtly prohibited by U.S. presidents in executive orders since the mid-1970s,[85] but there are indications that it may have been authorized since that time at high levels within the U.S. government. (Some executive orders are classified and theoretically could super-

sede earlier unclassified ones.) A manual developed for the Nicaraguan *contras* by one or more of their CIA advisers, for example, urges
that Sandinista officials be "neutralized" as part of a "selective use of
violence for propaganda purposes."[86] In addition, former CIA general
counsel Stanley Sporkin reportedly concluded in the early 1980s that
violent actions taken against terrorists would not constitute assassination under U.S. law.[87] That opinion, reinforced by State Department
legal adviser Abraham Sofaer, may have served as the legal justification for "sensitive retaliation operations" launched against those
believed responsible for the 1983 bombings of the U.S. Embassy and
Marine compound in Beirut, and in response to the killings of other
Marines in El Salvador in 1985.[88] Those actions may in turn have
served as important precedents for the "targeted killings" of Al Qaeda
operatives throughout the world during the past decade.[89]

A few writers have gone on record as favoring the use of assassination in particular circumstances. David Newman and Tyll Van
Geel have argued that humanitarian concerns about the treatment
of foreign citizens by a dictator could provide a "compelling justification for assassination."[90] Angelo Codevilla also questioned the
logic of the explicit U.S. legal prohibition of assassination, suggesting
that the practice can be morally preferable to war:

> The military art, the very opposite of indiscriminate killing, consists
> of striking those people and things most likely to stop the enemy
> from continuing the war. Today, the specialization of weapons and
> tactics of war make it easier than ever to go after those whose death
> is most likely to stop the killing. Often, as in the Gulf War, there is no
> quarrel with the enemy country, only with its chief. In such cases, it
> is both futile and immoral to demolish a country in the hope that this
> will persuade the tyrant to give way. Why not kill the tyrant?[91]

Codevilla's assertion that it is unwise to prohibit assassination
tout court is also supported by numerous arguments in the Western
philosophical tradition justifying tyrannicide as a permissible (if
last-resort) means to a just end, but missing from Codevilla's argument are other considerations present in the tradition that weigh
against employing assassination as an isolated act. One important

concern is that unless tyrannicide is coupled with a wider effort to replace the entire regime, it will likely result in greater repression of the populace rather than less.[92]

An interesting example of an assassination contemplated as part of a coup d'état was one developed by the CIA and the State Department in negotiation with dissidents in the Dominican Republic in 1960 to overthrow that country's dictator, Rafael Trujillo. Without passing final judgment on the justification of that plan, it is interesting to note the moral reasoning reflected in a letter sent by Henry Dearborn, the de facto CIA station chief in the Dominican Republic, to his superior:

> From a purely practical standpoint, it will be best for us, for the Organization of American States, and for the Dominican Republic if the Dominicans put an end to Trujillo before he leaves this island. If he has his millions and is a free agent, he will devote his life from exile to preventing stable government in the Dominican Republic, to overturning democratic governments and establishing dictatorships in the Caribbean, and to assassinating his enemies. If I were a Dominican, which thank heaven I am not, I would favor destroying Trujillo as being the first necessary step in the salvation of my country, and I would regard this, in fact, as my Christian duty.[93]

For Dearborn, then, numerous consequentialist considerations supported an argument in favor of assassination in this case.

Neil Livingstone, an expert on terrorism and "low-intensity conflict," argued that "state-sanctioned terminations" can be justified against terrorists:

> Just as it is not a crime to kill the enemy during wartime, so too should it not be regarded as a crime or a morally reprehensible act when a nation, acting in concert with its obligation to protect its own citizens from harm, seeks out and destroys terrorists outside its borders who have committed or are planning to commit atrocities on its territory or against its citizens.[94]

Livingstone added, however, that assassination should be considered "only when the potential target cannot be brought to justice in a more conventional manner."[95] His caveat is an important one, in part because assassination by definition excludes due process of law in ascertaining the guilt or innocence of the "accused" as well as in applying an appropriate punishment if and when guilt is established.[96] The assassin in effect acts as prosecutor, judge, jury, and executioner combined; unlike a domestic citizen arrested and charged with a capital crime, the foreign target of an assassination is precluded from being represented by counsel before an impartial court.

In addition, even when the intelligence is accurate and timely and the weapons precisely target the right person, there may also be risks to noncombatants that ought to inform the choice of tactics and weapons, and that might argue against resorting to assassination at all. Even a gunshot at close range can injure or kill others near the target, and the risks of collateral harm increase tremendously when explosives or missiles are used. For example, many innocent Palestinians have been killed in Israeli targeted killings of terrorists,[97] and all fifty U.S. "decapitation" strikes against Saddam Hussein in March 2003 not only failed to kill him and his sons but killed at least forty-two innocent Iraqis and injured dozens more.[98]

U.S. military personnel sometimes ponder such issues in connection with sensitive "targeted killing" missions. Rick Kaiser, a U.S. Army colonel who served sixteen months in Afghanistan, wrote in an unpublished paper that when military lawyers authorize the "kill or capture" of particularly dangerous insurgents or terrorists, those individuals can be shot on sight even if temporarily unarmed. But Col. Kaiser reasoned that in light of potential collateral harms to innocent people, as well as his concern about moral qualms felt by soldier-snipers who often aren't privy to the evidence justifying the "kill or capture" ruling, it would be better in such cases to operate by an alternative rule in which capture is the default priority and killing is permitted only if capture fails or is impossible under the circumstances.[99]

Additional ethical concerns arise when assassination is intended to be covert. An assassination can be covert in one of two ways: 1) the victim is made to appear to die by accident or natural causes, as when the CIA planned to kill Patrice Lumumba with a biological weapon that would make him appear to die of a viral disease indigenous to the Congo;[100] and 2) the victim is obviously murdered but evidence is fabricated to focus suspicion on someone or some group other than the actual perpetrator—an extreme form of black propaganda. The latter case suggests the additional possibility of misguided retaliation against a third party by allies of the assassination victim, as well as the obvious risk of an escalation of violent retribution among competing political or ethnic groups, such as that which has torn apart the social fabric of Lebanon and Iraq in recent years. These considerations render highly dubious any justification of assassination in black propaganda form, except perhaps to sow dissention among competing factions within a terrorist group or brutal dictatorship.

One suspects, though, that the reason why many assassinations are intended to be covert is that they simply could not withstand a public assessment of their moral justification. Many of the CIA assassination plots investigated by the U.S. Congress in 1975 seem to belie any real consideration for the well-being of their intended victim's fellow citizens. Too often the death of a foreign leader was an end in itself rather than simply a possible outcome of a comprehensive effort to replace a bad government with one that respected human rights. Removing Fidel Castro, for example, would not by itself have diminished the Cuban regime's oppression of its citizens, yet numerous CIA plots were devised against Castro (with vigorous White House support, to be sure) apart from any coordinated plan to replace him with a viable and more liberal government.[101] The latter could also be said for the many assassination and coup plots against Saddam Hussein sponsored by the CIA during the 1990s: Even if one of them had succeeded, there were probably no Iraqi citizens in a realistic position to take over the government who would have been less brutal than he was or who could have consolidated power in the face of a likely countercoup by Saddam's sons and other Saddam loyalists. Sometimes the only way to contain or chasten a dictator is through the threat or use of massive military force.[102]

Moreover, in the CIA's efforts to assassinate Patrice Lumumba and Fidel Castro, it recruited underworld figures Sam Giancana, Santos Trafficante, and other less famous gangsters to accomplish what CIA officers apparently would not or could not.[103] One individual employed in this connection was described in an internal CIA memo in the following fashion:

> He is indeed aware of the precepts of right and wrong, but if he is given an assignment [that] may be morally wrong in the eyes of the world but necessary because his case officer ordered him to carry it out, then it is right, and he will dutifully undertake appropriate action for its execution without pangs of conscience. In a word, he can rationalize all actions.[104]

The Senate committee that investigated the assassination plots appropriately judged this type of rationalization to be "not in keeping with the ideals of our nation." The committee also wisely observed that employing underworld characters "gives them the power to blackmail the government and to avoid prosecution, for past or future crimes."[105]

Assassination is often thought to be capable of ending and preventing war and terrorist crimes. This is no doubt true in many cases, but like other forms of covert action, assassination has too often been proposed as an option well before other less morally objectionable measures have been tried. Recall that among the covert operations considered by the CIA in 1954 against Jacobo Arbenz of Guatemala was his assassination by means of a "silent bullet." It is a disturbing commentary on the quality of moral reasoning employed by CIA and other senior U.S. officials at that time that the only apparent reason why the assassination option was discarded was the fear of making Arbenz a martyr.

Franklin Ford concluded at the end of a grim but impressively thorough account of political assassination from ancient to modern times:

> The history of countless assassinations, examined with an eye to comparing apparent motives with actual outcomes, contains almost none that produced results consonant with the aims of the doer, assuming those aims to have extended at all beyond the miserable taking of a life. . . . Political murder is undeniably dramatic. It is also, given the impossibility of predicting with assurance the full range of

its consequences, a highly unreliable expedient. More important . . .
it is a means that twists and dehumanizes its own ends. History has
repeatedly demonstrated that assassination, including tyrannicide
conceived in the most unselfish spirit, has tended to ignore man's
hard-won regard for due process and to defeat the highest purposes
of political life.[106]

The power to kill without leaving incriminating tracks can easily
lead to the rationalization of great crimes, even ostensibly in the
interests of liberal democracy. This does not imply that assassination ought to be completely prohibited, but it does suggest that any
proposed covert action of this type be subject to rigorous, high-level
oversight, including that of Congress.

Americans should also recall the shock and sorrow that they experienced from the assassinations of their own leaders, from presidents Abraham Lincoln and John Kennedy to political figures Martin Luther King Jr. and Robert Kennedy, and imagine the outrage
they would have felt had any of those assassinations been proved
to be the work of foreign intelligence agencies. Surely they can understand why foreign citizens would have similar feelings about the
killing of their own leaders.[107] Assassinations of government officials
can even constitute acts of war.

In situations where terrorists are protected by foreign governments, or where a government seems powerless to find or arrest
those individuals (as in Pakistan today), it may be possible for covert
CIA or Special Forces teams to extract them quietly and bring them
to the United States for prosecution, but that option places many
U.S. personnel at risk and, if exposed, it may be impossible for the
U.S. government to deny plausibly. Targeted killings of terrorists
might in some cases pose fewer such risks, making it unwise to prohibit them completely.

NOTES

1. Trygve Lie was a Norwegian politician who served as UN secretary
general from 1946–1952. I first encountered his intriguing quote in the

mid-1980s when researching my doctoral dissertation but have unfortunately forgotten when and where Lie was said to have written or uttered it. The quote is widely attributed to him on the Internet, but no one else seems to know its precise origin, either.

2. Angelo Codevilla, "Covert Action and Foreign Policy," in *Intelligence Requirements for the 1980's: Covert Action*, ed. Roy Godson (Washington, D.C.: National Strategy Information Center, 1981), 86.

3. Jeff McMahan, "The Ethics of International Intervention," in *Political Realism and International Morality: Ethics in the Nuclear Age*, ed. Kenneth Kipnis and Diana Meyers (Boulder, Colo.: Westview, 1987), 75–101.

4. McMahan, "The Ethics of International Intervention," 83.

5. McMahan, "The Ethics of International Intervention," 91.

6. Charles Beitz, "Covert Intervention as a Moral Problem," *Ethics and International Affairs* 3 (April 1989): 49.

7. Quoted in John Ranelagh, *The Agency: The Rise and Decline of the CIA*, Rev. ed. (New York: Simon & Schuster, 1987), 95–96.

8. Ranelagh, *The Agency*, 95–96.

9. Ranelagh, *The Agency*, 95–96.

10. "Seven Leaders of European Communism," *New York Times Magazine*, 12 October 1947, 8–9.

11. Günther Nollau, *International Communism and World Revolution* (Westport, Conn.: Greenwood, 1975), 180. On 122–23, Nollau also notes that at the Comintern's Seventh World Congress in 1935, Togliatti proposed that an address of greeting be formally sent to "Comrade Stalin, the Leader, Teacher, and Friend of the proletariat and of the oppressed of the whole world."

12. Arnaldo Cortesi, "Togliatti Demands Welles Retract," *New York Times*, 20 May 1947, 11; "Proof of Soviet Aid to Rome Reds Seen," *New York Times*, 29 May 1947, 3.

13. These documents, declassified in 1975, are reprinted in Roy Godson, *American Labor and European Politics* (New York: Crane, Russak, 1976), 174–75, 188–89.

14. These strikes were widely reported in the U.S. press. See, for example, Arnaldo Cortesi, "One Is Killed, Many Hurt in Italy as Communist Riots Still Spread," *New York Times*, 16 November 1947, 1, 28. See also a recently declassified CIA analysis of "The Current Situation in Italy" dated 16 February 1948, in *The CIA under Harry Truman: CIA Cold War Records*, ed. Michael Warner (Washington, D.C.: CIA Center for the Study of Intelligence, 1994), 181–89.

15. Arnaldo Cortesi, "Italian Red Makes Threats of Force," *New York Times*, 8 September 1947, 5; "Italian Red Chief Charges United States Is Preparing for War," *New York Times*, 15 September 1947, 1, 5; Arnaldo Cortesi, "Arms Cache of Partisans Is Found in Milan; Italian Police Say Reds Planned to Kill Foes," *New York Times*, 28 April 1948, 8.

16. On Italy, see "Czech Parallels Outlined in Italy," *New York Times*, 1 March 1948, 7, and Arnaldo Cortesi, "Fear of Red Coup Drives Lira Down," *New York Times*, 6 March 1948, 5. Paul Ginsborg, *A History of Contemporary Italy: Society and Politics, 1943–1988* (New York: Penguin, 1990), 116, portrayed the mood of most of the Italian press at the time: "[T]he Czech events were a warning of what would happen in Italy if the Popular Front [a combination of the Communist and Socialist parties] won, for the Communists were incapable of abiding by the rules of democracy, and their victory was but a prelude to dictatorship."

17. Trevor Barnes, "The Secret Cold War: The CIA and American Foreign Policy in Europe, 1946–1956. Part II," *Historical Journal* 25, no. 3 (1982): 663; Colby and Forbath, *Honorable Men: My Life in the CIA* (New York: Simon & Schuster, 1978), 109. Chapter 4 in Colby and Forbath is devoted to Colby's work for the CIA in Italy from 1953–1958. Colby later served in Vietnam and was director of Central Intelligence from 1973–1976.

18. Colby and Forbath, *Honorable Men*, 116–19, 125-27.

19. Colby appealed explicitly to these criteria in his 1989 essay, "Public Policy, Secret Action," *Ethics and International Affairs* 3 (April 1989). Beitz, "Covert Intervention as a Moral Problem," 50, note 12, argued that Colby's interpretation of self-defense was "extremely elastic."

20. Colby and Forbath, *Honorable Men*, 114.

21. See, for example, "Subversion by the CIA," *New York Times*, 20 February 1967, 36.

22. Lansing Warren, "France Expels Nineteen Russians as Instigators of Disorders," *New York Times*, 29 November 1947, 1, 11. See also Harold Callender, "French Police Seize Arms in Soviet-Run Refugee Camp," *New York Times*, 16 November 1947, 1, 29.

23. Ronald Filippelli, *American Labor and Postwar Italy, 1943–1953: A Study of Cold War Politics* (Stanford, Calif.: Stanford University Press, 1989), xii–xiii, 11, 112.

24. Roy Reed, "Goldwater Says CIA Is Financing Socialism in United States," *New York Times*, 27 February 1967, 1, 6.

25. Miles Copeland, *The Real Spy World* (London: Sphere, 1978), 235–237; Alfred McCoy, *The Politics of Heroin in Southeast Asia* (New

York: Harper & Row, 1972), 7, 16, 31, 44. McCoy's claims were based in part on interviews with former CIA officer Lucien Conein, who he said had numerous working contacts with the Corsican underground in Marseille and Vietnam during the 1950s and 1960s.

26. Godson, *American Labor and European Politics*, 120–21. Copeland, *The Real Spy World*, 237, claimed that the combined CIA-AFL–organized crime operations in France and Italy were "run so economically that they achieved a maximum of results with a minimum of brutality."

27. Braden was succeeded as head of the CIA's International Organizations Division by Cord Meyer, who later published a memoir, *Facing Reality*.

28. Thomas Braden, "I'm Glad the CIA Is 'Immoral,'" *Saturday Evening Post* 240, no. 10 (20 May 1967): 10. See also Hugh Wilford, *The Mighty Wurlitzer: How the CIA Played America* (Cambridge, Mass.: Harvard University Press, 2008), ch. 3.

29. Colby and Forbath, *Honorable Men*, 114–15.

30. See Louis Stark, "AFL for Creation of a 'Deminform'" (i.e., a democratic alternative to the Cominform), *New York Times*, 13 November 1947, 1, 9; id., "AFL Maps Backing of Marshall Plan," *New York Times*, 14 November 1947, 6; Kenneth Campbell, "AFL Joins Activity for French Labor," *New York Times*, 30 March 1948, 3.

31. "French Anti-Red Labor Group Short of Cash; Leaders Deny Receiving Subsidies from U.S.," *New York Times*, 31 March 1948, 14. A similar situation existed some years later when CIA officers working undercover for the American Federation of State, County, and Municipal Employees helped organize strikes in British Guiana against its Marxist prime minister from 1962–1963. Neil Sheehan, "CIA Men Aided Strikes in Guiana against Dr. Jagan," *New York Times*, 22 February 1967, 1, 17.

32. Colby and Forbath, *Honorable Men*, 120.

33. Leslie Gelb, "U.S., Soviet Union, China Reported Aiding Portugal, Angola," *New York Times*, 25 September 1975, 1, 22. A former CIA officer argued in a Spring 1992 confidential interview with me that no CIA funds were involved and that Gelb's story was thus erroneous.

34. Colby, "Public Policy, Secret Action," 69–71, mentioned that alternative but didn't say whether it was considered by U.S. officials during the 1940s or 1950s.

35. "Texts of Statement and Report on Covert CIA Aid," *New York Times*, 30 March 1967, 30.

36. Colby and Forbath, *Honorable Men*, 115, emphasis in the original.

37. Oriana Fallaci, "The CIA's Mr. Colby," *New Republic* 174, no. 11 (13 March 1976): 12–21.

38. Stephen Kinzer, *Overthrow: America's Century of Regime Change from Hawaii to Iraq* (New York: Times Books, 2006), ch. 8.

39. Kristian Gustafson, *Hostile Intent: U.S. Covert Operations in Chile, 1964–1974* (Washington, D.C.: Potomac, 2007), 1.

40. See George Benson, *Political Corruption in America* (Lexington, Mass.: D. C. Heath, 1978), and John Noonan Jr., *Bribes: The Intellectual History of a Moral Idea* (New York: Macmillan, 1984; Berkeley: University of California Press, 1987), chs. 15–20.

41. Noonan, *Bribes*, xi–xxiii, ch. 21. Also note the massive public outcry against political corruption that has occurred in such countries as Japan, Brazil, and Italy, belying the assumption that bribery is considered morally acceptable in such cultures.

42. Gustafson, *Hostile Intent*, 27–32, 113–38, 172–74, 205–7, 216–26. Apparently CIA officers in Chile initially opposed the 1970 coup attempt but then folded under pressure from the White House.

43. Steven David, *Third World Coups d'État and International Security* (Baltimore: Johns Hopkins University Press, 1987), 3.

44. David, *Third World Coups d'État and International Security*, 9–16. See also Edward Luttwak, *Coup d'État: A Practical Handbook* (New York: Penguin, 1968; Cambridge, Mass.: Harvard University Press, 1979), ch. 2.

45. Kermit Roosevelt, *Countercoup: The Struggle for the Control of Iran* (New York: McGraw-Hill, 1979), 51.

46. Barry Rubin, *Paved with Good Intentions: The American Experience and Iran* (New York: Oxford University Press, 1980), 79.

47. On purges of suspected Tudeh sympathizers in the armed forces, see "Red Ring Found in Iranian Army," *New York Times*, 24 February 1952, 3, and "Iranian Air Officers Held," *New York Times*, 28 February 1952, 4.

48. James Bill, *The Eagle and the Lion: The Tragedy of American–Iranian Relations* (New Haven, Conn.: Yale University Press, 1988), 54.

49. Bill, *The Eagle and the Lion*, 80. Roosevelt, *Countercoup*, 11, cryptically refers to Mossadegh as an "unwitting" ally of the Russians.

50. Bill, *The Eagle and the Lion*, 68, 70, 83; Rubin, *Paved with Good Intentions*, 66.

51. Mark Gasiorowski, "The 1953 Coup d'État in Iran," *International Journal of Middle East Studies* 19, no. 3 (August 1987): 277.

52. The British had previously been plotting a coup against Mossadegh, but when he got wind of it, he threw out all British diplomats. The British

thus sought CIA assistance because they had no one left in the country to carry out the plot themselves. Kinzer, *Overthrow*, 119. Kinzer noted on 123–24 that the coup proposal was actually opposed by the CIA station chief in Iran and many senior State Department officials, to no avail.

53. Roosevelt, *Countercoup*, 3, 11–12, 15, 93–94.

54. Gasiorowski, "The 1953 Coup d'État in Iran," 274. The extraordinary story of the CIA's fake "Tudeh" crowd is based on that author's interviews with five former CIA officers, 285, note 66. See also Kinzer, *Overthrow*, 127.

55. Roosevelt, *Countercoup*, 198–99; Kennett Love, "Shah, Back in Iran, Wildly Acclaimed; Prestige at Peak," *New York Times*, 23 August 1953, 1, 20.

56. Rubin, *Paved with Good Intentions*, 85.

57. Rubin, *Paved with Good Intentions*, 67–68; Bill, *The Eagle and the Lion*, 62–63, 72–78; Gasiorowski, "The 1953 Coup d'État in Iran," 276.

58. U.S. oil companies colluded to boycott oil from Iran following its nationalization of the AIOC in 1952, in part to dissuade expropriations in other countries, but also to gain access to oil sources from which they had previously been excluded. "In exchange for American support in overthrowing the Musaddiq [sic] government, the British [whose government had a majority stake in the AIOC] grudgingly permitted U.S. companies a 40 percent interest in Iranian oil." Bill, *The Eagle and the Lion*, 78–80.

59. Bill, *The Eagle and the Lion*, 94–97.

60. Stephen Schlesinger and Stephen Kinzer, *Bitter Fruit: The Untold Story of the American Coup in Guatemala* (Garden City, N.Y.: Doubleday, 1982), 12.

61. Schlesinger and Kinzer, *Bitter Fruit*, 83–97, 148.

62. Schlesinger and Kinzer, *Bitter Fruit*, 52–54.

63. Schlesinger and Kinzer, *Bitter Fruit*, 54, 105; Richard Immerman, *The CIA in Guatemala* (Austin: University of Texas Press, 1982), 79–82.

64. Schlesinger and Kinzer, *Bitter Fruit*, 91, 102.

65. On the many ties between the UFC and Eisenhower aides, see Immerman, *The CIA in Guatemala*, 124–25.

66. Schlesinger and Kinzer, *Bitter Fruit*, 102, 106–7. See also Stephen Ambrose, *Ike's Spies: Eisenhower and the Espionage Establishment* (New York: Doubleday, 1981), 218–24.

67. Schlesinger and Kinzer, *Bitter Fruit*, 120.

68. Immerman, *The CIA in Guatemala*, 49, 84–85.

69. Schlesinger and Kinzer, *Bitter Fruit*, 55–61.

70. Sydney Gruson, "Country Is Tense," *New York Times*, 7 February 1954, 25; Milton Bracker, "Guatemalan Reds Exploit Reforms," *New York*

Times, 3 March 1954, 11; Immerman, *The CIA in Guatemala*, 106. Kinzer indicated in *Overthrow*, 140, that Sydney Gruson was pulled out of Guatemala by the *New York Times* at the request of the CIA's Allen Dulles.

71. Kinzer, *Overthrow*, 136.

72. Schlesinger and Kinzer, *Bitter Fruit*, 112.

73. Schlesinger and Kinzer, *Bitter Fruit*, 110–11.

74. Schlesinger and Kinzer, *Bitter Fruit*, 115, 150.

75. Schlesinger and Kinzer, *Bitter Fruit*, 194–97.

76. Schlesinger and Kinzer, *Bitter Fruit*, 218–19; Immerman, *The CIA in Guatemala*, 198–200.

77. "The Text of Dulles' Speech on Guatemalan Upset," *New York Times*, 1 July 1954, 2.

78. Gregory Treverton, *Covert Action: The Limits of Intervention in the Postwar World* (New York: Basic, 1987), 79.

79. Kinzer, *Overthrow*, chs. 1–4.

80. "Congress, Senate, Select Committee to Study Governmental Operations with Respect to Intelligence Activities," *Alleged Assassination Plots Involving Foreign Leaders*, Interim Report #94-465, 94th Congress, 1st session, 1975, 181–87.

81. John Marks, *The Search for the "Manchurian Candidate": The CIA and Mind Control* (New York: W. W. Norton, 1979, 1991), 16–18, 119.

82. Christopher Simpson, *Blowback: America's Recruitment of Nazis and Its Effects on the Cold War* (New York: Weidenfeld & Nicolson, 1988), 153. See also Ambrose, *Ike's Spies*, 297.

83. Dale Andrade, *Ashes to Ashes: The Phoenix Program and the Vietnam War* (Lexington, Mass.: Lexington, 1990).

84. Marks, *The Search for the "Manchurian Candidate,"* 80–81.

85. David Newman and Tyll Van Geel, "Executive Order 12333: The Risks of a Clear Declaration of Intent," *Harvard Journal of Law and Public Policy* 12, no. 2 (Spring 1989): 440–41. The ban doesn't specify "foreign officials" or include the wartime caveat, but those qualifications seem to be consistent with the ban's intended scope. See Elizabeth Bazan, "Assassination Ban and E.O. 12333: A Brief Summary," *CRS Report for Congress*, 4 January 2002, and Catherine Lotrionte, "When to Target Leaders," *Washington Quarterly*, Summer 2003, 76–77.

86. "Tayacán," *Psychological Operations in Guerrilla Warfare*, with essays by Joanne Omang and Aryeh Neier (New York: Random House, 1985), 57–59. B. Hugh Tovar, in his 25 February 1992 letter to me, wrote (9), "'Neutralization' was not authorized at high levels [within the CIA],

and the individuals responsible for the [Nicaragua] manual were censured severely."

87. Bob Woodward, *Veil: The Secret Wars of the CIA, 1981–1987* (New York: Simon & Schuster, 1987), 362. Michael Kinsley quipped sarcastically in "We Shoot People, Don't We?" *Time*, 23 October 1989, 118, "What the assassination ban amounts to in practice is a rule against killing people whose names you know."

88. See Russell Watson, Nicholas M. Horrock, and Abdul Hajjaj, "Fighting Terror with Terror: An Abortive CIA Operation in Lebanon Is Uncovered," *Newsweek*, 27 May 1985, 32–33; William Cowan, "How to Kill Saddam," *Washington Post*, 10 February 1991, C2; Ed Offley, "El Salvador Raid in 1985 Revealed," and "Former Ranger Tells of Raid to Destroy Terrorist Camp," *Seattle Post-Intelligencer*, 15 June 1995, A1, A20, A21.

89. Bob Woodward, "CIA Told to Do 'Whatever Necessary' to Kill Bin Laden," *Washington Post*, 21 October 2001, A1; Barton Gellman, "CIA Weighs 'Targeted Killing' Missions: Administration Believes Restraints Do Not Bar Singling Out Individual Terrorists," *Washington Post*, 28 October 2001, A1; Thom Shanker and James Risen, "Rumsfeld Weighs New Covert Acts by Military Units," *New York Times*, 12 August 2002, A1; Robert Collier, "U.S. Forces Kill Top Al Qaeda Operative," *San Francisco Chronicle*, 5 November 2002, A1; Shaun Waterman, "Goss Says CIA Ban Excludes Terrorists," *Washington Times*, 25 March 2005, 5; Eric Schmitt and Mark Mazzetti, "Secret Order Lets U.S. Raid Al Qaeda," *New York Times*, 10 November 2008, A1.

90. Newman and Van Geel, "Executive Order 12333," 438. Cf. Lotrionte, "When to Target Leaders," 79–80.

91. Angelo Codevilla, "Get Rid of Saddam Hussein Now: The Moral Justification," *Wall Street Journal*, 25 February 1991, 8. See also Neil Livingston, "Should We 'Take Out' Terrorists?" *Counterterrorism and Security*, May–June 1991, 11–16. Livingston noted with some irony that Saddam Hussein began his career in the Iraqi Ba'ath Party as an assassin.

92. Theologian Dietrich Bonhoeffer, who participated in an unsuccessful attempt on Hitler's life in 1944, is said to have held that "the act of assassination must be coordinated with the plans of a group capable of quickly occupying, or remaining in, the key organs of the totalitarian dictatorship," a principle that resembles the *jus ad bellum* criterion of probable success. Larry Rasmussen, *Dietrich Bonhoeffer: Reality and Resistance* (Nashville, Tenn.: Abingdon, 1972), 145. Cf. Lotrionte, "When to Target Leaders," 81.

93. Henry Dearborn, letter to Thomas Mann, quoted in *Alleged Assassination Plots*, 195.

94. Neil Livingstone, *The War against Terrorism* (Lexington, Mass.: Lexington, 1982), 174–75.

95. Livingstone, *The War against Terrorism*, 175.

96. Laura Donohoe, "Assassinations Won't Make Us Safer," *San Jose Mercury News*, 22 November 2002.

97. Laura Blumenfeld, "In Israel, a Divisive Struggle over Targeted Killings," *Washington Post*, 27 August 2006, A1. Some U.S. and allied military officers have expressed similar concerns about innocent Afghan civilians killed in U.S. airstrikes intended to be precision killings of terrorists.

98. Human Rights Watch, *Off Target: The Conduct of the War and Civilian Casualties in Iraq* (New York: Human Rights Watch, 2003), 23.

99. Col. Richard Kaiser, "Wanted, Dead or Alive: The Moral Dilemma Faced in Killing or Capturing Terror Suspects," a paper written for my ethics and warfare class at the U.S. Army War College in May 2008, and summarized with his permission.

100. *Alleged Assassination Plots*, 13–70.

101. On the various plots against Castro, see *Alleged Assassination Plots*, 71–90, and Powers, *The Man Who Kept the Secrets*, ch. 9.

102. Kenneth Pollack, *The Threatening Storm: The Case for Invading Iraq* (New York: Random House, 2002).

103. *Alleged Assassination Plots*, 43–48, 74–77.

104. *Alleged Assassination Plots*, 46. Compare Machiavelli's dictum: "When the safety of one's country wholly depends on the decision to be taken, no attention should be paid either to justice or injustice, to kindness or cruelty, or to its being praiseworthy or ignominious." Niccolo Machiavelli, *Discourses on the First Ten Books of Titus Livius*, trans. Leslie Walker, S.J., cited in Quentin Skinner, *The Foundations of Modern Political Thought, Vol. I: The Renaissance* (New York: Cambridge University Press, 1978), 183.

105. *Alleged Assassination Plots*, 259.

106. Franklin Ford, *Political Murder: From Tyrannicide to Terrorism* (Cambridge, Mass.: Harvard University Press, 1985), 387–88.

107. Although President Kennedy authorized U.S. support in 1963 for a military coup against President Diem of South Vietnam, he and his advisers seem to have been deeply shocked when Diem and his brother were

summarily shot after their arrest. Apparently none of them had bothered to caution the plotters against killing Diem; perhaps the possibility of that outcome simply didn't occur to them. Kennedy's advisers later judged the coup to have been a "disaster," "a terrible, stupid thing," and the "worst mistake of the Vietnam War." Kinzer, *Overthrow*, chs. 7 and 9. Ironically, Kennedy himself was assassinated only a few weeks after Diem.

9

INTERROGATION

ruth \ *n* [Middle English *ruthe*, French *ruen*, to rue] 1 : compassion
for the misery of another 2 : sorrow for one's own faults : remorse

ruthless \ *adj* : having no ruth : merciless, cruel.[1]

A "FUNDAMENTALLY REPUGNANT PHILOSOPHY"

In our country's contemporary efforts to combat secretive terrorists using HUMINT, that is, intelligence collection via human
sources, we face some difficult ethical questions that have been
explored in other ways in previous chapters: Do ruthless enemies
warrant (i.e., justify, merit, or deserve) ruthless countermeasures?
Should we uphold high ethical standards even against unlawful
combatants who don't respect them? Or, to preserve what we value
most, are we morally justified in using tactics that strain or even
contradict those values? These questions also echo those of Carl
Friedrich in his classic study of raison d'etat:

> [O]nly those political theorists who subject government and politics
> to law and/or a transcendent moral order, who put justice ahead of
> or at least on a level with peace and order, are confronted with the
> problem of reason of state in its most perplexing form. For if the

constitutional order's survival is threatened by an enemy who does not acknowledge the validity of this law and moral order, what is the defender of the constitutional order permitted to do? How far may he go in violating the norms . . . he is supposedly bound to respect?[2]

Recall that this is not an entirely new challenge for Americans. Consider the following statements made by a special committee appointed by the president:

It is now clear that we are facing an implacable enemy whose avowed objective is world domination by whatever means and at whatever cost. There are no rules in such a game. Hitherto acceptable norms of human conduct do not apply. If the United States is to survive, long-standing American concepts of "fair play" must be reconsidered. We . . . must learn to subvert, sabotage, and destroy our enemies by more clever, more sophisticated . . . more effective methods than those used against us. It may become necessary that the American people be made acquainted with, understand, and support this fundamentally repugnant philosophy.[3]

As timely as such views sound to us today, they were actually written in reference to the *communist* threat more than 50 years ago in a report commissioned by President Dwight D. Eisenhower. Similar statements could also have been made earlier in U.S. history, for example, in reference to the Nazi threat of the 1930s and 1940s, or in response to anarchist bombings and assassinations during the late 1800s. President Abraham Lincoln weighed U.S. constitutional rights against national security during the Civil War, for example, when he suspended the writ of habeas corpus. In fact, the question of whether such rights should ever be infringed in the interest of security goes at least as far back as the Alien and Sedition Acts of 1798.[4]

Like our predecessors, we are now facing very serious threats to our country from enemies who violate all of the contemporary laws of war and traditional principles of military chivalry. In the wake of the 9-11 attacks, a view quickly developed within the U.S. government and much of the general public that at least some prior restraints on the conduct of intelligence and military personnel needed to be modified or even abandoned to obtain information that might be vital to preventing another devastating terrorist strike. Since then there have been many indications that U.S. government personnel—primarily Central Intelligence Agency (CIA) clandestine service officers but also military intelligence and special forces—were given permission to use more forceful and aggressive tactics than had previously been allowed, including interrogation methods intended to produce acute pain and fear, and renditions of detainees to countries notorious for using torture, all of which are problematic under international treaties, to say the least.[5]

Obviously members of Al Qaeda and similar groups have treated U.S. citizens and other innocent people in ruthless ways and fully intend to do so in the future. What then is morally permissible for us to do in preventing them from carrying out their plans? Given 1) the global expressions of revulsion that accompanied the revelations of abuses at Abu Ghraib, 2) the overwhelming support in Congress for the Detainee Treatment Act of 2005, and 3) President Barack Obama's executive order of 22 January 2009, "Ensuring Lawful Interrogations," the question of torture might seem moot at this point. But there are some important lines of analysis that have yet to be sufficiently explored." And if the United States were to experience another 9-11, the ethical questions would certainly arise again, and we'd need to be prepared to address them with solid facts, reflections, and arguments. A recent survey suggests that 49 percent of U.S. military personnel and 63 percent of the general public believe that it would at least be occasionally ethical to use torture against suspected terrorists.[6]

In this chapter, I examine some empirical, nonconsequentialist (deontological), consequentialist (teleological), and character (aretaic) factors bearing on intelligence interrogation techniques, which often play a role in HUMINT. More specifically, this chapter explores: 1) Nonmoral questions about the effectiveness of torture in interrogations, for example, does it ever "work" in the sense of producing accurate intelligence? 2) What does the law require? What have we pledged to do in relevant international treaties? 3) If the law were silent on torture, or if we were to reconsider our treaty obligations, how should we sort out the moral rights involved? Is a right not to be tortured absolute or something less strict than that? 4) What would be the probable consequences of legalizing torture in intelligence interrogations? Would the likely harms from that outweigh its potential benefits?

I personally feel greatly ambivalent and torn about the contending moral considerations at stake here, but I concur with law professor Sanford Levinson's sense of our urgent contemporary need to wrestle with the ethics of torture: "We are staring into an abyss, and no one can escape the necessity of a response."[7]

DOES TORTURE EVER WORK?

The empirical, nonmoral question of whether torture ever works as a method of intelligence interrogation is obviously important to the moral controversy, since if torture never worked, then it would be silly to use it in HUMINT.[8] Unfortunately, experts seem to be divided on the empirical question of whether torture can be effective.

On the one hand, a legal historian concluded from a study of centuries of torture in Europe that it's a highly unreliable way of producing accurate confessions.[9] A CIA interrogation manual written in 1963 and declassified in 1997 also surmised, "Intense pain is quite likely to produce false confessions, concocted as a means of escaping from distress."[10] The U.S. military and Federal Bureau of Investigation (FBI) have for decades taught their interrogators that torture is not effective in eliciting truthful statements.[11] And recent experiments with volunteers on the effects of isolation and sensory deprivation (conditions forcibly inflicted on some of our country's detainees since 9-11 but that don't necessarily constitute torture per se) indicate that significant memory loss and suggestibility can occur after only 48 hours, meaning that statements made by detainees subjected to such treatment are likely to be unreliable and misleading, even if they intend at that point to cooperate with their captors.[12]

A detailed memoir titled *The Interrogators*, written by an Army noncommissioned officer who served in military intelligence in Afghanistan, suggests that the most reliable interrogation methods are those echoing classic police and detective work: building rapport with the subject to foster trust; offering incentives for cooperation; gathering independent evidence without the suspect's knowledge; identifying discrepancies between the suspect's story and the stories of his accomplices and other witnesses; deceiving the suspect into thinking you know more than you do; and catching the suspect in lies that he or she can't sustain.[13] Such methods can be effective even against committed terrorists and have the added virtue of not crossing the line into torture.

On the other hand, the CIA interrogation manual suggests that physical coercion as well as sensory deprivation and verbal threats can sometimes be effective against a recalcitrant subject.[14] It also quotes a separate study indicating that "most people who are exposed to coercive procedures will talk and usually reveal some information that they might not have revealed otherwise."[15] In recent years, the CIA sought legal authorization—quietly at first, but later openly—to use "enhanced interrogation techniques" (e.g., "waterboarding" or simulated/controlled drowning) beyond those approved in military interrogation manuals, presumably because it believes such techniques to be effective in at least some cases.[16]

The U.S. military also reportedly employs techniques that border on torture as well as cruel, degrading, and inhumane treatment in the Survival, Evasion, Resistance, and Escape (SERE) training that it requires for some troops, indicating that the military believes them to be effective in "breaking" at least some detainees. Those techniques were apparently copied from ones used against American POWs during the wars in Korea and Vietnam, and at least some of the same techniques were adopted by U.S. interrogators at Guantanamo Bay in Cuba and in Afghanistan and Iraq, all with the authorization of senior civilian leaders and attorneys for the Department of Defense, the Department of Justice, the office of the vice president, and the CIA.[17]

Of course, "breaking" someone's will to resist doesn't necessarily mean that everything they say after that point is trustworthy. Indeed, the more acutely painful the torture is, the more likely the victim is to say anything (including lies) to end their ordeal. But there is some anecdotal evidence that torture can at least occasionally be effective in eliciting useful intelligence. A Sri Lankan army officer told writer Bruce Hoffman that torture induced some Tamil Tiger detainees to reveal details about planned terrorist acts.[18] Mark Bowden claimed that torture enabled Lebanese and CIA officers to identify who blew up the U.S. Embassy in Beirut in 1983.[19] And Alan Dershowitz has argued,

> The tragic reality is that torture sometimes works, much though many people wish it did not. There are numerous instances in which torture has produced . . . truthful information that was necessary to prevent harm to civilians. The *Washington Post* recounts a case from 1995 in which Philippine authorities tortured a terrorist into disclosing information that may have foiled plots to assassinate the pope and to crash eleven commercial airliners carrying approximately 4,000 passengers into the Pacific Ocean. . . . It is precisely because torture sometimes does work and can sometimes prevent major disasters that . . . the U.S. government sometimes "renders" terrorist suspects to nations like Egypt and Jordan.[20]

Even if those reports are true, that obviously doesn't prove that torture is always reliable or even most of the time. Like doctors who continue to use treatments they're comfortable with well after they've been scientifically proven to be less effective than other treatments, some intelligence officers might persist in practicing torture due to laziness, lack of creativity, or willful ignorance of the relative advantages of more humane methods.[21]

But then, *no* method of interrogation is guaranteed to work with every subject, and if intelligence personnel have already tried less questionable methods on a suspected terrorist without success, they might see torture as a last resort, a technique that might just work when other means have failed. As Andrew McCarthy, a former U.S. attorney who has prosecuted Islamic terrorists, has noted:

> Unfortunately, zealots inspired by Islamic militancy and willing to immolate themselves in suicide assaults are not likely to share their secrets under the comparatively mild duress of humane captivity.[22]

It's still an open question whether torture is ever necessary, let alone more effective than humane interrogation methods, in producing timely and reliable intelligence. But apart from moral and legal concerns, it's hard to see why any interrogator would want to deny herself a potentially useful HUMINT tool, especially if the stakes were very high and time were of the essence, as in a "ticking bomb" situation or its analogues.

Assuming that torture might at least occasionally work, what does the law require?

LEGAL RESTRICTIONS ON COERCIVE INTERROGATION

Since the law can sometimes permit or require unethical actions (e.g., racial discrimination under "Jim Crow" or South African apartheid), it can sometimes be ethical to break the law. But a prima facie obligation clearly exists to respect and obey laws that have been established by legitimate political bodies, as well as treaties ratified by representative governments.

Contemporary international treaties prohibit torture as well as inhumane and degrading treatment of detainees or prisoners. The prohibition stated in the UN *Convention against Torture and Other Cruel, Inhuman, or Degrading Treatment or Punishment* (CAT) is clear, comprehensive, and absolute. In the convention, torture is defined as "any act by which severe pain or suffering, whether physical or mental, is intentionally inflicted on a person for such purposes as obtaining from him or a third person information or a confession."[23]

Moreover, the treaty permits no exceptions to its prohibition of torture, even in situations where government officials suspect that a detainee has information that could prevent the loss of many innocent lives. Hence, since the United States is a signatory to the CAT and during its ratification expressed no reservations about its absolute prohibition of torture, there is no basis for the opinion voiced by some Bush administration lawyers that waterboarding is legal for the CIA to use "under certain circumstances."[24]

However, after 9-11 some of the president's legal advisors claimed that Common Article 3 of the Geneva Conventions (which also forbids torture and inhumane treatment) did not apply to Al Qaeda suspects, a position that President George W. Bush formally announced in February 2002. And some of those same legal advisors subsequently defined "torture" under the CAT in a ridiculously narrow way and the president's authority as commander in chief in a ludicrously expansive way, suggesting that in that role he has constitutional authority to override federal statutes. Apparently as a result, some interrogation techniques that were previously considered illegal were approved by senior U.S. officials: stress positions, sleep deprivation, face-slapping, removal of clothing, exposure to cold, waterboarding, and threats of death.[25]

Incredibly, Harvard law professor Alan Dershowitz has suggested that a precedent for interrogational torture exists in *domestic* U.S. case law:

> In the 1984 case of *Leon v. Wainwright*, Jean Leon and an accomplice kidnapped a taxicab driver and held him for ransom. Leon was arrested while trying to collect the ransom but refused to disclose where he was holding the victim. . . . Several police officers threatened him and then twisted his arm behind his back and choked him until he told them the victim's whereabouts. Although the federal appellate court disclaimed any wish to "sanction the use of force and coercion by police officers," the judges went out of their way to state that this was not an act of "brutal law enforcement agents trying to obtain a confession." "This was instead a group of concerned officers acting in a reasonable manner to obtain information they needed . . . to protect another individual from bodily harm or death." Although the court did not find it necessary to invoke the "necessity defense," since no charges were brought against the policemen who tortured the kidnapper, it described the torture as having been "motivated by the immediate necessity to find the victim and save his life." If an appellate court would so regard the use of police brutality—torture—in a case involving one kidnap victim, it is not difficult to extrapolate to a situation in which hundreds or thousands of lives might hang in the balance.[26]

Note a major fallacy in the court's reasoning, though: Praising the motives of the police begs the question as to whether their treatment of the suspect constituted illegal torture. Unfortunately, that same fallacy appears in a highly influential memorandum written by an Army lawyer in Guantanamo in October 2002: According to her, numerous harsh interrogation techniques should be considered "legally permissible . . . because there is a legitimate governmental objective in obtaining the information necessary that the high value detainees on which these methods would be utilized possess."[27] In other words, the fact that interrogators intended to elicit valuable intelligence was thought to override the fact that the detainees would be intentionally made to suffer, in some cases severely.

In strong contrast to Dershowitz's domestic torture precedent, McCarthy has argued that since 1994, U.S. statutory law categorically prohibits all forms of torture, with no exception for intelligence interrogation.[28] And a highly detailed study of relevant laws and treaties claimed that, in the U.S. government's own words to the UN Committee on Torture in 1999,

> Every act constituting torture under the [Torture] Convention constitutes a criminal offense under the law of the United States. No official of the government, federal, state, or local, civilian or military, is authorized to commit or to instruct anyone else to commit torture . . . or other cruel, inhuman, or degrading treatment . . . ([even] during a "state of public emergency").[29]

However, that same study surmised that federal statutes didn't necessarily apply to U.S. detention centers outside of U.S. territory.[30] This may be the main reason why many terrorist suspects have been questioned at Guantanamo Bay in Cuba, Bagram Airbase in Afghanistan, and secret CIA detention centers, even though using such sites to evade U.S. law clearly contradicts the intent of the Torture Convention.[31]

To remove any ambiguities about U.S. obligations under the Geneva and Torture conventions, Congress enacted the Detainee Treatment Act of 2005. The point of this legislation was further reinforced in June 2006 by the Supreme Court in its ruling in *Hamdan v. Rumsfeld*. The White House was thus forced to accept (at least publicly[32]) that the Torture Convention and Common Article 3 of the Geneva Conventions do apply to the conflict with Al Qaeda, and that anyone detained by the United States anywhere in the world should not be subjected to cruel, inhuman, or degrading treatment.[33]

As a result, the U.S. Army's revised *Field Manual (FM) 2-22.3: Human Intelligence Collector Operations*, issued in September 2006, affirms the importance of respecting the Geneva Conventions and the Detainee Treatment Act, not only when questioning enemy prisoners of war, but even when interrogating suspected insurgents and terrorists (categorized as "unlawful enemy combatants"). The manual also reminds army personnel that they can be prosecuted under the Uniform Code of Military Justice (UCMJ) for cruelty, assault, and so forth.[34]

Although *FM 2-22.3* does not explicitly refer to the Torture Convention, its regulations appear to be consistent with it for the most part. (A separate military manual on counterinsurgency issued in December 2006 does cite that treaty specifically.[35]) In light of the notorious uses of beatings, sexual humiliations, and intimidating guard dogs that occurred at Abu Ghraib and elsewhere,[36] *FM 2-22.3* specifically prohibits the following:

> Forcing the detainee to be naked, perform sexual acts, or pose in a sexual manner. Placing hoods or sacks over the head of a detainee; using duct tape over the eyes. Applying beatings, electric shock, burns, or other forms of physical pain. Waterboarding. Using military working dogs. Inducing hypothermia or heat injury. Conducting mock executions. Depriving the detainee of necessary food, water, or medical care.[37]

However, some of the interrogation techniques that are authorized elsewhere in *FM 2-22.3* seem to be in tension with at least the spirit of the Geneva and Torture conventions. For example, sleep deprivation—which can disorient a resistant subject[38] and impair his or her ability to stick to a consistent story—is apparently permitted by the manual, within limits: Detainees must be allowed at least "four hours of continuous sleep every 24 hours."[39] But there's no stipulation as to how many days such a regimen can legitimately be sustained; some reports indicate detainees to have undergone daily twenty-hour interrogations for many weeks in a row.[40] Prolonged sleep deprivation can actually be life threatening.

An additional Army-approved approach referred to as "Fear Up" involves identifying a preexisting fear or creating one in the source's mind to link the reduction of that fear to his cooperation. The manual cautions, "The HUMINT collector must be extremely careful that he does not threaten or coerce a source," lest he violate the UCMJ.[41] But the line separating "Fear Up" from illegal threats is perilously thin (especially in regard to a "Fear Up Harsh" variant).[42]

Another method, "Pride and Ego Down," is "based on attacking the source's sense of personal worth. . . . In his attempt to redeem his pride, the source will usually involuntarily provide pertinent information in attempting to vindicate himself."[43] Although this technique is hard to clearly distinguish from treatment that would classify as degrading, *FM 2-22.3* candidly states, "The HUMINT collector must remember that his goal is collecting information, not concern with the psychological well being of the source. He will be concerned with the latter only insofar as it helps him obtain the former."[44]

While neither "Fear Up" nor "Pride and Ego Down" qualify as torture under the law, since they don't rise to the level of inflicting severe pain or suffering, they may qualify as inhuman or degrading under both the Geneva and Torture conventions. Conversely, whatever U.S. law and military regulations currently permit or require, it obviously does not exhaust the moral issues at stake. Although the claim of some of the president's advisors that he may unilaterally override a treaty without the consent of the Senate[45] is highly dubious, in theory the president acting *with* the Senate could formally abrogate the CAT and other relevant treaties, if they concluded that strict adherence to them would endanger our nation's security. We might also imagine hypothetically, what if the law were silent on torture? How should we construe the relevant moral concerns and sort out any conflicts among them? The remaining sections of this chapter address these questions.

IS A MORAL RIGHT NOT TO BE TORTURED ABSOLUTE?

Torture and other cruel, inhuman, or degrading treatment share the following essential characteristics: 1) They involve an intentional infliction of suffering in another person, 2) They occur without that person's informed consent, and 3) They are not intended to promote that person's welfare. The second condition is essential to distinguish cruelty from, say, painful medical experiments that people might freely volunteer to undergo solely to help others. Condition three is needed to exclude painful medical treatments given to children or the mentally retarded for their own good but without their informed consent, since they lack that capacity. But any actions characterized by all three conditions are prima facie immoral, because they are clearly in tension with moral principles basic to virtually every serious normative theory today: compassion or concern for the well-being of others (entailing nonmaleficence or "nonharm"), and respect for human autonomy, dignity, and equality. By implication, a right not to be tortured would seem to be among the most fundamental of human rights, possibly even stronger (as some argue) than the right not to be killed.[46]

If a moral right not to be tortured were *absolute*, then there could be no legitimate exceptions to a rule against torture. This ethical stance is implied in the Geneva and Torture conventions and explicitly affirmed by such organizations as Amnesty International and Human Rights Watch, and many legal scholars and moral philosophers.[47] The U.S. military's 2006 *Counterinsurgency* manual echoes this view: "Torture and cruel, inhuman, and degrading treatment is never a morally permissible option, even if lives depend on gaining information."[48] Alberto Mora, a former general counsel to the U.S. Navy, was one of the earliest and most insistent voices inside the Bush administration opposing the adoption of harsh interrogation methods. In Senate testimony in June 2008, he publicly attacked that decision, in part on the basis of fundamental rights implied in the U.S. Constitution:

> The United States was founded on the principle that every person—not just each citizen—possesses certain inalienable rights that no government, including our own, may violate. Among these rights is unquestionably the right to be free from cruel punishment or treatment, as is evidenced in part by the clear language of the

Eighth Amendment and the constitutional jurisprudence of the Fifth Amendment and Fourteenth Amendment. If we can apply the policy of cruelty to detainees, it is only because our founders were wrong about the scope of inalienable rights.[49]

An absolute right not to be tortured is especially compelling in light of the horrifying testimony of torture victims at the hands of ruthless dictatorships during the past century. We need to retain the sense of revulsion and terror that torture evokes, even while examining it philosophically.

Consider also the scope and significance of the *jus in bello* rule of noncombatant immunity: The underlying principle here is that people who pose no physical threat to others should not be harmed in war; this evinces the Latin root of the word *innocent*, that is, nonthreatening. The principle of noncombatant immunity not only prohibits direct and intentional attacks on civilians, it also forbids harming soldiers who have either surrendered or been incapacitated by their wounds. Respect for this fragile principle might be seen as the most important way to prevent international conflicts from becoming total wars of annihilation, nothing more than a grim series of atrocities. So any step taken to qualify the complete prohibition on torturing detainees is very alarming in the context of military ethics and law. This is one reason why many military lawyers strenuously objected to the recommendations of Bush administration civilian legal advisors David Addington, John Yoo, Jay Bybee, William Haynes, Alberto Gonzales and others to authorize harsh interrogation techniques.[50]

However, although it disturbs me to say this, I'm not convinced that torture in interrogation is necessarily or always immoral, because an absolute right not to be tortured would entail that nothing that anyone might intentionally do to others could justify torturing them, even actively plotting mass murder, which strikes me as an absurd ethical stance.

Imagine that a senior member of Al Qaeda is arrested and refuses to cooperate with his captors.[51] (Readers might imagine being the CIA officers in charge of interrogating notorious Al Qaeda operatives Abu Zubaydah, Ramzi bin al-Shibb, or Khalid Sheik Mohammed soon after their capture.) In spite of his having instigated the murder of scores of innocent people, and more importantly his probable involvement in planning many more killings, let's also imagine that he claims an absolute right not to be tortured and demands to be treated accordingly. Ignoring for a moment the *legal* rights accorded to detainees under the Geneva and Torture conventions, I have great difficulty accepting the plausibility of absolute *moral* claims or demands made by people who have shown complete contempt for the basic rights and well-being of others, especially if they have knowledge of ongoing plans to commit mass murder.[52] I'm thus led to hypothesize that a moral right not to be tortured may be something less than absolute, that it might be more sensible to consider it a prima facie right instead, that is, a right that is clearly established and usually ought to be upheld but that can be trumped by other moral considerations under certain circumstances.[53] Let me explain.

THE RIGHT NOT TO BE TORTURED AS PRIMA FACIE

A prima facie right not to be tortured might be qualified in a couple of ways: 1) Perhaps the right could be *overridden* by the rights of innocent people not to be murdered, if torture were thought to be the only way to obtain information needed to prevent their murders. That sounds intuitively plausible, but it might also rationalize the torture of *innocent* people to save other innocents, which would be fundamentally unjust. Indeed, we would become no better than terrorists if we intentionally tortured the innocent, so I would strongly urge drawing a bright ethical line there. 2) Alternatively, perhaps a moral right not to be tortured could be *forfeited*,[54] as in the case of captured Al Qaeda leaders. This is similar to a deontological rationale for capital punishment: We rightly assume that every person has a prima facie right not to be killed, but we might nonetheless also claim that even that basic right can be forfeited by individuals who commit murder or conspire to do so.[55]

Although torture in both 1 and 2 would be morally troubling, to say the least, only in 2 would it not be clearly unjust. In other words, while torture would certainly *harm* an Al Qaeda leader, it wouldn't necessarily *wrong* him. (The same could be said of executing a murderer.) By contrast, torturing the innocent would *both* harm and wrong them.[56] Thus, I contend, only those who could plausibly be said to have forfeited their right not to be tortured could legitimately be subject to that appalling treatment; and, I further stipulate, only if necessary to prevent serious harms to innocent people, when more humane interrogation methods are highly unlikely to produce that result or have already failed.[57]

But concluding that someone has forfeited their right not to be tortured might seem to imply that there are no moral limits on what their interrogators might be allowed to do. This is so disturbing, even regarding would-be mass murderers, that we must look more closely at the right in question and other ethical concerns beyond that.

Perhaps some rights can be forfeited in part but not wholly, to some extent but not completely. For example, when we send convicted criminals to prison, we intentionally deprive them of some of their rights, but not all of them. Even criminals sentenced to death are protected from "cruel and unusual punishments" under the U.S. Constitution, without any obvious logical, moral, or legal contradiction. Similarly, even if terrorists could not credibly claim moral immunity from torture entirely, they would presumably retain a prima facie right not to be subjected to all possible forms of torture, or to be tortured merely out of vengeance or spite, or to amuse their captors, or to be tortured long after they could plausibly know any "actionable" intelligence.[58] (There is a parallel here to the *jus in bello* principle of proportionality.) Hence, even if torture were warranted in certain cases, it could not justifiably be conducted in utterly ruthless fashion.

There is another argument in favor of torturing suspected insurgents or terrorists, which, in spite of being full of holes, needs to be addressed if only because many U.S. leaders accept it uncritically.[59] The argument goes something like this: 1) During SERE training, we force our own troops to undergo severe physical and mental abuse to enable them to resist such methods if captured in hostile territory, like North Korea.[60] Since 2) we don't consider that unfair to our own troops, then 3) it's not unfair to treat enemy detainees any differently.

This argument is unsound. First, it assumes that the abuse that we force upon our own soldiers is useful to them, that we need to torture them to enable them to resist torture in the future by their enemies, which is highly doubtful to me. Second, even if that empirical assumption were credible, at least our own troops "consent" in a general way to whatever training is deemed necessary by their superiors to prepare them for dangerous roles they've more or less freely chosen. No one outside of the U.S. military, least of all a captured foreign combatant, has consented even remotely to SERE-like abuse at our hands.

Techniques apparently authorized and used in SERE training include stress positions, waterboarding (at least in Navy training), slapping of the face and abdomen, shoving heads against walls and onto floors, solitary confinement, cramped confinement, inducing exhaustion, sensory deprivation, sensory overload, sleep disruption, manipulation of diet, and "degradation." I'm personally very troubled by the fact that that any of our troops are subjected to such treatment, even ostensibly for their own good. I also worry about the potential moral corruption of the officers and noncommissioned officers expected (and trained) to inflict such suffering and indignity on their comrades. Somewhat ironically, part of the stated rationale for those extremely harsh SERE methods is to reinforce the military Code of Conduct, more specifically to help troops avoid giving up information that would betray other personnel, military plans, and so forth, and to help them "maintain dignity and honor."[61] But I find it hard to see how experiencing torture and degrading treatment at the hands of a fellow soldier could thereby teach the trainee any lessons about loyalty to country or devotion to comrades. On the contrary, it seems much more likely to induce alienation, mistrust, callousness, and cynicism about upholding high ethical standards.

Then again, I'm not an expert in the psychology of SERE training, and at least one Ph.D. in clinical psychology who oversaw Air Force SERE training, Jerald Ogrisseg, told Congress that it can be very useful to trainees who subsequently experience interrogation by enemy captors. He also claimed that SERE trainees are given a phrase that they can use to end the training whenever they might find it unbearable.[62] In theory, that could minimize the degree of brutality experienced (and inflicted), though trainees must surely feel compelled to endure as much as they possibly can and most likely feel guilt and shame if they "break" or quit.

INTELLIGENCE OFFICER VIRTUES AND VICES

More than 30 years ago in Senate testimony, a CIA officer stated paradoxically, "This is such a dishonest business that only honest people can be in it." He went on to say, "An intelligence officer . . . must be scrupulous and he must be moral . . . he must have personal integrity. . . . [He] must be particularly conscious of the moral element in intelligence operations."[63] Another career CIA officer told me,

> I have never seen the professional life of an intelligence officer as providing its own [separate] moral justification apart from fundamental ethical principles. Even [intelligence] tradecraft . . . can and should be made to conform to moral principles of decency, respect for individual rights, and consideration of the consequences of the action contemplated.[64]

Still another CIA officer assured me that high ethical standards play an important role in the evaluation and certification of clandestine service officers, who receive specialized tutorial training in ethical issues related to espionage, counterintelligence, and covert action.[65] I'm confident that when it comes to patriotism, courage, and selfless service, CIA officers exhibit those virtues as reliably as do our military personnel, physicians, nurses, police, and firefighters.

However, one of the professional skills uniquely required of intelligence officers (both civilian and military) who employ HUMINT is an ability to *manipulate* people. As chapter 7 on espionage details, the degree of manipulation can vary from the subtle blackmail threat latent in a financial relationship with an espionage agent to more obviously coercive measures. The element of control in intelligence operations is directly related to suspicion of the loyalty of the agent. Suspicion is a professional virtue for intelligence officers, especially for those who work in security and counterintelligence, since in theory anyone thought to be trustworthy may in fact be secretly serving the enemy.

A CIA analyst wrote that the agency's clandestine service officers (who recruit spies overseas) are "painstakingly trained in techniques that will convert an acquaintance into a submissive tool, to shred away his resistance and deflate his sense of self-worth."[66] The practice of interrogation is a significant component of intelligence work but also illustrates manipulation in its rawest form. William Johnson, a former CIA counterintelligence officer, offered a glimpse of the ethical risks involved: "Interrogation is such a dirty business that it should be done only by people of the cleanest character. Anyone with sadistic tendencies should not be in the business."[67] We are reminded, though, of the ease with which people can come to rationalize callousness and cruelty in dealing with perceived enemies. Given the natural human capacity for aggression, combined with the wrong set of biases, incentives, and peer pressures, many ordinarily decent people can succumb to sadism or callous cruelty (recall my analysis in chapter 4, Anticipating and Preventing Atrocities in War).

But torture is not necessarily something conducted solely by sadists. In the interrogation of terrorist suspects, for example, an intelligence officer might well be driven by the motive of preventing harms to innocent people. That officer might take no great pleasure in inflicting pain or fear but nonetheless considers it a regrettable but necessary means of seeking enough details about a terrorist plot to intervene.

What is it about interrogation that Johnson considered "dirty"? Not the presence of inflicted physical pain, which he regarded to be not only morally dubious but counterproductive.

> [P]hysical pain is not relevant in interrogation. Anxiety, humiliation, loneliness, and pride are another story. . . . The person who enjoys

hurting is a lousy interrogator in even the most human situation. But the humane person who shrinks from *manipulating* his subject is also a lousy interrogator. . . . The interrogator, like a priest or doctor, must have a talent for empathy, a personal need to communicate with other people, a concern for what makes other people tick even when he is putting maximum emotional pressure on them.[68]

In everyday moral parlance, empathy is related to compassion, but in intelligence work, the other is considered to be a potential threat to people and interests that the intelligence officer is sworn to protect. "Knowing one's enemy" in this role means understanding the other, but not in the interest of enhancing his or her freedom or well-being: On the contrary, empathy becomes a manipulative tool.

Would authorizing the torture of suspected terrorists, even with strict limits, inevitably corrupt the consciences and character of the personnel we asked to conduct it? There is something so obviously and intrinsically appalling about torture that anyone who hopes to remain a person of integrity—an admirable person—would not use more than the minimum degree of force necessary to obtain vital information. In other words, even if we could show that the person being interrogated had forfeited his right not to be tortured, an ethical interrogator would not consider that a "blank check." Then again, having the sort of compassion that I would consider part of the "standard equipment" of a person of conscience (see chapter 1) might make a professional interrogator less effective than someone who was less benevolent or who could train himself to suppress his compassion when questioning a detainee.

Former Army interrogator Tony Lagouranis worried initially after his arrival in Iraq that his compassion for detainees might make him a poor interrogator, but over time he developed a tendency to use increasingly harsh methods out of frustration when unable to persuade certain detainees to reveal what he thought they knew. He and his peers became obsessed with dominating detainees, achieving power and control over their will.[69] This suggests a psychological slippery slope potentially facing any interrogator, but especially one who resorts to harsh techniques.

Consider what it would take to create a training program for personnel to become authorized to conduct torture. Presumably we would be logically and practically compelled to authorize a broad range of "scientific" experiments on the relative effectiveness of various forms of torture in interrogation,[70] as well as psychological assessments to determine who among the group of prospective interrogators would be most effective at certain techniques. These projects might require the participation of medical doctors at various stages, which would represent an extreme departure from their core professional ethic of nonmaleficence.[71] The American Psychiatric Association (APA) has ruled that "psychiatrists should not participate in or otherwise assist or facilitate the commission of torture of any person." In addition, the APA has stipulated:

> Psychiatrists who become aware that torture has occurred, is occurring, or has been planned must report it promptly to a person or persons in a position to take corrective action. . . . No psychiatrist should participate directly in the interrogation of persons held in custody by military or civilian investigative or law enforcement authorities, whether in the United States or elsewhere. Direct participation includes being present in the interrogation room, asking or suggesting questions, or advising authorities on the use of specific techniques of interrogation with particular detainees.[72]

Similarly, while the American Medical Association permits its physician members to "perform physical and mental assessments of detainees," it further specifies that "[t]reatment must never be conditional on a patient's participation in an interrogation." Moreover, "[p]hysicians must neither conduct nor directly participate in an interrogation, because a role as physician–interrogator undermines the physician's role as healer."[73]

Like medical doctors, some CIA and military interrogators themselves might object to being expected to employ torture,[74] seeing it as a violation of their professional or personal ethic. This issue would no doubt generate heated debate among intelligence officers and perhaps necessitate establishing a "conscience clause" to permit objectors to opt out. Although the claim that "Americans don't torture, period" was never comprehensively true, it clearly represents an important ideal or core value that many conscientious professionals would be unable to abandon.

However, Michael Skerker has suggested that the moral character of an interrogator trained and authorized to use coercive methods is under no greater risk than that of military personnel in special operations who learn to kill at close quarters with their bare hands.[75] In other words, Skerker implies that since special operators do not typically become murderers as a result of their training or missions, neither should we expect interrogators inevitably to lose their moral integrity. Then again, we might also expect interrogators who use torture to suffer Post-Traumatic Stress Disorder (PTSD) at least as frequently as soldiers who have killed in close combat, and we have learned from our ongoing conflicts in Afghanistan and Iraq that PTSD is much more common (afflicting 20–25 percent of troops returning from combat) than previously anticipated.[76] So this would also need to be counted among the probable costs of authorizing torture.

OTHER POTENTIAL CONSEQUENCES OF LEGALIZING TORTURE IN HUMINT

I must now acknowledge that my earlier example of the captured Al Qaeda leader, like the standard "ticking bomb" scenario, assumes greater knowledge of the identity and intent of the subjects of interrogation than their captors typically have. In other words, allowing any torture in interrogation runs the risk in practice of subjecting entirely innocent people to horrific and wholly unjust suffering.[77] Individuals are sometimes erroneously detained by counterinsurgency forces, for instance, as a result of false accusations made against them by fearful or resentful neighbors, or based on flimsy circumstantial evidence, or when rounded up for questioning with other locals to satisfy some arbitrary quota or misguided metric of productivity.[78] Anyone like me who questions whether a right not to be tortured is absolute must take into account the incredibly unjust harms to the innocent that could easily occur if the practice of torture were officially permitted at all. Lagouranis concluded from his experiences interrogating Iraqi detainees:

> Once we accepted that any prisoner might be holding information that could save lives, we gladly used everything in our toolbox on everyone. This resulted in an expansion of the class of people who could be tortured. Now it included people who had been picked up for questioning but were not suspected of being insurgents, and it included people who were picked up on hunches—people against whom we had no solid evidence—and it included relatives of our real targets. . . . I see the spread of torture to these groups as natural and inevitable. At the time, I barely noticed it happening.[79]

In the end, I don't believe it's possible to eliminate the chance of accidentally torturing the innocent if interrogational torture were permitted legally, even if conducted by the most conscientious and skilled interrogators. Even one instance of such an act would be a horrific tragedy. But would it be possible to limit that risk significantly, short of a blanket prohibition? And if so, would that be morally acceptable, along the lines of the *jus in bello* rule of proportionality that permits indirect harms to noncombatants as long as they are not directly and intentionally targeted?

Alan Dershowitz has famously proposed requiring intelligence and law enforcement personnel to obtain a "torture warrant" (like a search warrant) from a judge before being allowed to use torture on a terrorist suspect. He argued that this would make the practice of torture—which he believes is inevitable—both more accountable and less frequent.[80] Andrew McCarthy further suggested that judicial authorizations for torture would be more effectively regulated by means of a centralized "national security court," a single tribunal made up of federal judges.[81]

Although the proposals of Dershowitz and McCarthy are clearly inconsistent with the Geneva and Torture conventions, they are worth careful consideration, but they have provoked vociferous condemnation from many circles. Ethicist Jean Bethke Elshtain called

Dershowitz's torture warrants "a stunningly bad idea,"[82] but like law professor Oren Gross, she nonetheless asserted that some forms of coercive interrogation might be morally justified in certain cases. Elshtain and Gross prefer to keep the legal ban on torture intact, while allowing government officials to plead "necessity" if prosecuted for torturing terrorist suspects.[83] Their approach echoes one advocated in 1978 by philosopher Henry Shue:

> Does the possibility that torture might be justifiable in some of the rarefied situations [that] can be imagined provide any reason to consider relaxing the legal prohibitions against it? Absolutely not. . . . An act of torture ought to remain illegal so that anyone who sincerely believes such an act to be the least available evil is placed in the position of needing to justify his or her act morally . . . to defend himself or herself legally. . . . If the situation approximates those in the imaginary examples in which torture seems possible to justify, a judge can surely be expected to suspend the sentence.[84]

Similarly, former Justice Department lawyer John Yoo argued that U.S. interrogators can legitimately appeal to "necessity" in defending their use of harsh techniques against terror suspects, in spite of our treaty obligations to the contrary.[85]

But Sanford Levinson pointed out a contradiction inherent in the legal position suggested by Shue, Elshtain, Gross, and Yoo:

> [T]his scarcely avoids legitimizing at least some acts of torture. What else, after all, is conveyed by accepting the possibility of acquittal, suspension of sentence, or gubernatorial and presidential pardons of what would be perceived as "morally permissible" torture? State officials would then be giving their formal imprimatur to actions that the various conventions condemn without exception.[86]

If we *openly* permit torture, even under highly restricted legal criteria a la Dershowitz and McCarthy, will we lose all of what little remains of our credibility in the international community on human rights? I would assume so. Alberto Mora, the previously cited former general counsel to the U.S. Navy, notes that our country's adoption of harsh interrogation methods beginning in 2002 had significant negative effects on our relationships with allies:

> As [U.S. allies] came to recognize the dimensions of our policy of cruelty, political fissures between us and them began to emerge because none of them would follow our lead into the swamp of legalized abuse, as we should not have wished them to. These fissures only deepened as awareness grew about the effect of our policies on fundamental human rights principles, on the Geneva Conventions, on the Nuremberg precedents, and on the incidence of prisoner abuse worldwide. Respect and political support for the United States and its policies decreased sharply abroad. . . . International cooperation, including in the military, intelligence, and law enforcements arenas, diminished as foreign officials became concerned that assisting the United States in detainee matters could constitute aiding and abetting criminal conduct in their own countries.[87]

Would we want other countries to follow our example if we legalized torture? Presumably they would be logically permitted to do so in relevantly similar circumstances, so we'd be hard-pressed to persuade them not to imitate us. But their systems of legal checks on abuses of power would not necessarily be as robust as ours, so the number of innocent people tortured around the world would probably grow.[88] As Tom Malinowski of Human Rights Watch has argued:

> One reason the Abu Ghraib scandal has been so harmful is that the United States was revealed to be using, and even justifying, interrogation methods that the U.S. government continues to call torture when they are employed in other countries. The United States has been a powerful voice for victims of torture and human rights abuses around the world. When it violates the principles it preaches to others, its moral authority diminishes, and repressive governments find it much easier to resist American calls for change. Sure, State Department officials can continue to urge Saudi Arabia and Egypt and Algeria to treat people humanely, but when the governments of these countries can quote U.S. government memoranda to defend their brutal actions, what can an American diplomat say in response?[89]

In addition, legalizing torture by U.S. intelligence officers would almost certainly undermine our efforts to "win hearts and minds" in countries where we're battling insurgents.[90] Would our own personnel be placed at greater risk of torture if captured or kidnapped overseas? Detainee abuses at Abu Ghraib almost certainly served to motivate hundreds if not thousands of Iraqis to kill U.S. troops. An Iraqi interviewed by Mark Danner in November 2003 (months before those abuses were publicized) vividly and passionately anticipated that result:

> For Fallujans it is a *shame* . . . for the foreigners to put a bag over their heads, to make a man lie down with your shoe on his neck. This is a great *shame*, you understand? This is a great *shame* for the whole tribe. It is the *duty* of that man, and of that tribe, to get revenge on this soldier—to kill that man. Their duty is to attack them, to *wash the shame*. The shame is a *stain*, a dirty thing; they have to *wash* it. No sleep—we cannot sleep until we have revenge. They have to kill soldiers.[91]

If we permitted *only* CIA officers to use torture within the limits advocated by Dershowitz and McCarthy, we might theoretically be able to limit risks to our *military* personnel by continuing to forbid them from ever using it, as columnist Charles Krauthammer suggested.[92] But it is difficult to imagine how that bright line could be maintained in counterinsurgency, since CIA officers would inevitably want to interrogate some individuals detained by soldiers, and obviously, if harsh CIA methods were publicized, retribution would likely occur against both U.S. military personnel and civilians.

The serious concerns discussed in this section weigh heavily against changing our laws to permit torture under any circumstances. Even if terrorists have in effect forfeited their moral right not to be tortured, and even if torture might prevent some terrorist attacks, there may still be overriding consequentialist reasons *not* to legalize torture in HUMINT. By analogy, even if we regard some crimes to be so heinous as to deprive their perpetrators of the right not to be killed, we might nonetheless refrain from instituting capital punishment, or establish a moratorium on further executions, out of concern, say, for the risk of inadvertently executing innocent people falsely convicted from sloppy police work or the testimony of false witnesses. I don't feel qualified to assess in sufficient detail the likely consequences of prohibiting or permitting torture, but such matters are eminently worthy of continuing reflection and public debate.

A MACHIAVELLIAN TEMPTATION

We treat detainees humanely.

—Donald Rumsfeld, former Secretary
of Defense, February 2002

We do not torture.

—President George W. Bush, November 2005

We don't torture people.

—George Tenet, former Director of
Central Intelligence, May 2007

Niccolo Machiavelli wrote in *The Prince*, "It is good to *appear* merciful, truthful, humane, sincere, and religious; it is good to *be* so in reality. But you [the head of state] must keep your mind so disposed that, in case of need, you can turn to the exact contrary."[93] In theory we might adopt a quasi-Machiavellian policy of pretending to prohibit torture while secretly practicing it.[94] Indeed, the temporary existence of a number of secret CIA detention facilities where Al Qaeda leaders were subjected to harsh interrogation techniques, combined with analogous military practices at Guantanamo and other locations, in contrast to the Bush administration's repeated public condemnations and denials of torture, indicates that our government actually adopted a version of the Machiavellian ethic.[95]

We can no longer credibly claim that Americans never torture. The evidence now overwhelmingly shows that some military and civilian interrogators after 9-11 used methods that clearly constituted torture as well as cruel, inhuman, and degrading treatment, and moreover that they were authorized to do so (in terms of "aggressive" and "enhanced" interrogation techniques or "counterresistance strategies") by top civilian officials in the Department of Defense, the Department of Justice, and the CIA, and by their respective military chains of command. But since those decisions and events represented a clear violation of U.S. laws in relation to the Geneva and Torture conventions, they may also have violated the U.S. Constitution, since they occurred without the consent of the Senate, which was required to ratify those treaties in the first place.

In March 2008, Congress passed a bill intending to limit CIA interrogation techniques to those approved in the military's 2006 HUMINT manual, which among other things would have prevented CIA officers from using waterboarding. But President Bush vetoed the bill, reasoning that it would have denied the agency some effective tools in dealing with suspected terrorists: "We have no higher responsibility than stopping terrorist attacks," he said. (But isn't upholding the rule of law just as important?) He added, "And this is no time for Congress to abandon practices that have a proven track record of keeping America safe."[96] Thus President Bush seemed to think that he could authorize such harsh techniques as waterboarding even while continuing to claim that the United States doesn't use torture. (Curiously, if Congress truly opposed that idea, why was it unable to override his veto?) As a result, prior to the inauguration of Barack Obama as President in January 2009, we had a bizarre and quasi-Machiavellian policy, at least in regard to nonmilitary interrogations, one that was inconsistent with our stated values and legal obligations under the Geneva and Torture conventions.

In my view, if any U.S. president would seek to authorize CIA or military personnel to use harsh interrogation methods against suspected terrorists and insurgents, he or she must first open a public dialogue with the Senate about abrogating the relevant treaties or otherwise modifying our existing pledges to uphold them comprehensively, as well as reflect very carefully on what that would entail for our country's core legal and ethical principles. Given the Senate's overwhelming endorsement of the Detainee Treatment Act of 2005 and its condemnation in 2007–2008 of the CIA's use of waterboarding, it is unlikely in the near future to take seriously any proposal to modify our existing treaty obligations. And President Obama is highly unlikely to propose any such change: One of his first executive orders ("Ensuring Lawful Interrogations") prohibited the CIA and other federal personnel from using any techniques on detainees that are not allowed by the Army's interrogation manual, Common Article 3 of the Geneva Conventions, or the Torture Convention. Obama's order also repudiated all of the legal interpretations of interrogation issued by the Justice Department under President Bush from 2001 to 2009.[97]

However, if U.S. citizens were to become victims of a terrorist attack on par with or exceeding the carnage of 9-11, that could well renew the national debate about the ethics of coercive HUMINT interrogation. If our leaders were to consider adopting (again) what amounts to torture in our efforts against terrorists, though, they must be forthright in doing so. Even Dershowitz qualified his advocacy of torture warrants thusly:

> Even the defense of necessity must be justified lawfully. The road to tyranny has always been paved with claims of necessity made by those responsible for the security of the nation. Our system of checks and balances requires that all presidential actions, like all legislative or military actions, be consistent with governing law. If it is necessary to torture in the ticking bomb case, then our governing laws must accommodate this practice. If we refuse to change our law to accommodate any particular action, then our government should not take that action.[98]

At the very least, unless and until our president and Senate are willing to formally renounce our treaty obligations that prohibit torture and other cruel, inhuman, and degrading treatment, our interrogators should stay clear of any methods that even contradict the spirit of those treaties. Fortunately, as indicated early in

226

this chapter, there are many *humane* interrogation techniques that skilled military and civilian intelligence personnel know how to use effectively, methods that they can rely on in the overwhelming majority of cases to elicit the intelligence that may be desperately needed to save scores of innocent lives.

NOTES

1. *Merriam-Webster's Collegiate Dictionary*, 10th ed. (Springfield, Mass.: Merriam-Webster, 1996).

2. Carl Friedrich, *Constitutional Reason of State: The Survival of the Constitutional Order* (Providence, R.I.: Brown University Press, 1957), 65–66.

3. "Report of the Special Study Group on the Covert Activities of the Central Intelligence Agency," 143–44; mentioned in chapter 5, "The CIA's Original 'Social Contract.'"

4. Geoffrey Stone, *Perilous Times: Free Speech in Wartime, from the Sedition Act of 1798 to the War on Terrorism* (New York: Norton, 2004); Daniel Farber, *Lincoln's Constitution* (Chicago: University of Chicago Press, 2003). On the Espionage Act of 1917 and Sedition Act of 1918, see also Daniel Patrick Moynihan, *Secrecy: The American Experience* (New Haven, Conn.: Yale University Press, 1998), ch. 2.

5. Don Van Natta, "Questioning Terror Suspects in a Dark and Surreal World," *New York Times*, 9 March 2003, A1; Mark Bowden, "The Dark Art of Interrogation," *Atlantic Monthly*, October 2003, 51–76; Dana Priest and Joe Stephens, "The Secret World of U.S. Interrogation," *Washington Post*, 11 May 2004, A1; James Risen, David Johnston, and Neil A. Lewis, "Harsh CIA Methods Cited in Top Al Qaeda Interrogations," *New York Times*, 13 May 2004, A1; Seymour Hersh, "The Gray Zone," *New Yorker*, 17 May 2004, 38ff.; John Hendren, "Officials Say Rumsfeld OK'd Harsh Interrogation Methods," *Los Angeles Times*, 21 May 2004, A13; John Barry, Michael Hirsh, and Michael Isikoff, "The Roots of Torture," *Newsweek*, 24 May 2004, 26–34; Human Rights Watch, *The Road to Abu Ghraib*, June 2004; Mark Danner, *Torture and Truth: America, Abu Ghraib, and the War on Terror* (New York: New York Review of Books, 2004); David Johnston, "In Remote Prison, Disputes Flared over Interrogations," *New York Times*, 20 September 2006, A1; Craig Whitlock, "Jordan's Spy Agency: Holding Cell for the CIA," *Washington Post*, 1 December 2007, A1; Mark Mazzetti, "CIA

Secretly Held Al Qaeda Suspect, Officials Say," *New York Times*, 15 March 2008, A6; Philippe Sands, *Torture Team: Rumsfeld's Memo and the Betrayal of American Values* (New York: Palgrave Macmillan, 2008); Jane Mayer, *The Dark Side: The Inside Story of How the War on Terror Turned into a War on American Ideals* (New York: Doubleday, 2008).

6. Pew Research Center for the Public and the Press, "Iraq and the War on Terrorism," 24 November 2005, http://people-press.org/reports/display .php3?PageID=1019 (23 November 2008).

7. Sanford Levinson, "Contemplating Torture: An Introduction," in *Torture: A Collection*, ed. Sanford Levinson (New York: Oxford University Press, 2004), 39.

8. I have not seen any controlled scientific studies examining this directly—any such study would obviously violate the ethical guidelines standard in human subjects research. But U.S. military personnel who had endured torture and degrading treatment as POWs in Korea and Vietnam were extensively debriefed after their return to the United States as to their reactions to interrogation tactics. Albert Biderman, "Communist Attempts to Elicit False Confessions from Air Force Prisoners of War," *Bulletin of the New York Academy of Medicine* 33, no. 9 (September 1957): 616–25; Theresa Dillon, "Educing Information Bibliography (Annotated)," in *Educing Information: Interrogation Science and Art*, ed. Russell Swenson (Washington, D.C.: National Defense Intelligence College, 2006), 311–28. Later in this chapter, I discuss how insights derived from our POWs influenced U.S. military training for troops at risk of capture and how they were eventually offensively employed against detainees at Guantanamo and elsewhere.

9. John Langbein, "The Legal History of Torture," in *Torture*, ed. Levinson, 93–103.

10. N.a., "KUBARK [CIA] Counterintelligence Interrogation," July 1963, 94.

11. U.S. Army, *Field Manual (FM) 34-52: Intelligence Interrogation* (1992), 1-8, and *FM 2-22.3: Human Intelligence Collector Operations* (2006), 5-21. Pagination in such manuals typically uses the format "chapter-page," that is, 1–8 means page eight in chapter 1, 5–21 means page 21 in chapter 5, and so on. On FBI interrogation policies, see Sands, *Torture Team*, and Mayer, *The Dark Side*. Human Rights First, "How to End Torture and Cruel Treatment: Blueprint for the Next Administration," October 2008, 5, asserted, "Intelligence experts agree that abusive interrogation practices actually impede efforts to elicit actionable intelligence, and that noncoercive,

rapport-building techniques provide the best opportunity for obtaining accurate and complete information." But as my subsequent comments suggest, the implication that intelligence experts would unanimously concur with such claims is incorrect and misleading.

12. "Total Isolation," a documentary that aired on BBC TV, 22 January 2008, www.bbc.co.uk/sn/tvradio/programmes/horizon/broadband/tx/isolation/ (23 November 2008). See also "Alone in the Dark," *BBC News*, 21 January 2008, http://news.bbc.co.uk/2/hi/uk_news/magazine/7199769. stm (23 November 2008).

13. Chris Mackey [pseud.] and Greg Miller, *The Interrogators* (New York: Little, Brown, 2004). See also Tony Lagouranis and Allen Mikaelian, *Fear Up Harsh: An Army Interrogator's Dark Journey through Iraq* (New York: New American Library, 2007), 34, 38. On the accuracy of Lagouranis's narrative, see Laura Blumenfeld, "The Tortured Lives of Interrogators," *Washington Post*, 4 June 2007, A1: "Stephen Lewis, an interrogator who was deployed with Lagouranis, confirmed the account, and Staff Sgt. Shawn Campbell, who was Lagouranis's team leader and direct supervisor, said Lagouranis's assertions were 'as true as true can get. It's all verifiable.' John Sifton, a senior researcher for Human Rights Watch, said the group investigated many of Lagouranis's claims about abuses and independently corroborated them."

14. "KUBARK Counterintelligence Interrogation," 82–94.

15. Paul Hinkle, "The Physiological State of the Interrogation Suspect as It Affects Brain Function," in *The Manipulation of Human Behavior*, Albert Biderman and Herbert Zimmer, eds., (New York: Wiley, 1961), 83.

16. On 5 February 2008, CIA director Michael Hayden said during Senate testimony that the agency had used waterboarding on three Al Qaeda detainees in 2002–2003; he also urged senators not to force the CIA to use only Army-approved interrogation techniques; Mark Mazzetti, "Intelligence Chief Cites Al Qaeda Threat to U.S.," *New York Times*, 6 February 2008, A1. Reports differ as to when the Justice Department first authorized the CIA to use waterboarding: Joby Warrick, "CIA Tactics Endorsed in Secret Memos: Waterboarding Got White House Nod," *Washington Post*, 15 October 2008, A1, implied that it occurred in 2002, while Scott Shane, "Waterboarding Is Focus of Justice Department Inquiry," *New York Times*, 23 February 2008, A1, suggested that legal approval may not have been forthcoming until 2005. Former CIA interrogator John Kiriakou said that waterboarding induced Abu Zubaida to provide information that disrupted several attacks: Joby Warrick and Dan Eggen, "Waterboarding Recounted:

Ex-CIA Officer Says It 'Probably Saved Lives' But Is Torture," *Washington Post*, 11 December 2007, A1.

17. M. Gregg Bloche and Jonathan Marks, "Doing unto Others as They Did unto Us," *New York Times*, 14 November 2005, A21, claimed that SERE techniques are "based on studies of North Korean and Vietnamese efforts to break American prisoners," and are "intended to train American soldiers to resist the abuse they might face in enemy custody." William Safire, "Waterboarding," *New York Times Magazine*, 9 March 2008, 16, noted that in 1976, Navy trainees were reported to have been subjected in training to "waterboard" torture, which resembled a technique used against U.S. POWs by North Korean captors in the early 1950s. See also Sands, *Torture Team*, especially on the paper trail implicating high officials in the Bush administration, Scott Shane, "China Inspired Interrogations at Guantanamo," *New York Times*, 2 July 2008, A1, and Mayer, *The Dark Side*, chs. 7, 8, and 10.

18. Bruce Hoffman, "A Nasty Business," *Atlantic Monthly*, January 2002, 49–52.

19. Bowden, "The Dark Art of Interrogation."

20. Alan Dershowitz, *Why Terrorism Works: Understanding the Threat, Responding to the Challenge* (New Haven, Conn.: Yale University Press, 2002), 137. He mentioned other ostensibly successful uses of torture on 139–40 and 249–50. See also Jerome Slater, "Tragic Choices in the War on Terrorism: Should We Try to Regulate and Control Torture?" *Political Science Quarterly* 121, no. 2 (2006): 202.

21. Lagouranis claimed in *Fear Up Harsh* to have observed many Army interrogators in Iraq who routinely resorted to harsh methods out of laziness.

22. Andrew McCarthy, "Torture: Thinking about the Unthinkable," *Commentary*, July–August 2004, 17. I'm grateful to my former student, Lt. Col. Doug Galipeau, for bringing this article to my attention.

23. United Nations Office of the High Commissioner for Human Rights, *Convention against Torture and Other Cruel, Inhuman, or Degrading Treatment or Punishment*, www.unhchr.ch/html/menu3/b/h_cat39.htm (23 November 2008), adopted by the General Assembly on 10 December 1984, and ratified by the United States on 21 October 1994.

24. Dan Eggen, "The White House Defends the CIA's Use of Waterboarding in Interrogations," *Washington Post*, 7 February 2008, A3, and "White House Pushes Waterboarding Rationale," *Washington Post*, 13 February 2008, A3; Mark Mazzetti, "Letters Give CIA Tactics a Legal Rationale," *New York Times*, 27 April 2008, A1.

25. U.S. Office of Legal Counsel, "Re: Standards of Conduct for Interrogation," a memorandum for Alberto Gonzales, 1 August 2002, was apparently largely written by John Yoo but signed by Jay Bybee. Subsequently, Jerald Phifer, "Request for Approval of Counterresistance Strategies," 11 October 2002, advocated the use of certain stress positions, exposure to heat and cold, and a technique that appears to be waterboarding; Donald Rumsfeld approved most of them on 2 December 2002, then rescinded that decision on 15 January 2003; those documents are reprinted in Danner, *Torture and Truth*, 115–68 and 181–83. The second "torture memo," U.S. Office of Legal Counsel, "Re: Military Interrogation of Alien Unlawful Combatants Held Outside the United States," 14 March 2003, was also written by John Yoo but for William (Jim) Haynes II, the general counsel for Rumsfeld at the Defense Department. See also Barry, Hirsh, and Isikoff, "The Roots of Torture"; Neil Lewis and Eric Schmitt, "Lawyers Decided Bans on Torture Didn't Bind Bush," *New York Times*, 8 June 2004, A1; Kathleen Clark and Julie Mertus, "Torturing the Law," *Washington Post*, 20 June 2004, B3; Adam Liptak, "Legal Scholars Criticize Memos on Torture," *New York Times*, 25 June 2004, A14; David Johnston and James Risen, "Aides Say Memo Backed Coercion for Al Qaeda Cases," *New York Times*, 27 June 2004, A1; Ruth Wedgwood and R. James Woolsey, "Law and Torture," *Wall Street Journal*, 28 June 2004, A10; Douglas Jehl and Eric Schmitt, "Army's Report Faults General [Sanchez] in Prison Abuse," *New York Times*, 27 August 2004, A1; R. Jeffrey Smith and Dan Eggen, "Gonzalez Helped Set the Course for Detainees," *Washington Post*, 5 January 2005, A1; Eric Lichtblau, "Gonzales Says '02 Policy on Detainees Doesn't Bind CIA," *New York Times*, 19 January 2005, A17; Human Rights Watch, *Getting Away with Torture? Command Responsibility for the U.S. Abuse of Detainees*, April 2005; Brian Ross and Richard Esposito, "The CIA's Harsh Interrogation Techniques Described," *ABC News*, segment aired 18 November 2005, http://abcnews.go.com/Blotter/Investigation/story?id=1322866 (23 November 2008); Mark Mazzetti, "'03 U.S. Memo Approved Harsh Interrogations," *New York Times*, 2 April 2008, A1; David Johnston and Scott Shane, "Memo Sheds New Light on Torture Issue," *New York Times*, 3 April 2008, A19. Mayer, *The Dark Side*, provides the most comprehensive account of these developments.

26. Dershowitz, *Why Terrorism Works*, 253.

27. Diane Beaver, "Legal Brief on Proposed Counterresistance Strategies," 11 October 2002, in Danner, *Torture and Truth*, 176.

28. McCarthy, "Torture," 22.

29. U.S. report to the UN Committee on Torture, quoted in Association of the Bar of the City of New York, "Human Rights Standards Applicable to the United States' Interrogation of Detainees," 2003, 70.

30. "Human Rights Standards Applicable to the United States' Interrogation of Detainees," 11. By contrast, Abraham Sofaer, "No Exceptions," *Wall Street Journal*, 26 November 2005, 11, argued that the CAT applies to any territory under U.S. jurisdiction.

31. Rosemary Foot, "Torture: The Struggle over a Peremptory Norm in a Counterterrorist Era," *International Relations* 20, no. 2 (June 2006): 138, 141; Mayer, *The Dark Side*, 230.

32. But see Charlie Savage, "Bush Could Bypass New Torture Ban," *Boston Globe*, 4 January 2006, A1. Michael Skerker reminded me in August 2007 that the president's signing statement left doubts as to whether he intended to uphold the Detainee Treatment Act. Skerker's concern was reinforced in October 2007, when Attorney General Alberto Gonzalez was revealed to have secretly ruled as lawful in 2005 a number of harsh interrogation techniques that were clearly intended by Congress to be illegal. Scott Shane, David Johnston, and James Risen, "Secret U.S. Endorsement of Severe Interrogations," *New York Times*, 4 October 2007, A1.

33. Joel Brinkley, "Rice Is Challenged in Europe over Secret Prisons," *New York Times*, 7 December 2005, A1; Scott Shane, "Terror and Presidential Power: Bush Takes a Step Back," *New York Times*, 12 July 2006, A20. See also President Bush's executive order of 20 July 2007, "Interpretation of the Geneva Conventions Common Article 3 as Applied to a Program of Detention and Interrogation Operated by the Central Intelligence Agency."

34. *FM 2-22.3: Human Intelligence Collector Operations*, vi-viii, 5-13 to 5-27, and appendix A.

35. *U.S. Army/Marine Corps Counterinsurgency Manual*, 251.

36. Danner, *Torture and Truth*, 26–49; Human Rights Watch, *The Road to Abu Ghraib*; Josh White, "Soldiers' 'Wish Lists' of Detainee Tactics Cited," *Washington Post*, 19 April 2005, A16; Tim Golden, "In U.S. Report, Brutal Details of Two Afghan Inmates' Deaths," *New York Times*, 20 May 2005, A1; Adam Zagorin and Michael Duffy, "Inside the Interrogation of Detainee 063," *Time*, 20 June 2005, 26–32; Josh White, "Documents Tell of Brutal Improvisation by GIs," *Washington Post*, 3 August 2005, A1.

37. *FM 2-22.3: Human Intelligence Collector Operations*, 5-21.

38. Randy Borum, "Approaching Truth: Behavioral Science Lessons on Educing Information from Human Sources," in *Educing Information*, ed. Swenson, 33–34.

39. *FM 2-22.3: Human Intelligence Collector Operations*, M-10. Lagouranis said in *Fear Up Harsh*, 85, that during part of his tour in Iraq, the Interrogation Rules of Engagement did not specify four *continuous* hours of sleep each day, so his supervisor told him to "break those four hours into five pieces" when interrogating a certain pair of suspected insurgents. Lagouranis further stated (86–90) that he and his peers took turns executing that exhausting regimen every day for four straight weeks with those detainees, combining sleep deprivation with stress positions and exposure to cold, rendering them extremely weak and disoriented. Those detainees apparently never provided any useful intelligence, though, even after being menaced by growling and lunging guard dogs (107–11). An earlier but similarly relentless, lengthy, and brutal interrogation at Guantanamo of Mohammed al-Qahtani, an Al Qaeda suspect captured in Afghanistan in November 2001, was first publicized in Zagorin and Duffy, "Inside the Interrogation of Detainee 063." Sands, *Torture Team*, convincingly documented the direct and immediate influence of decisions by Secretary of Defense Donald Rumsfeld on techniques used in interrogating al-Qahtani.

40. David Luban, "Torture, American-Style," *Washington Post*, 29 November 2005, B1; Sands, *Torture Team*.

41. *FM 2-22.3: Human Intelligence Collector Operations*, 8-10.

42. Mackey and Miller, *The Interrogators*, 276–77, narrated an example of an incident in Afghanistan involving an army intelligence officer.

43. This wording is from *FM 34-52: Intelligence Interrogation* (1992), 3-15 and 3-16; the comparable text in *FM 2-22.3: Human Intelligence Collector Operations* is on 8-13. "Pride and Ego Down" strikes me as a highly dubious way of eliciting cooperation from a subject. Lagouranis said in *Fear Up Harsh*, 82, "I'm not sure why interrogators think insults and humiliation produce results." But he immediately went on to describe an encounter with a large and imposing Iraqi detainee who surprisingly broke down after Lagouranis berated him as "illiterate and stupid, besides being fat and lazy." So perhaps Pride and Ego Down does sometimes "work."

44. *FM 2-22.3: Human Intelligence Collector Operations*, 8-12.

45. Bybee, "Re: Standards of Conduct for Interrogation," 146–49; Yoo, "Re: Military Interrogation of Alien Unlawful Combatants Held Outside the United States," 4–6, 18–19.

46. Henry Shue, "Torture," *Philosophy and Public Affairs* 7, no. 2 (1978), reprinted in *Torture*, ed. Levinson, 47–60. See also Roy Dixon, "Rejecting the Torturer," in Joint Services Conference on Professional Ethics, *Moral Obligation and the Military* (Washington, D.C.: National Defense University

Press, 1988), 141–63, and David Sussman, "What's Wrong with Torture?" *Philosophy and Public Affairs* 33, no. 1 (2005): 1–33.

47. Sussman, "What's Wrong with Torture?"; Association of the Bar of the City of New York, "Human Rights Standards Applicable to the United States' Interrogation of Detainees," 9–10. See also Ariel Dorfman, "The Tyranny of Terror: Is Torture Inevitable in Our Century and Beyond?" and Jean Bethke Elshtain, "Reflection on the Problem of 'Dirty Hands,'" in *Torture*, ed. Levinson, 3–18 and 77–89, respectively.

48. *U.S. Army/Marine Corps Counterinsurgency Manual*, 251.

49. Alberto Mora, statement before the U.S. Senate Armed Services Committee, 17 June 2008.

50. Barry, Hirsh, and Isikoff, "The Roots of Torture"; Josh White, "Military Lawyers Fought Policy on Interrogations," *Washington Post*, 15 July 2005, A1; Barton Gellman and Jo Becker, "The Unseen Path to Cruelty," *Washington Post*, 25 June 2007, A1; Eric Lichtblau and Scott Shane, "Gonzales, Loyal to Bush, Held Firm on War Policies, *New York Times*, 28 August 2007, A1; Sands, *Torture Team*.

51. Charles Krauthammer suggested a similar scenario in "The Truth about Torture," *Weekly Standard*, 5 December 2005, but although he approved of using torture in such cases, he didn't say whether he thinks anyone has a prima facie right not to be tortured or whether that right can be forfeited or overridden.

52. Analogously, I have argued elsewhere that people convicted of violent felonies can be said to have forfeited their otherwise equal claim to a major organ transplant: "Should Violent Felons Receive Organ Transplants?" *San Jose Mercury News*, 31 January 2002, and "Tough Choices on Heart Transplants," *Santa Clara Magazine*, Fall 2002, 32.

53. Recall my discussion of prima facie duties in chapter 1, based on W. David Ross, *The Right and the Good* (New York: Oxford University Press, 1930).

54. This claim was persuasively defended by Stephen Kerhnar, "For Interrogational Torture," *International Journal of Applied Philosophy* 19, no. 2 (Fall 2005): 230–34.

55. Joel Feinberg, *Rights, Justice, and the Bounds of Liberty* (Princeton: Princeton University Press, 1980), 239.

56. Fritz Allhoff, "An Ethical Defense of Torture in Interrogation," in *Ethics of Spying: A Reader for the Intelligence Professional*, ed. Jan Goldman (Lanham, Md.: Rowman & Littlefield, 2005), 129–32, briefly considered the possibility that a terrorist might forfeit a right not to be tortured, but

he quickly abandoned that train of thought in favor of the idea that the terrorist (like everybody else) has an "inalienable" right not to be tortured, which would nonetheless be overridden by the rights of his intended victims. Allhoff thus ignored the problem that his argument also would justify torturing *innocent* people, if their rights were overridden by the rights of a larger number of innocent people. A deeper problem with Allhoff's argument is his muddled grasp of utilitarian and deontological theories. Slater, "Tragic Choices," 203–4, took "the innocence problem" very seriously, but elsewhere (212), he claimed that in a "supreme emergency," such as an impending weapons of mass destruction attack, "there can be no limits at all," which could imply that even the intentional torture of the innocent might be justified (a position I reject).

57. Here I concur with Slater, "Tragic Choices," 211, on the importance of restricting torture exclusively to "last-resort" scenarios.

58. Compare the limits proposed by Allhoff, "An Ethical Defense of Torture in Interrogation," 132–35, and by Skerker, "Interrogation Ethics in the Context of Intelligence Collection," in *Ethics of Spying*, ed. Goldman, 161.

59. I have personally heard many U.S. military officers of various ranks and in different settings voice this argument.

60. Bloche and Marks, "Doing unto Others as They Did unto Us."

61. See the excerpts from the Joint Personnel Recovery Agency, "Physical Pressures Used in Resistance Training and against American Prisoners and Detainees," 25 July 2002, made public in a hearing of the U.S. Senate Armed Services Committee on 17 June 2008.

62. Jerald Ogrisseg, statement before the U.S. Senate Armed Services Committee, 17 June 2008. Ogrissig also testified that the Air Force would never use waterboarding in its SERE training, because in his view no one could be trained to endure it.

63. Testimony of "Michael Mulroney," in Congress, Senate, Select Committee to Study Governmental Operations with Respect to Intelligence Activities, *Alleged Assassination Plots Involving Foreign Leaders*, Interim Report #94-465, 94th Congress, 1st session, 1975, 436, note 27.

64. B. Hugh Tovar, letter to the author, 25 February 1992.

65. James Barry, letter to the author, 24 January 1992.

66. E. Drexel Godfrey Jr., "Ethics and Intelligence," *Foreign Affairs* 56, no. 4 (April 1978): 631.

67. William Johnson, "Tricks of the Trade: Counterintelligence Interrogation," *International Journal of Intelligence and Counterintelligence* 1, no. 2 (1986): 104.

68. William Johnson, *Thwarting Enemies at Home and Abroad: How to Be a Counterintelligence Officer* (Bethesda, Md.: Stone Trail, 1987), 33, 32, italics in the original. See also Ralph White, "Empathy as an Intelligence Tool," *International Journal of Intelligence and Counterintelligence* 1, no. 1 (1986): 57–75.

69. Lagouranis, *Fear Up Harsh*, 40–47, 127, 244–46. See also Josh White, "Soldiers' 'Wish Lists' of Detainee Tactics Cited," *Washington Post*, 19 April 2005, A16.

70. As I noted earlier and as Mayer, *The Dark Side*, extensively documented, some U.S. military and civilian interrogators applied at Guantanamo and in Afghanistan and Iraq what had been learned from years of internal SERE training about how to break the will of detainees, so perhaps we already have "scientific" torture-training programs in place.

71. Jonathan Marks, "Doctors of Interrogation," *Hastings Center Report*, July–August 2005, 17–22; Michael Gross, *Bioethics and Armed Conflict: Moral Dilemmas of Medicine and War* (Cambridge, Mass.: MIT, 2006), ch. 7.

72. American Psychiatric Association, "Psychiatric Participation in Interrogation of Detainees," May 2006, www.psych.org/Departments/EDU/Library/APAOfficialDocumentsandRelated/PositionStatements/200601.aspx (23 November 2008).

73. American Medical Association, "Physician Participation in Interrogation," June 2006, www.ama-assn.org/ama1/pub/upload/mm/38/i-06ceja.pdf (23 November 2008).

74. I'm indebted to John Hawkins for suggesting that point.

75. Skerker, "Interrogation Ethics in the Context of Intelligence Collection," ed. Goldman, 162. A similar claim was made three decades ago by former CIA officer Arthur Jacobs in a letter to *Foreign Affairs* 56, no. 5 (July 1978): 867–75. See also John Langan, "Moral Damage and the Justification of Intelligence Collection from Human Sources," *Studies in Intelligence*, Summer 1981, reprinted in *Ethics of Spying*, ed. Goldman, 104–13.

76. Dana Priest and Anne Hull, "The War Inside: Troops Are Returning from the Battlefield with Psychological Wounds, but the Mental Health System That Serves Them Makes Healing Difficult," *Washington Post*, 17 June 2007, A1.

77. Skerker concluded in "Interrogation Ethics in the Context of Intelligence Collection," "There is inadequate empirical data on error rates in interrogations in police settings and no publicly available material to my knowledge on interrogations performed by American intelligence officers" (142). Thus we probably have no way of knowing how many innocent

people have been inadvertently subjected to coercive U.S. interrogation methods. But in 2003, military intelligence officers estimated that "between 70 percent and 90 percent of the persons deprived of their liberty in Iraq had been arrested by mistake," "Report of the International Committee of the Red Cross on the Treatment by the Coalition Forces of Prisoners of War and Other Protected Persons by the Geneva Conventions in Iraq during Arrest, Internment, and Interrogation," February 2004, in Danner, *Torture and Truth*, 257.

78. Lagouranis, *Fear Up Harsh*, 74: "We had a lot of prisoners who were fingered by informants, [e.g.] turned in by neighbors. Usually, this was their way of settling a grudge." On indiscriminate detention of Iraqis to fulfill arbitrary quotas or on the basis of flimsy testimony or evidence, see 149, 187, 192–97, 219–20. He also quoted a Marine lieutenant colonel in charge of a detention facility as saying, "Anyone who comes into this prison is guilty, and if I let them out it's because of overwhelming evidence of innocence." Lagouranis commented, "I was absolutely floored. We'd come here to spread democracy and the rule of law, but ended up inverting our own values. Even the Iraqi police interrogators with whom we worked were appalled [by] our system of justice, or lack of it, and they ridiculed the lectures from the Marines about how fair, humane, and just the Americans were" (197–98).

79. Lagouranis, *Fear Up Harsh*, 246.

80. Dershowitz, *Why Terrorism Works*, 158–61. In a more recent article, "Tortured Reasoning," in *Torture*, ed. Levinson, 259–60, Dershowitz noted that he developed the idea of a torture warrant while teaching in Israel in the 1980s.

81. McCarthy, "Torture," 24.

82. Elshtain, "Reflection on the Problem of 'Dirty Hands,'" 83.

83. Elshtain, "Reflection on the Problem of 'Dirty Hands,'" 85–87, and Oren Gross, "The Prohibition on Torture and the Limits of the Law," in *Torture*, ed. Levinson, 229–32.

84. Shue, "Torture," 58–59.

85. Yoo, "Re: Military Interrogation of Alien Unlawful Combatants Held Outside the United States," 74–80.

86. Levinson, "Contemplating Torture," 36. See also Dershowitz, "Tortured Reasoning," 272–77.

87. Mora, statement before the Senate Armed Services Committee. Mora illustrated those points by adding that "allied nations have refused on occasion to train with us in joint detainee capture and handling operations

because of concerns about U.S. detainee policies," and that "senior NATO [North Atlantic Treaty Organization] officers in Afghanistan have been reported to have left the room when issues of detainee treatment have been raised by U.S. officials, out of fear that they may become complicit in detainee abuse."

88. Ironically, our own legalization of interrogational torture would probably reduce our need to "outsource" it to other countries via "extraordinary renditions," but the global incidence of torture would likely increase anyway, as our ability to persuade other countries not to employ it would decline.

89. Tom Malinowski, "Banned State Department Practices," in *Torture: Does It Make Us Safer? Is It Ever OK?*, ed. Kenneth Roth and Minky Worden (New York: Human Rights Watch, 2005), 141.

90. Malinowski, "Banned State Department Practices." See also my article, "Why Hearts and Minds Matter: Chivalry and Humanity, Even in Counterinsurgency, Are Not Obsolete," *Armed Forces Journal* (September 2006), and *U.S. Army/Marine Corps Counterinsurgency Manual*, ch. 7.

91. Danner, *Torture and Truth*, 1, emphasis in the original.

92. Krauthammer, "Truth about Torture."

93. Niccolo Machiavelli, *The Prince*, trans. and ed. Robert Adams (New York: Norton, 1977), 50, emphasis added.

94. Bowden argues in "The Dark Art of Interrogation," 76, "Torture is a crime against humanity, but coercion is an issue that is rightly handled with a wink, or even a touch of hypocrisy; it should be banned but also quietly practiced." His intended distinction between torture and coercion is unclear, though, especially as he equated "coercion" with "torture lite."

95. Priest and Stephens, "The Secret World of U.S. Interrogation"; Risen, Johnston, and Lewis, "Harsh CIA Methods Cited in Top Al Qaeda Interrogations"; Shane, Johnston, and Risen, "Secret U.S. Endorsement of Severe Interrogations"; Sands, *Torture Team*; Mayer, *The Dark Side*.

96. Steven Lee Myers, "Bush's Veto of Bill on CIA Tactics Affirms His Legacy," *New York Times*, 9 March 2008, A1. Senator John McCain supported the president's veto, which is surprising in light of his earlier firm stance against the use of harsh interrogation methods by the military, and his own previous experience of being tortured by the North Vietnamese.

97. Executive Order no. 13491, "Ensuring Lawful Interrogations," 22 January 2009, http://www.whitehouse.gov/the_press_office/Ensuring_Lawful_Interrogations/ (13 February 2009).

98. Dershowitz, *Why Terrorism Works*, 153.

10

CONCLUDING REFLECTIONS

Blessed are the peacemakers.

—Matthew 5:9

You have patiently followed my lead through an often complex series of moral trails under partly cloudy skies. I'll now review a few of the landmarks identified during our journey and point the way toward the territory of peacemaking (which unfortunately I cannot afford to explore here in depth).

As you'll recall, I have argued that good ethical decision making cannot be reduced to a short checklist or model. Fundamentally, it requires a rich range of *moral emotions*, including empathy toward others' suffering and well-being, a sense of fairness and outrage against injustice, a desire not to incur shame and guilt from doing evil, and so forth. But because some of our gut-level feelings and judgments can be rooted in biased perceptions and ignorance (e.g., racism or sexism), we need to be able to reflect on whether they're sensible; this demands *mindfulness and self-awareness*. Good ethical decisions can also depend on *imagination*, both in anticipating the consequences of alternative actions/policies for everyone they'll significantly affect, and in creating new and better options. Sound ethical reasoning sometimes entails *hard intellectual work* to research relevant facts and probabilities, to identify which moral duties are at stake, and to determine whether an ethical argument satisfies the canons of logic. And converting ethical reasoning to action may require *courage* to oppose powerful countervailing social, organizational, economic, or political pressures.

In some situations, when sufficient time is available before a decision must be made, people of integrity—warriors and spies included—will need to draw upon all of those traits and skills. In other instances, though, split-second decisions will not permit sophisticated analysis. We can educate and train people to make good decisions even in those cases, but at that point, they'll be relying on largely unconscious intuitions and judgments, not a deliberate decision-making model.

All of us are bound to recognize and uphold a number of objective and strong (albeit prima facie) ethical principles, including compassion for others and respect for their autonomy and dignity. Such principles do not entail strict pacifism or forbid secret intelligence operations entirely, but they do require anyone in a position to authorize war, espionage, covert action, or coercive interrogation to at least give concerted attention to *alternative* actions that might more completely reflect our most important moral obligations.

What we desperately need, but too often lack, are elected officials who comprehend and take seriously the ethical principles at stake in their employment of military and intelligence assets. And at least as essential are senior leaders in our military, intelligence, and diplomatic communities with the wisdom, integrity, and courage to dissuade elected officials from launching unjust wars or cavalierly abandoning longstanding moral values and legal standards bearing on the conduct of military and intelligence personnel. Such leaders must also be mindful of the tendencies of otherwise decent people to resort to cruelty in such highly stressful situations as combat and interrogation, and to obey superior orders to commit atrocities even when doing so deeply violates their consciences. Those tendencies have profound implications for the content of professional training and education programs and for inculcating a habit of emotional mindfulness in every warrior and spy.

Regarding the ethics of war, I have claimed: 1) All people have a prima facie right not to be killed. This right can only be forfeited if they intentionally try to kill innocent people or while they are combatants in war. 2) Given the immense destruction and loss of life that war usually brings, all nonviolent means of realistically achieving just objectives should be tried first. 3) War should only be waged when necessary to protect the rights and welfare of the innocent. 4) Innocent civilians should not be directly targeted. 5) Weapons and tactics should not be used against military targets in ways that are certain to cause civilian casualties, unless it is the only way to protect one's own soldiers or civilians. Even then, harms to enemy civilians should be minimized. 6) Captured soldiers should not be tortured or summarily executed but treated humanely. 7) Each side should be held accountable for any atrocities committed by its military forces. Similar principles and rules arose in the Western just-war tradition and have been incorporated into international treaties, for example, the Hague, Geneva, and Torture conventions, but such tenets are not unique to the West or to Christianity in particular: Every major religious tradition has developed comparable ones. It ought to be possible for people of all faiths to work in concert to implement them, without first having to agree on which views of God are best.

Concerning intelligence operations, although I think that the Central Intelligence Agency (CIA) can credibly claim a firm social contract with the American people, legitimate intelligence goals cannot justify any and all means. Many espionage and covert action techniques remain morally problematic despite their employment in the service of a worthy cause by a justified profession. To manipulate people into becoming espionage agents, to employ harsh interrogation techniques, or to deceive foreign citizens via covert action infringes the prima facie rights of autonomous, rational adults, which can only be overridden or trumped by more important prima facie duties or rights. Although the concept of "national interest" implies the tacit consent of domestic citizens—and permits us to criticize CIA covert actions in Guatemala and Iran that narrowly served the interests of private corporations—it cannot unequivocally warrant coercive intelligence methods, in part because it cannot be assumed to satisfy the tacit or even hypothetical consent of foreign citizens.

The use of human agents—voluntary and nonvoluntary—is intended to provide information believed to be unobtainable through other methods. Clandestine collection of intelligence using human agents (HUMINT) remains crucial in penetrating hostile intelligence agencies (counterespionage); in monitoring the existence, movements, proliferation, and elimination of weapons of mass destruction; and in monitoring and subverting international terrorism and narcotics trafficking. But the risks inherent in all espionage activities suggest that for the sake of the agent alone, efforts should be made to determine before the agent is recruited that the information needed cannot be ascertained by less problematic methods. In addition, since after an agent is recruited the agent–officer relationship takes on a life and momentum of its own, care must be taken to avoid situations where innocent third parties would be harmed or justice obstructed in the interest of preserving the agent's identity and continued service.

Recruiting voluntary agents has the advantage of involving no deception about the identity and general motives of the recruiter. Furthermore, a just cause can be served by intelligence officers and voluntary agents working together to undermine an unjust regime or destroy a terrorist organization like Al Qaeda. But such agents usually deserve not to be deceived about the risks involved in the operations they are asked to carry out. Nor should the fact that their work is secret tempt their handlers to treat them as expendable, to allow them callously to be sacrificed to Realpolitik or the shifting winds of diplomacy.

The chief advantage of employing a false-flag approach or blackmail in certain situations is that intelligence-gathering objectives can be pursued even where foreign citizens are highly unlikely to voluntarily serve as CIA agents, but such methods raise very difficult ethical questions. False-flag methods by definition deceive the agent as to the identity of the recruiter and thus hide from the agent the full risks inherent in his or her tasks as well as their true purposes. Blackmail is blatant coercion. It is difficult enough to justify its use against known criminals; it is all the more so when it arises out of the calculated entrapment of a previously innocent person who merely happens to have probable access to sensitive information desired by the CIA. Finally, to the extent that false-flag and blackmail tactics seek to "stretch" the agent's conscience, they can result in the corruption of the agent, in addition to his or her victimization.

These primarily deontological concerns about espionage are challenged, though, by the consequentialist reply that if one rules out an espionage source or method, one may thereby eliminate the possibility of knowing certain kinds of vital information. It's not difficult to construct hypothetical cases in which having particular information about the intentions of a tyrannical regime or a terrorist cell could mean the difference between life and death for many people, cases that would therefore question the validity of strict prohibitions on deceptive and coercive intelligence methods or the use of criminals as agents.

However, having stared long and hard into the abyss of interrogational torture, I've concluded that even if terrorists have in effect forfeited their moral right not to be tortured, and even if torturing them might prevent some terrorist attacks, there seem to be overriding consequentialist reasons *not* to legalize torture in HUMINT, especially the risk of accidentally torturing innocent people who have been falsely implicated as terrorists.

Although human societies throughout history have sometimes waged total war against their enemies, faith communities can nurture firmly rooted habits and dispositions of compassion and nonviolence, reducing the likelihood and severity of war by dispelling the ignorance, fear, and hatred that too often inspire and escalate it. Many people in diverse cultures have devoted their lives to nonviolence in exemplary ways, modifying their behavior through personal meditation and reflection, engaging in countless small acts of kindness, working patiently at cultural exchange and quiet diplomacy,[1] and fostering public political activism (including nonviolent civil disobedience) in support of basic human rights. Such activities are fully consistent with the just-war principles of proportionality (especially its last-resort component) and right intention; indeed they seem to be required by them.[2] In practice, though, they are often exhibited more commonly by strict pacifists than by just-war proponents (including me, I must confess).

But there have also been many admirable diplomats, military and intelligence officers, and development-agency personnel who have engaged in creative and dedicated peacemaking, some in ways that rival those of the most inspired pacifists. On the military side, such initiatives have included limiting the use of deadly force (or using nonlethal weapons), even in situations where it might otherwise be assumed to be the quickest and most effective way to neutralize a threat; monitoring and managing the emotional states of soldiers to minimize the likelihood of atrocities in war; meeting with local families to express remorse for killings of their loved ones, even when their deaths were sincerely unintended by U.S. forces; building and securing schools and hospitals in conflict zones; and convening meetings between bitter ethnic or religious enemies to discuss concerns and negotiate compromise solutions to disputes. Soldiers who do such things deserve to be called peacemakers as much as their pacifist counterparts do.

Our species evolved eons ago in Africa in ways that make it unwise for us to think that we can ever do away with strong military and intelligence capabilities if we hope to preserve our respective national communities. But our human nature also responds favorably to conciliatory words and gestures from real or perceived enemies,[3] permitting us to sometimes put aside old grievances, resolve conflicts, and consciously forego the use of deception, conspiracy, and bloodshed when not truly needed to ensure our defense.

Although a cogent theory of peacemaking need not be highly abstract, the practice of peacemaking can require considerable creativity, patience, determination, and courage. (This subject clearly deserves at least a whole chapter dedicated exclusively to it, but I must limit myself here to a very few general points.) Ideally, peacemakers understand such basic human needs and interests as security and respect, which are shared across cultures,[4] but they also learn enough about the relevant communities' histories and distinct cultures to be able to honor their legitimate (or at least deeply held) grievances and aspirations, without thereby raising their expectations to unrealistic heights. They systematically identify traditional and emerging leaders having power and influence over the issues at stake, assessing the motives and agendas of each as to whether they're likely to help or hinder a nonviolent resolution of disputes. They carefully establish their own credibility as trustworthy mediators with the key political players. They tactfully nurture constructive dialogue between the major antagonists, promoting mutual respect for the interests of their counterparts. And they enable the parties to take ownership of the peacemaking process themselves so as not to make them dependent on an external mediator.[5]

Peacemaking is a noble and vital calling, one whose virtues and skills all of us—even warriors and spies—should strive to inculcate in ourselves and practice within our diverse spheres of influence.

NOTES

1. Marc Gopin, "The Practice of Cultural Diplomacy," 22 November 2002, www.gmu.edu/departments/crdc/docs/culturaldiplomacy.html (23 November 2008).

2. John Howard Yoder, *When War Is Unjust: Being Honest in Just-War Thinking*, Rev. ed. (Maryknoll, N.Y.: Orbis, 1992), 72–75.

3. Frans de Waal, *Peacemaking among Primates* (Cambridge, Mass.: Harvard University Press, 1989), chs. 2 and 6.

4. Abraham Maslow, *Motivation and Personality*, 3rd ed. (New York: HarperCollins, 1987); Roger Fisher, William Ury, and Bruce Patton, *Getting to Yes: Negotiating Agreement without Giving In*, 2nd ed. (New York: Penguin Books, 1991), ch. 3.

5. Chester Crocker, Fen Osler Hampson, and Pamela Aall, eds., *Leashing the Dogs of War: Conflict Management in a Divided World* (Washington, D.C.: U.S. Institute of Peace Press, 2007) is a remarkably comprehensive collection of scholarly essays that details these and many other practical peacemaking strategies. See especially Louis Kriesberg, "Contemporary Conflict Resolution Applications," 455–76.

ABOUT THE AUTHOR

David L. Perry is director of the Vann Center for Ethics at Davidson College in North Carolina, where he teaches ethics courses as a full professor, fosters extracurricular discussions of contemporary ethical issues, and leads interdisciplinary workshops on integrating ethical concerns across the curriculum. From 2003 to 2009, he was professor of ethics at the U.S. Army War College in Carlisle, Penn¬sylvania, where he taught ethics and warfare, strategic leadership, critical thinking, and other courses for military colonels and their civilian counterparts. He previously taught biomedical ethics, business ethics, and other courses in philosophy and religion at Seattle University and Santa Clara University, and was a management consultant in corporate ethics at the Ethics Resource Center in Washing¬ton, DC. Although he's published over 40 articles, this is his first book. He earned a B.A. in religion from Pacific Lutheran University, and A.M.Div. and Ph.D. degrees from the University of Chicago Divinity School. He shares his home with two big labs, Bud and Curly, who evince no interest in moral philosophy but are also blissfully ignorant of the sad history of human conflict.